DATE DUE

WHAT PRICE PARENTHOOD?

What Price Parenthood?

ethics and assisted reproduction

edited by
Courtney S. Campbell
The Hastings Center

Dartmouth

Aldershot · Brookfield USA · Hong Kong · Singapore · Sydney

Published by
Dartmouth Publishing Company Limited
Gower House
Croft Road
Aldershot
Hants GU11 3HR

Dartmouth Publishing Company Limited
Distributed in the United States by
Ashgate Publishing Company
Old Post Road
Brookfield
Vermont 05036
USA

A CIP catalogue record for this book is available from the British Library

Library of Congress Cataloging-in-Publication Data
What price parenthood? : ethics and assisted reproduction / edited by
  Courtney S. Campbell.
     p. cm.
   Includes index.
   ISBN 1-85521-224-2 : $55.95
   1. Human reproductive technology–Moral and ethical aspects.
 I. Campbell, Courtney S., 1956–
 RG133.5.W48 1992
 176–dc20   91-5167
                                                                       CIP

Printed and bound in Great Britain by
Ipswich Book Company Ltd.

Contents

Feminist Perspectives on Assisted Reproduction

International Perspectives on Assisted Reproduction

Introduction

The new technologies of assisted reproduction have been simultaneously a cause for celebration and alarm. They have promised liberation from the procreative destinies consigned to us by nature and held out the prospect of parenting for many infertile couples and individuals. Yet every biomedical breakthrough seems also to be haunted by the spectre of a Huxleyan *Brave New World*, with its chilling depiction of mass production reproduction. In this respect, the new reproductive technologies have forced individuals, families, professionals, and society to confront enduring questions about the quest for parenthood, the kinds of family bonds—genetic, biological, or social—that we value, the relation (and separation) of reproduction and sexuality, and the balance between private choices and societal responsibility. This volume of essays and case studies that first appeared in the *Hastings Center Report* on in vitro fertilization, embryo freezing, and surrogate parenting illumines the difficult value choices imposed on us by the powers and possibilities of the new reproductive technologies. The collection has been organized to provide the reader with a sense of the evolving ethical debates from a variety of philosophic, policy, and cultural perspectives.

In Vitro Fertilization

Although as Huxley's writing attests, "test tube" babies have long been a possibility in the imagination, only in the last two decades has biomedical research sufficiently perfected procedures and techniques to permit fertilization by human gametes to occur outside the womb, and subsequently to apply these techniques in clinical practice. In vitro fertilization (IVF), designed principally to alleviate female infertility, involves extracting an egg (or eggs) from a woman, fertilization by sperm in a laboratory culture, and transfer of the newly formed human embryo to the uterus for the duration of gestation. Some have raised philosophical and theological objections to this entire process on the grounds that it separates reproduction from sex or that the technological interventions violate the integrity of natural processes. However, much of the ethical discussion of the early 1970s focused on essentially a technical consideration about IVF: Would a child conceived through IVF be exposed to undue risks? Or would the technical manipulations risk offspring who would be abnormal in some respect?

The scientific response to the ethical question arrived with the birth of Louise Brown in England in 1978, and as so often occurs with biomedical breakthroughs, both ethics and the law struggled to catch up. The first set of essays present reflections on the moral and human significance of Louise Brown's birth. The issues under debate by Paul Ramsey, Stephen Toulmin, Marc Lappé, and John Robertson have continued to set the philosophical parameters in subsequent discussions of the ethics of IVF: Should the procedure be considered under a paradigm of experimental research or of therapy? What balance should be sought between the severity and probability of risks to early embryos, infertile women, and to prospective parents, and the anticipated benefits of IVF? How adequate are biological and sociological models of disease when biomedical technology can transform the givenness of infertility into a disease susceptible of cure? Finally, is IVF morally similar to other societally tolerated methods of assisted reproduction, such as artificial insemination, or is it so distinctive that, as Ramsey suggests, it represents "another long step for mankind" to a brave new world of technologically determined reproduction?

Once the in vitro genie was out of the bottle, however, the central concern was not *whether* to proceed, but *how*, and this prompted the regulatory response of control and limitation. As Margaret O'Brien Steinfels observes, a U.S. government Ethics Advisory Board convened in the immediate wake of Louise Brown's birth assumed the inevitable use of IVF as a treatment for infertility and provided a "yes, with conditions" endorsement for researchers while not committing the government to public funding support. As a consequence, control and management of IVF was left to the private sector. Frank H. Marsh and Donnie J. Self outline the medical criteria used by the first private IVF clinic in the U.S. to screen patients for selection into the program. "Patients" were initially limited to heterosexual couples with a stable marriage, but the ethical grounds for excluding unmarried couples and single women, irrespective of sexual orientation, would eventually become a point of substantial controversy.

The Norfolk clinic also required that financial expenses be paid for by the couple, a question that is at the heart of the case study, "Baby Making and the Public Interest." Who should pay for treatment of infertility—the patients, insurance companies, government? The social justice and economic implications of our quest for parenthood remain in search of a satisfactory solution.

Embryo Freezing

As access to IVF gradually became more widespread, it soon became clear that the success story of Louise Brown could not be replicated in every instance. More often than not, fertilized eggs either failed to implant or aborted spontaneously subsequent to implantation. Rather than repeating the invasive laparoscopy procedure following each failure, researchers began to employ a method of superovulation, by which several eggs were retrieved and fertilized simultaneously. This solution to a technical problem, however, thrust IVF technology into the crucible of controversy over the moral status of the human embryo because it left in its wake a host of complex ethical questions over the use of what biologist Clifford Grobstein calls "spare" embryos.

Advisory commissions in Australia, the United Kingdom, and the United States have all maintained that the developing human embryo is deserving of moral respect, even if not of the full moral status and legal rights of persons. Yet as the essays by Grobstein, David T. Ozar, and Andrea Bonnicksen reveal, the scientific, ethical, and clinical conundrums broached by the availability of extra embryos are not readily resolved. Grobstein proposes that, whether implanted in multiples, frozen for later use, used in research, or donated to others, spare embryos can only promise to enhance the general prospects of success with IVF. Ozar examines the extent of our obligations to unused frozen embryos and contends that they should be preserved in a frozen state, rather than discarded, until they can be implanted in a volunteering woman or can no longer survive implantation. Technical and ethical constraints notwithstanding, Bonnicksen notes that over time embryo freezing has become such a routinized part of the entire IVF process that its ethical dimensions are now seldom questioned.

IVF and embryo freezing force us to confront not only the value of the human embryo, but also questions of decision-making authority and criteria for justifiable decisions. If we ask the procedural question, "Who should decide?" about the disposition of the embryo, we are likely to respond, "the parents," but as George J. Annas observes, it is part of the nature of assisted reproduction to render our conceptions of "parenting" systematically ambiguous. Depending on the etiology of its conception, a child may well have five "parents" by birth—a genetically related mother and father, a gestational mother, and a rearing or social mother and father. In testimony originally presented before the U.S. Congress, Annas maintains that the new methods of reproduction require new laws to give legal meaning to the concept "parent" and to protect embryos from exploitation.

The need for legal adjudication with respect to frozen embryos became manifest in a 1989 Tennessee case, *Davis v. Davis*, in which a divorced couple contested the custody of seven embryos that had been frozen while they were married and participants in an IVF program. John Robertson, an expert witness in the case, writes that prospective parents embarking on IVF should give an advanced directive regarding the disposition of frozen embryos should contingencies such as death, divorce, illness, disability, or financial reversal render the couple unavailable or unable to agree at some future point. Both Robertson and Annas object to the rationale for the decision in *Davis*, which awarded custody of the embryos to the woman for purposes of implantation on the grounds that embryos are "persons." Even if there is widespread consensus about the value and respect owed to the human embryo, then, ambivalence and controversy over the scope of this obligation continues to underlie many current conundrums of assisted reproduction.

Surrogate Parenting

The distinctive feature of assisted reproduction through surrogate parenting arrangements is not technology, for in many instances, surrogacy requires no more technology than artificial insemination; rather, surrogacy is characterized by the involvement of a woman who may not wish to rear a child but is willing to assume the burdens of gestation. Even while in vitro fertilization and embryo freezing programs have continued to expand, commercial surrogacy, in which payment is made to the pregnant woman, has been the subject of very critical ethical scrutiny and, in some jurisdictions, of legal prohibition. Why has this been the case?

The values about women embedded in the practice of commercial surrogacy have been one source of ethical and policy objections. For some critics, surrogacy is degrading to women, insofar as surrogates are valued only for their reproductive capacities, and to their bodies, which are used as a means for someone else's ends. The economic dimensions of surrogacy are often viewed as unduly coercive and as exploitative of women, particularly the financially indigent. The prospect of giving up the child at birth seems, moreover, to require the pregnant woman to distance herself psychologically from one of the most intimate of experiences, pregnancy, bonding, and birth.

The impact of commercial surrogacy on the kinds of fundamental relationships society values has been another source of criticism, with some opponents contending that toleration of the practice will foster the commercialization of motherhood and support views that children are "property," thus giving symbolic legitimacy to "baby selling." And, like the other methods of assisted reproduction, surrogacy may risk a loss of our moral bearings about the meaning of "family," "parent," or "mother." What identity can be given to maternity, for example, when the parenting of a child may involve the contribution of an ovum from a genetic mother, a uterus and nourishment through birth from a gestational mother, and rearing from a social, adoptive mother? Surrogacy may seem to rend asunder what nature had joined together.

Others, however, have maintained that restrictions on surrogacy, whether through moral suasion or legal regulations, are no less demeaning to women as moral agents. Indeed, prohibition of surrogacy has been held to represent an unjustifiable paternalistic infringement on the reproductive rights and autonomy of women, and supporters of commercial surrogacy have maintained that such restrictions may set a dangerous precedent for state regulation and control of who has the right to reproduce. In addition, given the rising rates of infertility in many societies among those of childbearing age, and the long queues for adoption, surrogacy can be an available option for couples who might otherwise be childless.

The ethical casuistry of surrogacy has appropriated diverse analogies to adjudicate between these competing moral positions. John Robertson sees the essence of surrogate motherhood as "intentional conception for adoption." It therefore poses no distinct moral issues from other parenting practices already resolved and societally accepted, even if some, such as adoption, artificial insemination, or blended families, deliberately compartmentalize biologic and social parenting. Herbert T. Krimmel, in testimony before the California State Assembly, finds the adoption analogy superficial, and instead

strongly critiques surrogacy through a marketplace model: Since surrogates will conceive children because of their utility to others, the practice risks transforming our view of children from unique individuals to "commodities or items of manufacture." Despite this critique, as George Annas notes, in several early 1980s court cases testing the legality of commercial surrogacy, commerce and contracts seemed to trump concern for the best interests of the child.

The social and ethical limits of this contractual paradigm were glaringly revealed in the internationally famous case of "Baby M." The child's mother, Mary Beth Whitehead, refused to relinquish Baby M to the biological father, William Stern, in violation of their contractual agreement. A custody dispute ensued that ultimately reached the New Jersey Supreme Court, which invalidated surrogate contracts. That strategy, Annas believes, will effectively deter commercial surrogacy, a practice that he feels too closely assumes the form of baby bartering. "There are, in a civilized society, some things that money cannot buy."

Public policy in the United Kingdom carried that sentiment one step further, passing criminal sanctions on third-party beneficiaries of commercial surrogacy under the 1985 Surrogacy Arrangements Act. Diana Brahams, however, challenges the fairness and the consistency of imposing such sanctions while noncommercial surrogacy is unrestricted, and advocates a regulatory approach for both forms of surrogacy. In ethical and policy disputes over any surrogacy arrangement, we may nevertheless wish that our culture was gifted with the wisdom of Solomon.

Assisted Reproduction and Feminist Ethics

While women are often held up as the principal beneficiaries of methods of assisted reproduction, the particular role of procreation, pregnancy, and birth as constitutive features of women's lives and self-identities have made artificial insemination, surrogacy, and in vitro fertilization the objects of acute concern among feminists. There is no common, general feminist perspective on assisted reproduction but rather a diversity of positions ranging from acceptance to ambivalence to antagonism. This diversity reflects, however, differences in emphasis and meaning of some common feminist ethical themes.

Among these themes are the moral primacy of *experience*, and particularly the experience of powerlessness; the value of human *embodiment*; the *social context* of moral choices; the *relational character* of human experience; and personal *empowerment* or control of one's life, including control of reproductive choices. Feminist critiques of assisted reproduction will therefore focus on the nature and purposes of technological intervention on the female body, the embeddedness of social and cultural values that foster the scientific quest for facilitating parenthood, the role of technology as an intermediary for transmitting these values, the capacity of assisted reproduction to rupture or create valued relationships, and the disparities in power present in society, and especially experienced by patients before biomedicine, that threaten self-determination and empowerment over reproductive choices. Indeed, every opportunity for expanded choice opened by technology simultaneously increases the medicalization of pregnancy and childbirth.

This paradox, and the cultural context of reproductive choice are prominent in the essays by Paul Lauritzen, Maura Ryan, Janice G. Raymond, and Christine Overall. Reflecting on personal experience with infertility, Lauritzen observes that patient access to assisted reproduction comes at the cost of ceding control to the medical profession, while Ryan's critique centers on the excessively individualistic and asocial presuppositions of arguments that appeal to procreative liberty to support assisted reproduction.

Reproductive choice is further diminished because the cultural idealization of fertility and parenthood causes reproductive technologies to be experienced as coercive rather than empowering. Like Diana Brahams, Raymond is critical of the "unexamined hallowing of altruistic surrogacy," which she sees as having little to do with money, and everything to do with cultural expectations about pregnant women as society's "archetypal altruists." These expectations create pressures of conformity that structure women's reproductive choices, particularly within families, as almost predetermined and morally meaningless.

Although fertility therapy or implantation of multiple embryos may enhance the prospects of success with IVF, as Grobstein suggests, it also risks an unwanted consequence, multiple gestation. The technological "out" in such a situation may be selective termination of some of the developing fetuses. As Christine Overall notes, however, this simply exemplifies how women are left to the mercy of technology rather than empowered to control their reproductive actions: "The technological 'solutions' to some forms of female infertility create an additional problem of female hyperfertility—to which a further technological 'solution' of selective termination is then offered."

International Perspectives

The concern with context and the cultural embeddedness of moral values and choices is equally evident in the approaches of particular countries to questions of assisted reproduction. While different ethical and policy answers may be rendered on reproductive technologies according to the particular country, several themes converge to form common philosophical, professional, and policy parameters for debate. A first theme concerns the scope of procreative autonomy and privacy: There is crosscultural acceptance that many decisions about reproductive choices are properly the domain of the persons involved; at the same time, privacy shields donors of gametic materials, leaving vexing questions about the desires of offspring to learn of their genetic identity. A second concern is the medicalization of reproduction. In many instances, the medical profession has both *promoted* development of assisted reproductive methods and *controlled* access by "medical indication" policies. Third, a societal commitment to develop these technologies will often be a piece of a much larger debate over the allocation of societal resources and priorities within health care. This becomes especially evident in societal approaches to insurance coverage and the extent of financial reimbursement to patients. Finally, a common cultural concern is whether the scientific quest to remedy infertility will inevitably push on to research on embryos and genetic manipulation.

Can and should this quest be limited by professional norms, recommendations by advisory bodies, or even legislation? Who finally controls technological reproduction and for what purposes are the technologies to be used? It is hoped this collection will aid the reader in formulating his or her own answers to these unavoidable questions of our contemporary ethos.

Courtney S. Campbell
Associate for Religious Studies
The Hastings Center

In Vitro Fertilization: Four Commentaries

INTRODUCTION *Whatever else one may think of it, the birth of Louise Brown was surely the medical media event of the year. The combination of medical wizadry and the relief of individual suffering continues to thrill most of the people most of the time. Rumors of the death of the "idea of progress" have been greatly exaggerated.*

Louise Brown's safe delivery was also the media ethics event of the year. "Ethicists" found their phones ringing with unwonted frequence. "Was the work of Drs. Edwards and Steptoe moral?" the journalists wanted to know. The resulting quotes that found their way into the press fell, roughly, into two classes. There were those cited as saying in vitro fertilization

was wrong and one more step toward a Brave New World, and those who said it really isn't much of an ethical issue at all. Much of the same flavor, in more detail, will be found in the symposium that follows.

If one were to ask which of those two viewpoints seems to have carried the day, both the popular and scientific early returns would seem to indicate the latter. An important variable in the debate, which flourished first in the early seventies, has been the question of safety. The apparent good health of Louise Brown has done much to remove that question from the ethical equation. If the issue continues to be argued, as it should, it will have to be set on a higher and more subtle terrain.

A similar phenomenon presented itself in the case of prenatal diagnosis and is probably now presenting itself with recombinant DNA research—ethical arguments heavily dependent upon dangers to human subjects were forced to give way before track records of safety. And a moral should be obvious: if scientists are ingenious enough to carry out the research in the first place, they will probably be clever enough to figure out how to do it safely. That should set some minds at ease. But it would be a misfortune if it set all minds at ease: the larger and more important questions of the ends of medicine and our right to manipulate human nature remain as alive as ever.

—Daniel Callahan

1 Manufacturing our Offspring: Weighing the Risks

by PAUL RAMSEY

Pope Pius XII once warned against reducing the cohabitation of married persons to the transmission of germ life. This would, he said, "convert the domestic hearth, sanctuary of the family, into nothing more than a biological laboratory" (*Acta Apostolicae Sedis* 43:850 [1951]). That quaint language was spoken about artificial insemination. The Pontiff feared the nemesis of humanity under the fluorescent light of laboratories. He warned

of this in 1951—eons ago!

For more than a decade, medical teams have been racing to bring to birth a baby fertilized in a laboratory. The British team of Steptoe and Edwards is the winner. "Brown" is an ordinary name; the father is a railway worker, the mother a Lancashire housewife. Baby Louise Brown is not so ordinary. On the advice of the gynecologist Patrick C. Steptoe an agent has been hired, supposedly to protect the Browns from undue pressure and to guarantee the newborn Brown a good start in life. To

the fluorescent light of the laboratory has been added the media spotlight.

The Possibility of Damage

The first question to be raised concerns damage to the new Brown from these procedures in their entirety. In a 1974 scientific article the other member of the winning team, Robert G. Edwards, a physiologist at Cambridge University, asserted, "If there is no undue risk of deformity additional to those of natural conception, and publicity is avoided, the children should grow up and develop normally and be no more misfits than other children born today after some form of medical help" (R. G. Edwards, "Fertilization of Human Eggs in Vitro: Morals, Ethics and the Law," *The Quarterly Review of Biology*, 49:1 [March 1974], 3-26). Here Edwards raised two points: how we were to estimate "undue" additional risks of deformity (and whether *any* such risks should be imposed) and the psychological damage that may result if publicity is not avoided.

On the first point, Edwards argues for

Hastings Center Report, October 1978

fifteen pages that there is no risk of deformity from the procedure. I understand why the risks are very low. The developing life (the blastocyst, not yet called the embryo) that is manipulated is a cluster of cleaving cells. These cells have "totipotency." As yet none is on its way to becoming, say, blood, or has "clicked-off" its potency for becoming, say, a liver cell or a bone. At this point in human development the individual (like an earthworm) can renew itself even if momentarily injured. After differentiation into various tissues and organs, the embryo and fetus is more vulnerable to irreversible damage; for example, from thalidomide taken by the mother during pregnancy.

However small, there is still risk of induced injury. The question of "undue" additional risk remains at the heart of the moral question whether human genesis should ever have been attempted in this way. Having carefully built the case for no undue risk in his article, Edwards then spends four pages warning all participants in this procedure that they are liable to "wrongful life" suits for tort compensation. As defendants, all the participants would have to prove that any damage did not result from manipulating the blastocyst. (Among the parties liable, and to be warned, is the "semen donor," not only the husband—which shows that the procedure is not intended to be used only to the good end of overcoming a married woman's oviduct blockage.)

I was stunned by this contradiction in a single article by an eminent scientist because heretofore I had supposed that only theologians were reputed to "fudge" in their arguments. In any case, the knowledge that one may induce injury, though not predictable, cannot be excluded. This seems to me to be significant in a conclusive moral argument against the experiments that have gone on for more than a decade. Moreover, if the new Brown is normal as announced, this will prove only that this kind of human genesis is now and for the future not to be condemned for this reason. Such success will not show that all the past trials at irremovable possible risk (including baby Brown's) were for that period of time excusable.

I once expressed the "macabre 'hope'" that the first child conceived by laboratory fertilization would prove to be a bad result—and that it be well advertised, not hidden from view. That might halt the practice! Edwards missed my irony, failing to note that I also said: "I do not actually believe that the good to come from public revulsion in such an event would justify the impairment of that child. But then for the same reasons, neither is the manipulation of embryos a procedure that can possibly be morally justified"—even if the result happens to be a Mahalia Jackson. (Paul Ramsey, "Shall We 'Reproduce?' ", *Journal of the American Medical Association,* 220:11 [June 12, 1972], 1482). A small risk of grave induced injury is still a morally unacceptable risk.

The Damage of Publicity

Concerning the second source of possible grave damage—publicity—I do not know whether or why Edwards changed his mind. Perhaps there was only a breakdown of communication between him and Steptoe who advised that Louise Brown be capitalized from birth. One can speculate, however, as follows concerning the dilemma the winning team faced. They needed to prove their accomplishment to the scientific community and to the world at large. A British doctor had announced previously that there were one or more babies already born in Europe by this procedure. He offered no proof, and was disbelieved. Nobody wins a Nobel prize for science that way.

If the Steptoe-Edwards team wanted both to advance science and/or their scientific reputations and to protect the next Brown from damaging publicity, they should have tried to create a new "institution" for doing both. The British Medical Association could have been asked to appoint a monitor who could now certify the team's achievement while at the same time avoiding publicity focused upon the subjects (the Browns) with whom the scientist-physician have achieved their success.

In the absence of this anticipatory solution, there was no other recourse than to try to control the publicity and to enable Louise Brown to garner the revenues. This baby will be hailed or stigmatized all her life as the first laboratory-fertilized progeny to be birthed in all human history. Think of the enormity of that reputation! If this child is not physically or psychologically damaged from its beginning, socio-psychological ruin seems invited. If she is the world's best tennis player or if she becomes a juvenile delinquent, the outcome will be explained or excused by her unique genesis. Mahalia Jackson had a more obscure and normal passage into maturity. So also did the parents Brown, and Drs. Steptoe and Edwards. What now have they visited upon this child?

We are told that this sort of "assisted pregnancy" is a "far cry" from Aldous Huxley's pharmacological, genetic, and womb-free paradise. This is true for the moment. Women with fallopian tube blockage now will be able with their husbands to have children. That is all.

Doris Del Zio says that she only wanted a child, although the press begins to report or insinuate that Doris and John Del Zio now say that they might have been the "first." Destructive prevention of that notoriety could also be cause for damage claims in our commercial civilization. Clearly, however, Doris's egg and John's sperm and the cultured blastocyst (if such it was) belonged to them and to no one else. On the other hand a physician is not a patient's plumber. He has professional standards, and is held to them by review committees.

Still there is more to be said about medical and public policy than that a woman's infertility can be "cured." This medical technology is another "long step for mankind" toward Aldous Huxley's "Brave New World." Host "mothers" with wombs-for-hire are immediately possible. Nothing technically limits the fertilization to the husband's sperm. We already have sperm banks. Egg banks will be next. People will be able to go to either to select. Bearing the child can be arranged by contract and financial payment. The consequences to come from opening of the human uterus to medical technological control are not likely to contribute to the emancipation of women.

There is still more. We are not limited to human progeny growing with their own natural genetic endowments. We are not limited to the child Lesley Brown has or Doris Del Zio wanted. Gene splicing soon can be done before the blastocyst or embryo is transferred to the womb of the woman—any woman. "The procedures," Edwards and David Sharpe wrote in a 1971 scientific article, "open the way to further work on human embryos in the laboratory" (R. G. Edwards and D. J. Sharpe, "Social Values and Research in Human Embryology." *Nature* 231 [May 14, 1971] 87-91).

The authors do not mean only benign attempts to correct genetic defects. They also mention cloning and the creation of "chimeras" by importing cells from other blastocysts (perhaps from other species). These creations also need women to carry them through pregnancy. Noting that the first principle of medical ethics—Do no harm—permits the alleviation of infertility, and that this "has been stretched to cover destruction of fetuses with hereditary defects," Edwards and Sharpe ask rhetorically whether the first principle of medical ethics can be stretched to justify "the more remote techniques of modifying embryos"?

Even more ominous is the announced claim that scientists have the "right" to "exercise their professional activities to the limit that is tolerable by society . . . as lay attitudes struggle to catch up with what scientists can do." Publics must be "helped to keep pace." In short, science does not operate within the ethics of a wider human community. It is a scientific ethic, or whatever can be done, that should shape our public philosophy. Let laggards beware.

True, in his 1974 article, Edwards stated that there is "hardly any point in making chimeras until some clinical advantage can be shown to accrue from the method." But he also speaks of "sexing blastocysts" before transfer. His remedy for the problems this remedy will lead to is: "Imbalance of the sexes could probably be prevented by recording the sex of newborn children, and adjusting the choice open to parents." Scientist-kings will manage everything. His only reservation is that the use of "surrogate mothers" should be avoided at the present time until more is known about the interlocking psychological relationships among the parties. Edwards does not say how we can acquire such knowledge without (on his own terms) doing an unethical experimentation now in order to find out whether we ought to do it or not.

Finally, the human womb is a halfway technology. It is replaceable by more "perfect" artifices. Given recent advances in newborn intensive care units, only about twenty-two weeks remain to be conquered in which the human female must necessarily participate in procreation. Then "reproduction" can replace procreation, and we will come to Huxley's Hatcheries. His was a vision of society in which everyone was quite happy. The way there is also a happy one, and we go along that way always motivated by good ends, such as the relief of women's infertility.

For all the motherhood intended at present, the truth is that as C. S. Lewis wrote in *The Abolition of Man:* "The regenerate science . . ., would not do even to minerals and vegetables what modern science threatens to do to man himself" (New York: Macmillan, 1947, p. 49).

Readers may wish to perform the following experiment on themselves. Turn off the tube. Don't pick up the newspaper for two days. Instead, read *That Hideous Strength,* the third book in C. S. Lewis's science fiction trilogy (New York: Macmillan, 1946). The final assault upon humanity is gathering in Edgestow, a fictional British college town. The forces of technology, limited no more by the Christian ages, are trying to combine with pre-Christian forces, represented by Merlin the Magician whose body is buried on the Bracton College grounds. Only the philologist Ransom can save humankind from the powers of the present age concentrated in the National Institute of Coordinated Experiments (acronym NICE).

It is NICE that the Browns have a wonderful baby. Lewis need not have thought of his fictional college, Bracton. Cambridge University is NICE too. To give couples a baby sexed to their desires will be NICE. Every other step taken will certainly be NICE. Finally, *Brave New World* is entirely NICE. For everyone is happy. Only there is no poetry there. Nor will a baby ever be a surprise.

PAUL RAMSEY *is professor of religion at Princeton University and the author of* Ethics at the Edges of Life: Medical and Legal Intersections, *recently published by Yale University Press.*

2 In Vitro Fertilization: Answering the Ethical Objections
by STEPHEN TOULMIN

The phrase "test tube babies" had the power to make people's flesh creep long before Aldous Huxley's *Brave New World;* the medieval alchemist, for one, was often suspected of using his alembic to gestate an artificial homunculus. Yet, at the present time, complete gestation of a human embryo outside the body, as Huxley envisioned it, remains a speculative possibility.

Nonetheless, the anxieties associated with controversies over artificial insemination, human experimentation, genetic engineering, abnormal chromosomes, even abortion and the fetal "right to life," are still active in the public mind. Thus any innovation in techniques of fertility control that apparently moves in the direction of complete in vitro gestation arouses complex emotions, which can easily obscure the actual ethical issues involved.

If we are to discuss the ethics of in vitro fertilization in 1978, we must take care to do so precisely. In vitro fertilization in the Del Zio lawsuit in New York and the Brown case in England is a procedure that is first and foremost a *therapeutic procedure* analogous to the artificial insemination of a wife with the husband as donor. Its immediate purpose is to enable a married couple, who have been prevented from conceiving children because of physiological obstacles, to bear a child; the procedure is undertaken at the request of, and with the free consent of, the prospective parents.

3

In artificial insemination, a husband's sperm is procured by masturbation and then introduced by artificial means into the wife's uterus: there, zygosis occurs just as though the sperm had arrived through sexual intercourse, and implantation and gestation are free to proceed normally. With in vitro fertilization, sperm and ovum are removed from the husband and wife, and what is introduced artificially into the wife's uterus is a zygote formed in a laboratory dish: once the embryo transfer is made, however, implantation and gestation are free to proceed normally.

Are they likely to proceed normally? Or does this procedure involve ethically objectionable risks? The first question is a technical one; at first there seems no special reason why, once implantation has occurred, the resulting gestation should proceed differently from any other. Nor should the eventual risks to the wife—who is the only person clearly exposed to risk —be notably greater than those resulting from artificial insemination with the husband's sperm.

The second question is an ethical one, and is not much harder to answer: the foreseeable risks are certainly no greater than the prospective parents are absolutely entitled to assume and accept on their own responsibility. Any failure on the part of the attending physician to disclose material risks, or any damage suffered as a result of misuse or mishandling of the spermatazoa and ova involved could, of course, be the subject of a straightforward tort action by the parents, as they would be in the case of an incompetently performed artificial insemination.

Nor is there any evident reason to foresee that in vitro fertilization will give rise to an abnormally large number of deformed babies. The risks of deformity are by far the greatest after implantation and during the subsequent pregnancy. A significantly damaged zygote would be unlikely to implant in the first place. (During the initial subdivisions of an embryo's cells, no differentiation has yet taken place: simple physical division of the early embryo might result in the birth of identical twins, but deformity is no more likely than in any other pregnancy.)

On the face of things, then, the ethical question about in vitro fertilization in the present situation is almost rhetorical:

If there is no general ethical objection to procedures aimed at permitting a wife who is otherwise barren to become fertile, why should there be any special objection in this case? Married couples have a right to desire children; their physicians have a right (even a duty) to assist them in attaining that desire; so why should anyone else— particularly the state—have a right to intervene between them?

Answering the Objections

All the same, many people do feel that in vitro fertilization raises delicate ethical issues, and we need to look at these issues here, if only to see how far they are based on the failure to pay attention to the exact character of the situation. (Quite small differences may be morally crucial.) Let me take some sample issues and deal with them one at a time.

OBJECTION: In vitro fertilization involves ethically questionable biomedical research.

ANSWER: In the Del Zio case at any rate, the procedure was undertaken as innovative therapy, not as biomedical research at all. Under existing policy, it was not subject to review by the procedures in place for the ethical review of research protocols. Even if the procedure formed part of a research protocol, however, it is not clear why it should be regarded as ethically questionable by current standards. The basic reason for the ethical review of research protocols is to ensure that "research subjects" are not subjected to undue risks from procedures that have no therapeutic purpose, and that they give the fullest and best informed consent they can to the performance of such procedures. Given adequate consent procedures, patients are free to undergo, either within or outside the research context, therapeutic procedures (for example, chemotherapy or heart transplantation) involving major risks, of a kind that are simply not in question in the gynecological situation. There seems little doubt either about the quality of the Del Zios' consent, or about the therapeutic purpose of the procedure to which they consented.

OBJECTION: Even as innovative therapy, in vitro fertilization ought to have been subject to ethical review.

ANSWER: If that issue is to be raised, it cannot be raised about in vitro fertili-

zation in isolation. As a matter of social policy, a strong though not conclusive case can be offered for establishing formal procedures of "therapy evaluation" more or less analogous to those employed by the Food and Drug Administration in evaluating novel drugs and medical devices. But the goal of any such therapy evaluation would be to ensure that patients have full, accurate, and independent assurances about the safety and efficacy of therapeutic procedures, not to preempt their decision whether or not to undergo those procedures. (At present, the efficacy of a great many routine and fashionable procedures, such as coronary bypass surgery, has been less than fully evaluated.)

If in vitro fertilization shows signs of becoming a routine gynecological procedure, it would no doubt be desirable for its safety and efficacy to be given an independent evaluation. But there is no call to single it out for evaluation at the present stage, or to think that the Del Zios and other couples like them are in any greater need of "protection" than a great many other clients who undergo either standard or innovative treatments at the hands of physicians and surgeons.

OBJECTION: In vitro fertilization should be stopped for fear of what scientists may do next.

ANSWER: This is a pure "flesh-creeping" argument, of a kind that has been advanced against every innovation since the discovery of fire. In its present form, in vitro fertilization should probably be monitored, and even licensed, in whatever ways are appropriate to, say, artificial insemination and the operation of sperm banks; but there is no reason to anticipate any more serious misuse of the procedure than is already possible using stored sperm and artificial insemination.

If our existing institutions make it possible for us to live with artificial insemination, it is surely possible for us to live with current forms of in vitro fertilization. In any event, if in vitro fertilization becomes a straightforward low-risk procedure, banning it by legislation out of ill-defined fears of the future will merely deprive a whole class of currently barren women of their chief hope; and it will, as a result, encourage the development of "black market" or "bootleg" in vitro fertilization operations. In short, in vitro fertilization is a good case in which to refrain from legislative paternalism.

4

OBJECTION: In vitro fertilization may lead to unacceptable genetic manipulations.

ANSWER: Once again, there is no greater reason to fear that this will happen than there already is with artificial insemination and sperm banks. If we have effective ways of monitoring the existing means of fertility control such as artificial insemination, there is no reason why they should be any less effective for in vitro fertilization. (Not that a "mad scientist" would find it easy to manipulate the DNA of a human sperm or ovum without the woman's knowledge, and procure her unwitting collaboration in gestating a "monster"! This could happen already, using artificial insemination; but do we really take the possibility seriously? There are plenty of more likely—not to say, actual —misdeeds for our inflamed imaginations to contemplate.)

OBJECTION: There are no protections for the unborn child.

ANSWER: Until implantation has taken place, there is no "unborn child" to protect. After implantation, the embryo conceived with the help of in vitro fertilization is in no greater and no less need of protection than any other embryo. The fundamental point is simply this: at the time of implantation, the mother's uterine wall is indifferent to the location at which zygosis previously occurred, just as it is indifferent to the question whether a sperm reached the uterus through sexual intercourse or by artificial insemination. As for the supposed risk that a child conceived through in vitro fertilization will be born deformed, and so be entitled to claim "wrongful life," those fears are— as we saw earlier—without serious substance.

Evaluating Therapy: An Issue for the Future

Often enough, the most vigorous ethical and social debates focus attention on urgent political issues of which the cases under discussion are relatively unsatifacory illustrations. The Tuskegee syphilis scandal had nothing to do with "federally funded biomedical research," yet it played a major part in leading up to the ethical review of research protocols. Recombinant DNA aroused questions about public involvement in setting priorities for publicly funded research, though in it-

self it posed, at worst, some public health problems whose bacteriological risks were largely exaggerated; and so on. The present debate about in vitro fertilization may well be the catalyst needed to activate the whole political issue of therapy evaluation. People are asking, "How could this kind of thing have been done, in the name of therapy, without anyone else—even the hospital management in the Del Zio case— seemingly knowing about it?" (I have deliberately avoided discussing the specific rights and wrongs in the case. But the role of the hospital authorities does seem ethically hard to justify. They were clearly entitled to withdraw the physician's hospital privileges, if adequate grounds existed for doing so; but it was surely quite un-Hippocratic for them to vent their indignation with the physician on the Del Zios!) And, certainly, there are plenty of accepted therapeutic procedures that are in serious need of evaluation, since their efficacy and safety are open to serious question.

Still, in vitro fertilization in its present form scarcely seems a high-priority problem. By comparison with many routine and accepted procedures in medicine and surgery, its safety is barely in question. As to its efficacy: by comparison with other available ways of bringing help to otherwise infertile women, one can only say, "It may very well work, and it can scarcely do them much harm; so who are we to deprive them of that hope?"

STEPHEN TOULMIN, PH.D., *is a member of the Committee on Social Thought at the University of Chicago.*

3 Ethics at the Center of Life: Protecting Vulnerable Subjects

by MARC LAPPÉ

The Del Zio and Brown cases raise the issue of the propriety of human intervention at the very earliest stages of human life. As such, these two events could be seen as examples of what Paul Ramsey calls "ethics at the edges of life," where questions of human morality often stand out most starkly. I think the case of in vitro fertilization raises a broader set of issues that rests squarely in the center of our lives.

I would like to move any discussion away from the special case ethics of control of in vitro fertilization to the more general ethics issues of protecting vulnerable subjects from harm. Paul Ramsey, Leon Kass, and others addressed the ethical issues of pre-embryonic interventions at length in the early 1970s.* These re-

views followed on the heels of major breakthroughs in direct visualization and culturing of the human ova. By 1970, sufficient control of the fertilization process made the prospects for reimplantation of the fertilized ovum possible from a technical viewpoint.

In 1971, British researchers Robert Edwards and David Sharpe concluded in their essay "Social Values and Research in Human Embryology" (*Nature* 231 [May 14, 1971], 87-91), that the moral issues were largely secondary to the technical triumph of overcoming culturing

*See especially Leon R. Kass, "Babies by Means of In Vitro Fertilization: Unethical Experiments on the Unborn," *New England Journal of Medicine* 285: 1174-79, 1971; and Paul Ramsey, "Shall We 'Reproduce?' " *Journal of the American Medical Association* 220: 1346-50; 1480-85, 1972.

difficulties for human eggs. They and other experimental embryologists argued that it was simply a matter of time until the first human was born as a result of successful reimplantation. While Kass and Ramsey decried the "therapeutic" justifications for such procedures and stressed that the experimentation was nonconsensual (for the fetus), the research community generally disregarded their pronouncements as "uninformed" and naive moralizing.

The researchers failed to take account of a mounting public revulsion over fetal research generally. In the face of formal opposition, most notabably a 1972 *JAMA* editorial calling for a moratorium, and a 1975 HEW regulation prohibiting federal funding of such experiments unless approved by a national ethics advisory board, the efforts of the American research community toward in vitro fertilization were curtailed or at least redirected toward less volatile areas of human embryological studies.

Not so in England. There, if we are to believe newspaper accounts, numerous attempts at in vitro fertilization and reimplantation were made—but failed. And now, we have living proof of the first bona fide example of a successful reimplantation and birth.

The ethical considerations that Ramsey and Kass raised against in vitro experimentation were based on acknowledging the worth of potential human life, and respecting the absolute right of the unborn child to the voluntary consent to experimentation. Both adhered to the dictum that "We cannot ethically get to know how to do this procedure."

This reservation was obviously disregarded in England. Edwards and Patrick Steptoe, a gynecologist, defended the propriety of their work with naturalistic arguments, and generally did not ascribe any "rights" to the early embryo. Edwards argued (with some justification) that the early embryo is a wholly resilient and malleable subject, only distantly related in complexity and sentiency to the human form it will become nine months hence. The "subject" did not warrant special protections because it was not yet a *person* in the whole sense. "Risks" at this stage were considered minimal if not nonexistent.

Thus, both Edwards and Steptoe, and presumably Landrum Shettles (the prin-

cipal physician in the Del Zio case) felt justified in not observing any of the normal maxims of human experimentation, that is, perfecting the technique on closely related animals before trying them on humans. Soon-to-be-human "subjects" were thus not formally conferred rights of protection afforded other humans who participate in experimental procedures because they did not, in this view, deserve such protection.

Protecting Vulnerable Subjects

Irrespective of the standing that we legally or morally confer on the human embryo, we *have* acknowledged its vulnerability and I believe we must act accordingly. And it is at precisely this junction that the Del Zio and Brown events point directly to the ethical issue of risk-taking generally.

The original purposes of perfecting in vitro techniques—to study the physiology and maturation of critical organ systems, and to understand the processes where development goes wrong (teratogenesis), have been largely abandoned by these latter-day efforts to put technological innovation directly into clinical practice. And it is here that a major ethical omission has occurred.

Whatever we may say about the propriety of the aborted experiment in the Del Zio case (and here I must add that the defense's only morally tenable line of argument was that Dr. Vande Wiele acted in the interests of protecting the health and welfare of Mrs. Del Zio in disrupting the procedure), the fact remains that the potential risks to the as-yet-to-be developed human embryo were ignored. The decision of *when* to begin treating a potential person as a person is at the hub of this and every other argument pertaining to procreative decision making, from abortion to the locus of responsibility for fetal alcohol syndrome. While it is true that the *early* ovum and fertilized egg are resilient to interventions of this sort, this is not the case once development has moved forward toward organogenesis. And it is at this point in embryonic development (some two to four weeks after fertilization) that I would argue that its claims on us for protection originate.

Full recognition of the scope of the risks to prenatal life from maternal exposure to an extraordinary array of sub-

stances, chemicals, and drugs in the environment is still unfolding. And recognition of the extent to which these sources of external agencies contribute to mild and profound birth defects remains unknown, but with the recent recognition that even very small amounts of alcohol (perhaps as little as one or two drinks a day) pose a hazard to fetal development, we cannot be sanguine about the safety of the fetus.

It can be argued that as long as we do not provide guidance to help an informed public minimize the impact of potentially harmful agents during pregnancy, it is inconsistent to hold experimenters accountable for potentially risk-laden experiments. This is of course morally wrong: we do not allow the failure to act responsibly in one area to mitigate our responsibility in another. For instance, the drug companies, and secondarily the medical profession were seriously derelict in their responsibility to protect human life when they allowed diethylstilbestrol (DES) to be widely used on pregnant women in the late 1940s and early 1950s without first determining its teratogenic and carcinogenic hazards, even though review of such hazards was not yet mandated.

Limits on the Right to Procreate

These examples underscore a key task: to define the limits that can be placed on the expression of the human desire to procreate based solely on the need to have offspring. Here, it seems to me, the salient variables are the parents' intent and willingness to accept the burden of custodial care of upbringing should an infant be deformed or retarded, weighed against the acceptability of *knowingly* exposing a vulnerable, and obviously nonconsensual subject, to unknown risks.

In both instances, I have felt, along with Hans Jonas, that absolute vulnerability demands absolute protection. If a pregnancy cannot be conceived without possible risk to the fetus, then the parent has an absolute responsibility to ensure that he or she has taken reasonable steps toward protecting the fetus from those risks. Right now, of course, we tolerate violation of that norm all the time. Parents at risk for serious genetic disease or defect in their offspring are not expressly forbidden from procreating, nor is there any social sanction, explicit or otherwise, to prevent them

6

from doing so. Nor de we discourage pro-fertility interventions like ovulation-inducing hormonal treatments that have the likelihood of producing multiple births, and the resultant risk of prematurity and respiratory distress in the offspring.

We know only that a handful of fertilized eggs (perhaps as few as 40 to 50 percent) actually successfully implant and go to term. Who shall be responsible for monitoring and intervening in the rescue of those which *nature* condemns to failure? And in the past where we have placed a hand in the womb, we have caused more havoc than we have prevented—with the notable exception of the Rh-incompatible pregnancies. In the end we must admit that we have no overall policy on risk-taking for the unborn that would indict Mrs. Del Zio for undertaking, or Dr. Vande Wiele for subverting, the conception of an embryo at risk for defect or early death.

Perhaps we should take the Del Zio case as an example, not so much of human foible and dashed hopes, but as an instance of human hubris, where through our overreaching we set the stage for potential tragedy in the birth of a defective child, and in averting that tragedy, created another.

The lessons of the Del Zio case are thus valuable in what they tell us about our general failure to accord respect for the unborn rather what it reveals of the misery of a single person. The utility of these lessons will depend on recognizing that they are but a small subsample of the larger ethical issues in our overall failure to acknowledge responsibility for protecting the unborn from the hazards of the first nine months of life.

In this sense, the Del Zio and Brown cases reveal our continuing fascination with the bizarre at the expense of the everyday realities of human suffering. I feel that it is not at the fringes of life and death where the ethical dilemmas of human existence are played out, but at the *center*. There life unfolding in all its mystery is confronted by all too many untoward events as a result of the human drive to control nature.

MARC LAPPÉ, PH.D., *is Chief, Office of Planning and Evaluation, California State Department of Health Services, and former Associate for Genetics at The Hastings Center.*

4 In Vitro Conception and Harm to the Unborn
by JOHN A. ROBERTSON

The recent birth of Louise Brown raises the question of whether society ought to permit willing couples and doctors to use in vitro fertilization to overcome infertility. Although no law currently prohibits use of in vitro fertilization as a treatment for infertility, DHEW regulations prohibit institutions receiving federal research funds for conducting research involving implantation of human ova, unless the Ethics Advisory Board determines its "ethical acceptability." While further study is needed, ethical questions about this research seem less salient now that the technique has apparently produced a healthy baby.

Two justifications have been asserted for restricting in vitro conception as a means to relieve infertility. It is said that extra-utero conception, though not in itself harmful, might move us toward total artificial manipulation of reproduction, ending in Huxley's dehumanized hatcheries, where babies are "decanted" from bottles with predetermined characteristics. The problem of technologizing natural processes, however, is not unique to reproductive advances; it arises with most new biomedical capabilities, and appears no more a ground for restriction here than elsewhere. The slope may not be as slippery as feared—we can employ in vitro conception without also producing clones in artificial wombs. Moreover, practices antithetical to our values might, when they finally occur, be acceptable to future generations with very different value systems from our own.

The second justification asserts that relieving infertility through in vitro conception is morally impermissible because of the greater risk that the implanted cells will abort or produce defective children. In my view, this argument does not withstand scrutiny, and is therefore not a sufficient moral or legal ground for banning the procedure, though it would justify regulation to minimize the frequency of such outcomes.

This argument could be viewed as a plea for distributive justice for the aborted fetuses and deformed children resulting from these procedures. They bear significant burdens, without consent, in order to confer the benefits of parenthood on childless couples who cannot otherwise conceive. Generally, heavy burdens may not be imposed without consent or overriding justification. But consent is absent, and though relief of infertility is a worthy goal, it is insufficient to justify the suffering of aborted fetuses and deformed children. Treating them justly means that we must treat them as we treat other nonconsenting, incompetent persons, and must prohibit the use of procedures that harm them.

As a claim for distributive justice for aborted fetuses, the argument seems plainly insufficient, unless one believes that abortion is generally wrong. If one believes that pregnant women should have wide discretion to decide whether to abort, then the higher risk of spontaneous or induced abortion from in vitro conception techniques is not a sufficient reason for banning them. Public policy currently grants the pregnant woman autonomy over the abortion decision. She may override the interests of the fetus, at least until viability, for any reason she chooses. The state can no more stop women from conceiving because they might abort and hence harm fetal interests, than it can

7

stop abortion altogether. Given the current state of the law, a higher risk that fetuses conceived ex utero will abort should not preclude infertile women from conceiving by the only means available to them.

Prevention of Harm to Offspring

Prevention of harm to a deformed offspring, however, seems a more persuasive argument, for parents free to abort fetuses may not harm children. The parents, it is said, are a direct cause of the deformed child's suffering, because they choose to conceive in a manner that risks producing a deformed child. On utilitarian grounds these burdens cannot be justified, because the suffering of the child who lacks capacity for normal development and interaction is so much greater than the suffering of a couple who must remain barren.

The utilitarian argument seemed especially compelling while in vitro techniques remained experimental and the risk of deformity appeared great. If the magnitude and probability of deformity lessen as more babies are born, this argument loses force. As the teratogenic effects of the procedure decrease and prenatal detection of defective fetuses increases, the resulting satisfaction to parents made fertile may well outweigh the suffering of infants born deformed from in vitro conception.

But opposition to in vitro conception because of harm to offspring rests more on a deontological or rights position, than on a utilitarian calculus of burdens and benefits. On Kantian principles of respect for persons, the imposition of burdens without consent to benefit others is prima facie wrong, even if net utility is increased. Knowingly risking a deformed birth violates the right of the child, for it imposes harm without its consent, whether or not others are greatly benefited.

Both the utilitarian and rights position seem misconceived, however, for it is unclear how the deformed child has been harmed. At the time of the in vitro conception, there was no child with rights that could be violated. The parents have not caused a child who would otherwise be normal to be born defective, for there is no child to be harmed aside from the very act creating the risk of harm. The act creating the risk of injury also brings about the very being that is said to be injured. But for that act, the child would never have existed at all. From the child's

perspective, the only alternative to the action that allegedly violates his right not to be harmed is even less desirable, for it means no existence at all. One does not respect a person's rights by refraining from an activity that prevents his existence altogether.

It is difficult to escape the conclusion, shared by the courts in "wrongful life" cases, that a non-normal child has no cause of action against persons causing the abnormality if the alternative to their action is no life at all. On this view, human existence, however imperfect, is in most cases to the individual involved, preferable to nonexistence. Children deformed as a result of in vitro techniques at least are alive, and unless their lives are full of incessant pain, they are better off than if they were never conceived at all. The couple's choice of procreative technique thus does not violate the child's rights, and should not be banned on that ground. Indeed, under *Roe* v. *Wade*, such concern would not amount to the compelling state interest necessary to justify interference with procreative choice.

An opposite conclusion would, in other situations, lead to results that clearly do violate the rights of deformed persons. If it is better that such children not be born at all, rather than be born with less than full capacities, then it follows that once born, such persons would be better off dead than alive. Killing them would then be morally justified (or obligatory) as a means to promote their interests, for life in their condition is said to justify preventing their birth altogether. Most of us would recoil in horror at such a practice. Rather than serve their interests, killing deformed persons to save them from the suffering of a life with handicaps would, except in the rare case of irremediable suffering, be an intolerable violation of their rights, which the criminal law would punish.

This conclusion would also lead to intolerable results in the case of a couple who are heterozygote carriers of a genetic defect not diagnosable prenatally and who knowingly decide to take the one-in-four risk of conceiving a deformed child; in the case of a thirty-eight-year-old woman who rejects prenatal diagnosis for Down syndrome because she is morally opposed to abortion; and in the case of the pregnant woman exposed to rubella who also refuses to have an abortion. Have they

violated any right of the child who is born deformed, when the only alternative would have been no child at all? Does the risk of deformity justify depriving them of the chance to procreate? The logic of the argument against in vitro conception necessarily encompasses these cases as well. If the state may ban in vitro conception to prevent possible harm to resulting offspring, it may also require sterilization, amniocentesis, or abortion to prevent deformed births in other situations. Yet procreative autonomy in those other situations seems essential. No morally relevant ground distinguishes in vitro conception.

Opposition to in vitro conception because of possible harm to the offspring may stem in part from a perception that couples resorting to in vitro techniques callously sacrifice the interests of potential offspring in order to improve their own lot. But children born deformed from such procedures do not suffer alone. A couple plagued by infertility will also suffer greatly if in vitro conception yields a deformed birth. They have every incentive to minimize that possibility, for the burden on them is also great. As the risk of serious deformity increases, infertile couples will be reluctant to use these procedures. A choice to take that risk might involve love for the desired child as much as self-interest.

In any event, the state may regulate in vitro conception to minimize the frequency of abnormal births, even though it may not ban in vitro techniques altogether. Doctors who perform these procedures without informed consent, without a high degree of skill, or without exhausting other medical options, can be made legally liable. The state may encourage alternative methods of satisfying desires for parenthood, or choose not to fund the research necessary to make in vitro procedures more widely available. But it should not ban the use by willing, informed parties as a last resort to overcome infertility due to oviduct blockage, on the ground that a defective child may suffer who would not exist at all but for use of that technique.

JOHN A. ROBERTSON *is associate professor, University of Wisconsin Law School, and Program in Medical Ethics, University of Wisconsin Medical School.*

8

In Vitro Fertilization: 'Ethically Acceptable' Research

by MARGARET O'BRIEN STEINFELS

On March 16, 1979, the Ethics Advisory Board concluded that, with certain constraints, research on in vitro fertilization and embryo transfer (popularly referred to as test-tube babies) is ethically acceptable. The Board's recommendations to HEW Secretary Joseph Califano were the culmination of a long debate, involving: several years of discussion in scholarly and professional journals; a 1975 ban on government funding of such research on humans; the work of the National Commission for the Protection of Human Subjects on fetal research; and five months of hearings by the Ethics Advisory Board itself in ten cities. And then, of course, there was the catalytic event: the successful implantation by English researchers, Patrick Steptoe and Robert Edwards, of an egg fertilized in vitro and the subsequent birth of Louise Brown on July 25, 1978.

The thirteen-member Ethics Advisory Board, composed of seven physicians, two lawyers, one businessman, a member of a philanthropic organization, a philosopher, and a religious ethicist first took up the subject in September 1978.* In inviting testimony and holding public hearings across the country, the Board facilitated a wide-ranging public discussion—far more than with most research and medical issues—on in vitro fertilization and the transfer of the embryo to the mother's uterus. Its final report discusses the technical, ethical, legal, and public policy aspects of in vitro fertilization and embryo transfer and ends with five recommendations, stated in the form of conclusions (see box, p. 7). Although the conclusions are advisory and Secretary Califano can accept, reject, or modify them, it is probable that they will set the framework for whatever regulations are written, for any legislation that is passed, and for the kinds of practices that will evolve in the private

MARGARET O'BRIEN STEINFELS *is editor of the Hastings Center Report.*

sector. In fact, the Board expressed the hope that its general conclusions would "provide guidance to Institutional Review Boards and other groups who are asked to review research that will not be supported by HEW. . . ."

The Board's Deliberations

Following its five months of hearings, the Board began its own discussion on February 21 and agreed on a final draft at its March meeting. Perhaps the Board's final conclusions can best be understood by describing the two points returned to again and again in the two-day discussion in February.** First, the Board explicitly assumed that in vitro fertilization and embryo transfer is an inevitable step in the treatment of infertility. Apparently the many infertile couples who wrote to or testified before the Board conveyed the message that they were determined people, ready and willing to face any risk in order to have genetic offspring. This intensity of feeling was reinforced by the view of some Board members that private physicians were ready to carry out the procedure. In sum, there was no stopping therapeutic use in the private sector.

Second, the Board recognized that in vitro fertilization would further aggravate the debate over abortion now looming large in both the medical and political worlds. The abortion question might be

---

*Members: James C. Gaither, a San Francisco attorney, chairman; David A. Hamburg, president, Institute of Medicine, co-chairman; Henry W. Foster, Meharry Medical College; Donald A. Henderson, Johns Hopkins School of Hygiene and Public Health; Robert F. Murray, Howard University College of Medicine; Mitchell W. Spellman, Harvard Medical School; Daniel C. Tosteson, Harvard Medical School; Eugene M. Zweiback, Omaha, Nebraska, a physician; Sissela Bok, Harvard University, an ethicist; Richard A. McCormick, Kennedy Institute, Center for Bioethics; Jack T. Conway, United Way of America; Maurice Lazarus, Federated Department Stores, Inc.; and Agnes N. Williams, a lawyer.

**This information and the quotes that follow are drawn from a transcript of the meeting.

raised early in the procedure when unused fertilized eggs might be discarded or later when prenatal diagnosis might reveal a defective infant. Testimony to that effect signalled the potentially divisive political effects of federal funding for in vitro fertilization research, including a possible replay of the Hyde Amendment debate that ended in cutting Medicaid funds for abortion.

Mindful, perhaps, of the fact that ten years of ethical objections to in vitro fertilization and embryo transfer had not carried the argument against the procedure's development, the Board paid relatively little attention to the issues that have dominated the ethical discussion. The moral status of the fetus was cited as among the major difficulties the Board had to face, and there was a review of significant points in embryologic and fetal development at which lines against research might be drawn. Nonetheless, quite early in the discussion, the Board set aside that question. Similarly, what have been called "soft ethical issues" received almost no attention. For example, those that Leon Kass enumerated in his testimony: family bonds, lineage, and self-identity; total gestation outside the uterus; genetic manipulation; and commercial storage and banking of human ova and embryos. (*Public Interest*, Winter 1979, pp. 32-60.)

Although never phrased in these words, the Board's dominant quesion then became: how can determined couples be protected from unknown risks in undertaking in vitro fertilization without recommending public funds for research and clinical trials? Proceeding in the manner of a body that hopes to reach a consensus, the Board both acknowledged and finessed the issues on which it could not agree by careful attention to the wording of its conclusions.

Risks

It is very difficult to assess the risks of the procedure. Drs. Steptoe and Edwards have not yet published the data on their work and had declined an invitation to appear before the Board to discuss it. In an effort to learn more about the technical details the Board asked Professor R.V. Short (Director, Reproductive Biology Unit, University of Edinburgh), to prepare a summary of the presentation Steptoe and Edwards made at a meeting of the Royal College of Obstetricians on January 26, 1979.

His report raised the hope that the Steptoe/Edwards technique might resolve some ethical problems; if their method involved the fertilization of only one egg and its transfer as it seemed in their later attempts, undue manipulation or discard of unused, fertilized eggs might be avoided. On the other hand, the relatively large number of women (68) who underwent an even larger number of operations to retrieve ripe eggs contrasted with the small number of successful births (2), underlining the need for caution. Nor did the Board seem reassured by the nonscientific manner in which Steptoe and Edwards had presented and discussed their data. Dr. Eugene Zweiback remarked, "This is the most underwhelming piece of scientific data that I've ever seen. . . . if this is the tome on which the world is going to embark upon their clinical applications, I think we must be aware of that. . . . More questions are unanswered than are answered."

Out of that concern came the subsequent discussion of risk, first to the child and then to the couple. Since the risk question could not be answered with the technical information available, the Board recommended support of animal research (Conclusion 1) and the systematic collection, analysis, and dissemination of information on in vitro fertilization (Conclusion 4). In recommending that HEW should "consider support" of animal research, including nonhuman primates, the Board hypothesized that problems of safety, efficacy, and long-term adverse effects in humans might become apparent, although it recognized that therapeutic application in humans was likely to go on whether or not animal studies were done, and that the expense and difficulty of animal research, especially in nonhuman primates, might make it prohibitive.

Clearly, neither animal research nor data collection will give a reasonably quick answer to the harder questions: would anything in the fertilization and transfer process increase the likelihood of defective offspring? Would natural screening

and spontaneous abortion work in the same way as in a normally conceived pregnancy? Or would induced abortions become more likely? Were there long-term developmental and physical consequences for individual children conceived by the in vitro method? What might be the physical and psychological risks to the mother? Would there be increasing disrespect or coldness toward human life as the result of discarding fertilized eggs or developing embryos? Given all these risks—most of them unknown—how could couples be adequately informed of problems they might face?

Given that the Board's assignment came from HEW, this range of questions about risk was translated into the immediate, practical one: does the department and the government have a responsibility to protect infertile couples who are willing to undergo any degree of risk to have a genetic offspring? Does it have a duty, as well, to protect potential offspring?

Risk of the procedure, risk to the couple, and risk to the possible child underscored the importance of good research and adequate controlled clinical trials. Obviously, carrying out such a responsibility entails further research on in vitro fertilization. But how far does the government's responsibility, if any, extend? Simply making information of known risks available? Or supporting clinical trials to assure impartial and accurate information? But this would require government funding, which could put the government on a collision course with anti-abortion groups.

Separating the Questions

At this point a number of important distinctions were made. Professor Richard McCormick suggested that the question of in vitro fertilization be distinguished both from the question of government funding and from the priority such research ought to receive, if it is funded. Thus, for example, the Board might conclude that research on in vitro fertilization could proceed but recommend that, because of the objections of many citizens, government funds ought not support it.

As to the status of the embryo, the two ethicists on the Board joined in arguing, in McCormick's words, that "when we have doubts about the claims that human life makes upon us, we must give life the benefit, as a general rule." Professor Sissela Bok seconded that comment and went

on to articulate a set of distinctions that coincided with McCormick's concerns.

She suggested that different ethical stances might be taken when fertilization was followed by transfer and when it was not. Respect for life is more clearly seen when in vitro fertilization is coupled with embryo transfer, because an infertile couple is being helped to have a child. A defensible end or purpose of fertilization without transfer is not so clear because the intent is to discard or manipulate the fertilized egg or embryo.

Other members of the Board expressed greater support of fertilization with transfer than without: "I have less difficulty . . . pursuing . . . in vitro fertilization and transfer within the context of the husband-wife situation with an objective to achieve a normal child . . . I come down on the side of extreme reservation in the research area." But the concern about risk once again asserted itself. Dr. Zweiback:

I would go along with [Professor Bok] 100 percent if I was absolutely certain that in vitro fertilization with transfer was a very safe procedure. . . . But I cannot convince myself based upon the data that is available that it is truly so safe that I could recommend it . . . to a barren woman. . . . Perhaps in vitro fertilization without transfer is a logical step towards convincing myself and many other people that it is, indeed, a safe procedure. . . . I think for us to go and sanction fertilization with transfer and at the same time sanction against fertilization, per se, might indeed be hazardous to some people.

The tensions between the ethicists and other board members on the issues of respecting early human embryos and supporting research was clearly delineated in remarks by Dr. David Hamburg.

Much of the discussion . . . has revolved [around] a basic value of our society, the sanctity of life. I find myself genuinely perplexed, deeply perplexed, about how to apply that fundamental value in this context. . . .

One of the principal ways to advance the sanctity of life has been to understand more deeply the nature of life. Now when one comes to the question, to paraphrase that unfortunate officer in Vietnam, of destroying life in order to save it, we clearly draw the line in some fashion. We differ probably in what we mean by destroying lives, but there is a pretty broad consensus that we don't want to destroy life in order to deepen our understanding of it.

That brings us to another fundamental value about which I'm also perplexed . . . freedom of inquiry. . . . Obvious-ly, when it comes to applications, some applications are dangerous and some are less dangerous, and we have not been very discriminating about application. Our power today, of course, is greater for better and for worse than it has ever been in history, and the question of re-stricting freedom of inquiry in terms of this application is more vivid and poig-nant than it has ever been. But we have tended to hold the view, as a society, that this is another slippery slope, that is

From the Ethics Advisory Board's Final Report

SUMMARY

. . . In its deliberations on human *in vitro* fertilization, the Board confronted many ethical, scientific and legal issues.

A. After much analysis and discussion regarding both sci-entific data and the moral status of the embryo, the Board is in agreement that the human embryo is entitled to profound re-spect; but this respect does not necessarily encompass the full legal and moral rights attributed to persons. . . .

B. The Board is concerned about still unanswered ques-tions of safety for both mother and offspring of *in vitro* fertil-ization and embryo transfer; it is concerned, as well, about the health of the children born following such a procedure and about their legal status. Many women have told the Board that in order to bear a child of their own they will submit to what-ever risks are involved. The Board believes that while the De-partment should not interfere with such reproductive decisions, it has a legitimate interest in developing and dis-seminating information regarding safety and health. . . .

C. A number of fears have been expressed with regard to adverse effects of technological intervention in the reproduc-tive process. . . .

Although the Board recognizes that there is an opportunity for abuse in the application of this technology, it concluded that a broad prohibition of research involving human *in vitro* fertilization is neither justified nor wise. . . .

D. The question of Federal support of research involving human *in vitro* fertilization and embryo transfer was trouble-some for the Board in view of the uncertain risks, dangers of abuse and because funding the procedure is morally objec-tionable to many. In weighing these considerations, the Board noted that the procedures may soon be in use in the private sector and that Departmental involvement might help to re-solve questions of risk and avoid abuse by encouraging well-designed research by qualified scientists. . . .

CONCLUSIONS

CONCLUSION 1: The Department should consider support of carefully designed research involving in vitro fertilization and embryo transfer in animals, including nonhuman primates, in order to obtain a better understanding of the process of fertil-ization, implantation and embryo development, to assess the risks to both mother and offspring associated with such proce-dures, and to improve the efficacy of the procedure.

CONCLUSION 2: The Ethics Advisory Board finds that it is acceptable from an ethical standpoint to undertake research involving human in vitro fertilization and embryo transfer pro-vided that:

A. if the research involves human in vitro fertilization with-out embryo transfer, the following conditions are satis-fied:
1. the research complies with all appropriate provisions of the regulations governing research with human subjects (45 CFR 46);
2. the research is designed primarily: (A) to establish the safety and efficacy of embryo transfer and (B) to obtain important scientific information toward that end not reasonably attainable by other means;
3. human gametes used in such research will be ob-tained exclusively from persons who have been in-formed of the nature and purpose of the research in which such materials will be used and have specifi-cally consented to such use;
4. no embryos will be sustained in vitro beyond the stage normally associated with the completion of im-plantation (14 days after fertilization); and
5. all interested parties and the general public will be advised if evidence begins to show that the proce-dure entails risks of abnormal offspring higher than those associated with natural human reproduction.
B. in addition, if the research involves embryo transfer fol-lowing human in vitro fertilization, embryo transfer will be attempted only with gametes obtained from lawfully married couples.

CONCLUSION 3: The Board finds it acceptable from an ethi-cal standpoint for the Department to support or conduct re search involving human in vitro fertilization and embryo transfer, provided that the applicable conditions set forth in Conclusion 2 are met. However, the Board has decided not to address the question of the level of funding, if any, which such research might be given.

CONCLUSION 4: The National Institute of Child Health and Human Development (NICHD) and other appropriate agencies should work with professional societies, foreign governments and international organizations to collect, analyze and dissemi-nate information derived from research (in both animals and humans) and clinical experience throughout the world involv-ing in vitro fertilization and embryo transfer.

CONCLUSION 5: The Secretary should encourage the devel-opment of a uniform or model law to clarify the legal status of children born as a result of in vitro fertilization and embryo transfer. To the extent that funds may be necessary to develop such legislation, the Department should consider providing ap-propriate support.

to say, when you begin to restrict freedom of inquiry, you had better go very carefully.

The Board's final resolution of this deep-lying tension appears in the arduous formulation of Conclusions 2 and 3.

Reverting to the language of Secretary Califano's mandate, the Board found that "it is acceptable from an ethical standpoint to undertake research involving human in vitro fertilization and embryo transfer" under certain conditions (Conclusion 2); in addition the Board found "it acceptable from an ethical standpoint" for HEW to support such research (Conclusion 3).

"Acceptable from an ethical standpoint," in light of the Board's semantic clarifications, may mean both more and less than the words themselves suggest. The Board says: "This phrase is broad enough to include at least two interpretations: (1) 'clearly ethically right' or (2) 'ethically defensible but still legimately controverted'. . . . the Board is using the phrase in the second sense; . . . [and] wishes to emphasize that it is *not* finding that the ethical considerations against such research are insubstantial."

What does the Board mean by "ethically defensible"? Erudite treatises may ultimately clarify the matter. In the meantime, only questions can be raised about it. Does the Board mean that it has weighed the ethical arguments pro and con and found on balance that arguments in favor of in vitro research outweigh those against? It does not say so. What are the ethical considerations that make in vitro research ethically defensible? Is it protection of risk-assuming couples? The preponderance of the Board's deliberations would suggest so, but in concluding remarks, the Board writes, "where reproductive decisions are concerned, it is important to guard against unwarranted governmental intrusion into personal and marital privacy." But doesn't such a claim argue against both a protective and prohibitive role for government? Finally, has the Board, in using the phrase "ethically defensible," introduced a new criterion for analyzing ethical considerations in research, one that will be clarified only with further application?

These definitional problems notwithstanding, the Board went on in Conclusion 2 to set certain limiting conditions on human in vitro fertilization, (A) without embryo transfer (that is, when research would be primary), and (B) with embryo transfer (that is, when therapeutic application would be primary). These limiting conditions take account of the Board's view that "the human embryo is entitled to profound respect; but this respect does not necessarily encompass the full legal and moral rights attributed to persons." Thus such research must comply with the appropriate regulations governing research with human subjects and "no embryo will be sustained in vitro beyond the stage normally associated with the completion of implantation (14 days after fertilization)." When research on in vitro fertilization is to include embryo transfer the Board recommends that "embryo transfer . . . be attempted only with gametes obtained from lawfully married couples."

Conclusion 3 repeats the language of Conclusion 2: federal funding is acceptable from an ethical standpoint. However, the Board explicitly draws back from suggesting what level of funding, if any, such research should receive. By this strategem, the Board joined two concerns and left both to the political process: (1) the appropriateness of government funding in the face of ethical objections to in vitro fertilization research and (2) the priority in vitro fertilization research should hold when measured against competing needs. Yet having approved the research in the first place, the Board's thinking in Conclusion 3 seems to signal hesitation. But perhaps it is not so much hesitation as a political compromise by which the Board hopes to satisfy both proponents and opponents of the research. Proponents—researchers, physicians, and interested couples—can move ahead with the procedure; opponents will be satisfied with restrictions on government funding. The adoption of "Hyde amendment" strategies to avoid public conflict is certainly problematic, since it has not worked in the original instance; whether the Board was wise to do so with in vitro fertilization research remains to be seen.

Conclusion

The Board's task was not easy; nor are its conclusions likely to receive any award for cutting the Gordian knot of moral opposition to in vitro fertilization, government involvement in such research, and the strong desire for genetic offspring. Those who believe that in vitro fertilization and transfer is the first step toward human production in place of procreation are probably right in seeing nothing in the Board's conclusions or arguments that prevents the ultimate justification of surrogate mothers and the commercial banking of ova and, at some future date, of embryos. They are unlikely to share the Board's sanguine view that such development "may be contained by regulation or legislation. Other abuses may be avoided by the use of good judgment based upon accurate information. . . ."

On the other hand, those who believe that in vitro fertilization with embryo transfer is a logical and appropriate extension of medical therapy in the treatment of infertility will be unhappy about the Board's reluctance to endorse the procedure wholeheartedly and to urge federal support forthrightly, not only for research, but for therapeutic application in government-funded medical care programs. In the absence of funding, particularly for the poor, they will raise questions about the equal availability of a possibly useful therapy.

But, in addition to these substantive problems with the Board's conclusions, there is also a procedural issue. Is it appropriate for boards, such as the Ethics Advisory Board, when they are reviewing medical research, to be structured so that more than half of the members represent the medical and research community? The deliberations of this Ethics Advisory Board suggest that the "ethical questions" will be focused narrowly on those ethical issues that overlap with the concerns of researchers—in this case the problem of risk—to the exclusion of ethical or value issues that may be of concern to those outside the research community, for example, the "soft ethical issues" mentioned above or the increasing interventions in the process of human conception, gestation, and birth. Particularly if they are in the majority, the researchers' and physicians' ethical imperative—protect research subjects and patients from nonvalidated therapies—is likely to become the dominant imperative of the Board. But in the larger view, such an imperative is only one of many ethical considerations. Thus, one must ask whether a Board constituted largely of researchers and oriented to their ethical concerns can be relied upon to say "no" to research or whether they may not be overwhelmingly disposed to judge research as "ethically defensible" in the confusing way the Board has used that term.

In Vitro Fertilization:
Moving from Theory to Therapy
by FRANK H. MARSH and DONNIE J. SELF

On January 25, 1980, the nation's first therapeutic in vitro fertilization clinic received official sanction to commence its long-awaited operation. The state of Virginia issued a certificate of need authorizing Norfolk General Hospital to renovate space, enabling the Eastern Virginia Medical Authority to establish the clinic. The project had previously received approval from the Committee on Human Experimentation and Research of Eastern Virginia Medical School, after being the most closely scrutinized protocol ever processed by this institutional review board.

Two years have passed since the announcement by England's Patrick Steptoe of the birth of Louise Brown, the first of the "test-tube" babies. Since that time, philosophers, theologians, and others have debated the moral wisdom of in vitro fertilization. Their arguments, touching on a wide range of ethical issues such as the origins of life, experimentation, and sexual intimacy, have been either in support of or against the *concept* of in vitro fertilization itself. The actual methodology and criteria to be employed by a clinic, should the concept move to reality, has been largely examined and addressed only from a hypothetical "what if?" stance. The purpose of our article is to describe some aspects of the procedure being employed at the Norfolk Clinic as it moves ahead with therapeutic in vitro fertilization.

Medical Criteria for Patient Selection

The Norfolk Clinic's procedure includes not only highly sophisticated medical tech-

FRANK H. MARSH, J.D., PH.D., *is associate professor in the department of philosophy at Old Dominion University.*
DONNIE J. SELF, PH.D., *is associate professor in the department of family medicine at Eastern Virginia Medical School and the department of philosophy at Old Dominion University.*

nology, but a set of medical criteria for patient selection as well. At the Norfolk clinic, patient screening is an integral step in that selection. Thus, the initial screening of patients is seen not only as the first in a series of steps that will culminate in a successful pregnancy, but also as a necessary condition for carrying out the medical procedure.

The development of the criteria for patient selection has presented difficulties from medical, ethical, and legal viewpoints and will probably continue to do so because of what patients are requesting. For example, the screening is presently restricted to married couples, although discussions of potential scenarios involving single women and surrogate mothers have occurred.

Initially, the patient selection was to focus solely on those women who demonstrated fallopian tube demise because of any of a variety of medical complications such as pelvic inflammatory disease, bilateral salpingectomy after ectopic pregnancies, tuboplasty failure or unsuccessful tubal reanastomosis, congenital aplasia or hypoplasia of the fallopian tubes, or women with any other malfunctions that impair the normal physiology in transporting the oocyte from the ovary to the endometrial cavity.

However, due to the very nature of the treatment being proposed, it was felt that consideration in patient selection should include the husband as well, since the clinic was dealing with infertile couples. The man can have medical dysfunctions that contribute to the infertile state of a couple, and these dysfunctions were recognized as valid reasons to consider him in the screening process.

Ethical factors for including the father-to-be were just as important. The demands of confidentiality and informed consent required that the "patient" mean a married couple. The current criteria were developed for the couple. They are:

1. The couple must be both childless and married. The medical history must demonstrate clearly that there is no other possibility of achieving pregnancy by any other medically known means. In addition to the medical history, the couple must also demonstrate a stable marriage to the satisfaction of the attending physician. The latter condition is considered to be exclusively a clinical judgment and not a moral judgment.

2. Both the husband and the wife must be generally healthy and pass general physical examinations.

3. The woman must have a normal uterus and her ovaries must be accessible for the laparoscopic procedure.

4. There must be normal endocrine function and normal menstrual function.

5. The wife must be under thirty-five years of age, and at least twenty-five years of age. The best available medical evidence today indicates that normal fertility decreases significantly after age thirty-five. The rationale here is to assist the normal physiological function and to reduce difficulties and risks that are associated with pregnancies where the woman is over thirty-five years of age.

6. The couple must be able to pay for the treatment. The estimated cost of the procedure ($4,000) is not covered at present by most medical insurance programs. In fact, it has been expressly excluded by Blue Cross in the state of Virginia.

7. The couple must suffer from any one of the following dysfunctions:

a. Nonfunctioning fallopian tubes for any reason;

b. Infertility due to oligospermia (low sperm count, that is, below 20 million per ml.) The normal sperm count is in the range of 50-60 million per ml. Over 1 million couples suffer involuntary infertility due to oligospermic husbands. At present, it appears that it requires no more than 50,000 sperm to fertilize an egg in vitro: considerably less may even be sufficient. (This is in contrast to artificial insemination, which requires a larger than normal count.) In vitro fertilization should have significant application to oligospermia.

Hastings Center Report, June 1980

Furthermore, it may be the least complicated and most applicable area in that the women will generally have normal pelvises and readily accessible ovaries for laparoscopy.

c. "Hostile cervical mucus" syndrome, a condition in which the woman possesses antibodies or other unknown substances that interfere and render sperm inactive. Theoretically, a tube with a protective sheath could penetrate the mucus of the cervix so that when the protective sheath is withdrawn the tube containing the embryo for transplantation can then deliver the embryo directly into the uterus uncontaminated by the "hostile cervical mucus." Though it affects only a small percentage of patients, in vitro fertilization would be an extremely useful procedure to have available for them.

d. Normal infertility. This class—about 15 percent of all infertile couples—includes those in whom no identifiable cause of infertility can be discovered.

The Therapeutic Techniques

Through March 1980, a significant number of couples from among thousands inquiring have been selected as patients and are currently undergoing treatment at the Norfolk Clinic. Of these, several women have actually undergone the in vitro procedures. However, it should be noted that the clinic is a general fertility clinic, and the procedures are not restricted solely to in vitro fertilization. Other procedures are being pursued, such as in vivo fertilization, tubal surgery, AIH (artificial insemination husband), and AID (artificial insemination donor), treatment of endocrine disorders, and many other types of infertility treatment.

The in vitro method has been refined from that previously reported in the literature in that, rather than multiple oocytes or egg cells, a *single* oocyte is removed by laparoscopic technique and fertilized. This refinement eliminates superovulation, which results in the retrieval of many egg cells and causes hormonal imbalances and disrupted menstrual cycles. From an ethical viewpoint, the taking of a single oocyte responds in part to the arguments previously raised against selecting of eggs and discarding surplus embryos.

Briefly, the in vitro method followed at the clinic is: a single oocyte is removed by laparoscopic technique from an ovary. This egg cell is placed in a culture dish to which the sperm from the woman's husband are added. Here the fertilization takes place. Incubation occurs externally for about 36 to 48 hours until the embryo is in the 8-to-16 cell stage of development. At the time the 8-to-16 cell stage is reached, the embryo is placed through the cervix into the woman's uterus. The placing of the embryo into the uterus requires no anesthesia and presents virtually no risk to the woman.

The in vivo technique is identical to that of the in vitro technique with regard to egg cell retrieval. But then the single unfertilized ovum is immediately placed directly into the uterus for fertilization in vivo. The couple is instructed to have intercourse several hours just prior to the egg retrieval and transfer, so that sperm will be present in the uterus at the time of transfer, and to have intercourse again immediately following the procedure.

Only one public report has appeared on the progress of any of the women being treated at the clinic. This report, issued by the patient, indicated that an unsuccessful effort had been made to retrieve an egg and that no further attempts would be made. Whether any of the other implantations have been successful remains confidential. It is, however, expected that positive results will be announced at some point when a pregnancy is far enough along. However, if such reports are made, the couple probably will make the report themselves, for the medical school and hospital have a strict policy of not commenting on the details of work in progress. Since the women being treated may return to the prenatal care of their own obstetricians/gynecologists, the control of confidentiality will rest largely with the patient.

In setting up criteria for the screening procedure, the Norfolk Clinic was faced with another delicate subject—whether or not the woman should be required to accept amniocentesis. This issue was resolved by allowing the patient to choose, and thus removing what would have seemed to be a coercive step.

No doubt as more applicants are screened, other issues and problems will appear. Is it fair to exclude unmarried couples or single women from the procedure? If so, what particular place does marriage hold with in vitro fertilization that it does not seem to hold with "natural" pregnancies? The financial requirements also raise a difficult issue. Is a childless couple to be denied treatment simply because they can not afford it? An interesting comparison could be made here to the federal funding of Medicaid abortions. If in vitro fertilization is to be included within the concept of health care delivery rather than that of research, a host of other ethical questions will be raised about costs and payments.

As other clinics are set up around the country, they will undoubtedly look to the Norfolk experience for guidance—in both the medical technology and the ethical dimensions of in vitro fertilization, although it is not yet clear that all the appropriate questions have even been asked.

Case Studies in Bioethics

Case No. 540

A thirty-two-year-old California woman, Joan Travis, and her husband, David, had tried for over two years to have a baby. After seven months on a fertility drug, Mrs. Travis became pregnant and thereafter gave birth to six infants at Santa Clara hospital. The delivery was normal, but none of the babies survived more than eight days.

Mr. Travis participated in a group health insurance program through his employer. The policy normally pays for delivery and medical care of newborns, and the insurance carrier paid the hospital bill, which came to more than $50,000.

The cost of the delivery and subsequent care will cause an increase in premiums to all members of Mr. Travis's group health insurance plan next year. Because it is a joint employer-employee program, both will share the burden. His employer plans to pass on the additional cost by raising premiums. Nevertheless, Mrs. Travis maintains that she will take the same drug again in another attempt to have a child. Do the Travis's have a moral obligation to avoid taking a risk which would increase the insurance premiums of Mr. Travis and his co-workers? Does the insurance company have a moral obligation to pay the costs for the voluntarily assumed risk? Does every couple have the right to bear children, regardless of the cost to society?

Do couples have the right to bear children at any cost?

Baby Making and the Public Interest

by THEODORE TSUKAHARA, JR.

Group health insurance operates on the principle of risk pooling. Premium rates are based on the average risk profile of the group membership rather than on the specific risks faced by particular members. The scope of benefits, the size of the group, and the demographic characteristics of the members are factors which influence the premium calculations.

The inclusion of maternity benefits in a group policy is usually very expensive, especially if there are significant numbers of younger members in the group. The probability that maternity claims will be made against the insurance pool is very large. Thus, premiums paid by older members will reflect the higher risk of maternity claims even though the likelihood that they will require this coverage is very small. The economic effect is that older members bear part of the medical costs of younger members who will become parents.

In order to establish some measure of equity in access to the group insurance pool, normally some limitations are imposed on benefit payments. Typically, medical claims which arise from a previously existing medical condition will be subject to some restriction. For example, most policies would exclude payment for infertility treatment on that principle. Because individual decisions can affect the risks faced by individuals for particular benefits, it is important to include restrictions in group policies where the premiums are not tailored to risks individuals are willing to assume privately. Otherwise, some individuals will overconsume benefits and cause a real transfer of resources from others to them in the form of higher premium payments for all.

Most group health insurance programs recognize that the decision to have children is properly viewed as a private choice. To provide full insurance coverage for maternity-related medical expenses would give couples with a strong desire for large families an economic incentive to exercise their preference at the expense of couples with opposite tastes. Therefore, most policies attempt to be neutral and to provide coverage only for complications which arise from pregnancy which requires extraordinary medical intervention such as surgery. Maternity coverage is thus limited to the incremental costs over the amount required for a normal delivery. However, the Travis's insurance program did cover care for newborns and the company had a legal obligation to pay the hospital bill.

Joan and David have exhibited an intense desire to become parents. I assume their initial decision to undergo treatment for infertility was made after a complete discussion with their physician about the risks associated with the drug. In particular, I assume they were fully aware of the potential for multiple pregnancies and the associated reduction in the probability of survival of any newborns; I assume further that David was aware of the limited coverage provided by his group insurance program. Their decision to proceed without additional insurance indicates their willingness to accept the full psychological and economic costs of their decision.

In spite of their tragic losses, Joan and David are determined to try again to become parents. Even if the insurance company was obligated to make payments the first time, there appears to be a flaw in the group policy which must be rectified in order to protect the other members of the insurance pool from another large outlay on behalf of the Travis's. The policy must be rewritten.

In economic theory the absence of insurance for a risky choice is an example of market failure. The usual remedy is for the government to provide the required insurance. Thus, if Joan and David cannot insure against the possible financial losses which may result because no insurance is available, then economic justice suggests that they be assisted in coping with any financial losses that might arise. If insurance is available and they choose not to insure, then the Travis's should be responsible for any financial consequences resulting from their decision. They could argue that they could not afford the premiums. This information, however, should signal to them the magnitude of the risks associated with their desire for a child. Since Joan and David stand to gain directly from the joys of parenthood, they should· also be prepared to bear their fair share of the costs.

THEODORE TSUKAHARA, JR. *is associate professor of economics at Pomona College and Claremont Graduate School, Claremont, California.*

by SEYMOUR SIEGEL

The case of Mr. and Mrs. Travis involves one of the basic human rights —the right to bear children. This right is an integral part of our humanity, an expression of the innate desire to perpetuate the race and to somehow mitigate the threat of our mortality. The cry of Rachael (Gen 1:28)— "Give me children or I will die"—is a poignant expression of the fundamental importance of children to human existence. This consciousness is being altered in some circles today. However compelling the arguments concerning the threat of overpopulation, the shortage of economic means, the liberation of women—the basic thrust of human nature to contribute to the future remains powerful.

One of the purposes of governments and communal organization is to protect basic human rights. Governments are instituted among men to help us pursue happiness. There is no doubt that for the vast majority of mankind the opportunity to bear children is indispensable for the pursuit of happiness. Therefore, the community has a responsibility to make responsible parenthood possible.

In our age of astronomical medical care costs, governments and the com-

This factual case study is one of a series demonstrating ethical dilemmas in medicine and the life sciences. The series, "Case Studies in Bioethics," is selected and prepared by Robert M. Veatch.

munity have the responsibility to assure that parents can have children by guaranteeing that financial needs in connection with the birth will be met. There is no sure way of knowing in advance the precise amount of these costs. Some parents will require less; others much more. An insurance plan is a contract in which all parties involved are obligated to help the other individuals in the agreement to realize their legitimate health goals.

It is clear that the Travises will not be able to realize their aspiration to be parents unless they can have some assurances that economic barriers will not prevent their having children. It seems that their plea is: give us some assurance that if there are inordinate charges related to the birth of our children, we will be helped to pay, or we will have to forego the right to have our own offspring. It seems to me that the fellow insurees of Joan and David Travis have the responsibility to make it possible for all the members of the contract to have children—even where circumstances result in extraordinary costs. These costs will, to be sure, involve an additional

burden. But this is part of the price we pay for our living together in community.

This case is paradigmatic of the problem of individual rights against the demands of the community. This is especially important in the light of the increased demand that births be limited in response to the growing population problem. There is, of course, great merit in the efforts to limit the number of births in the world. However, the individual who wishes to have children does have the right to assert his privilege even against what is perceived by many to be the world's needs for population control. This does not mean that educational efforts trying to persuade people of the danger inherent in unlimited population growth should not continue. But it does not mean that no form of coercion, including economic coercion, should be applied.

The human birthright includes the right to give birth. The desire for propagation is one of the elementary forms of our humanness. To thwart this desire is to endanger something that adds to our human stature. As in many other instances, to do the good involves costs. However, I believe in this instance it involves a cost we should bear without bitterness, and even with good cheer.

SEYMOUR SIEGEL *is professor of theology, Jewish Theological Seminary, New York City.*

the hastings center REPORT

Institute of Society, Ethics and the Life Sciences

Volume 2, Number 1: February, 1972

Ethics of In-vitro Fertilization
Risk-taking for the Unborn

by MARC LAPPÉ

In the summer of 1959 I worked in the laboratory of embryologist Meredith Runner, then at the Jackson Laboratory in Maine. My supervisor was Dr. Alan Gates, who was among the first to demonstrate that mouse embryos could be flushed from the oviducts by a stream of saline, picked up in a tiny glass pipette, and reintroduced into the uterus of a suitable recipient without damage or loss of viability.

I can recall bending over the hot light of a microscope lamp and peering at two blastocysts that floated in a seemingly vast expanse of saline. A small glass bulb with an even smaller capillary pipette in it dangled at the end of a long rubber tube in my mouth, giving me a crude means of controlling the suction. In time, I was able to pull one of the embryos into the capillary end of the pipette, behind an air bubble needed to mark its position in the tube. I put the pipette aside and turned to look at the anesthetized white mouse at my side. Its right side was shaved down to the pink skin and swabbed with alcohol so that it looked translucent. A glistening red uterus, no wider than a piece of spaghetti, extruded from a slit in the

skin. Holding the uterus gently, I quickly punctured it with the tube, and blew in the speck of life. Fifteen days later a brown mouse was born from a white mother. I was sixteen years old.

Now, almost thirteen years later, I am a member of an Institute where some of my colleagues have questioned the ethical justifications for the very same procedure. But this time the experimental subject is man, and the stakes are considerably higher. As a laboratory student, I could have afforded to make mistakes with "my" mice, even taken the chance of severely damaging a developing embryo. The

---

Scientists have successfully fertilized a human egg in a test tube and seem on the verge of implanting such an egg in a womb where it will grow to full term.

Although proposed as a means of helping women who are barren because of blocked oviducts, the procedure is considered by some scientists to be such a major new step that the burden of proof should be on those who favor going ahead, rather than on those who would delay.

Here Dr. Lappé, an experimental pathologist and an Associate of the Institute, proposes conditions under which we might go ahead.

---

first physician attempting embryo transfers in human beings cannot take these risks; it is neither "his" embryo nor anyone else's. Or can he?

Those who oppose the development of the technologies needed for perfecting in vitro fertilization and implantation of human embryos question the propriety of perfecting technologies by experiments on the unborn. They ask if manipulation of such new (and by implication "innocent") life is not itself an abuse of power, and underscore the uncertainties of the procedures by citing the unknown depth of damage and hidden injuries to which such offspring might be subjected.

Is childbearing an inalienable right? The principal justification for attempting in vitro fertilization and reimplantation of human embryos (rather than, say, adoption or artificial insemination) has been to afford childless couples a means of having their *own* offspring. (In the United States, there are some two and a half million childless couples, a small proportion of whom would qualify for in vitro procedures.) If childbearing were an inalienable right, in vitro fertilization could be justified on the basis that there is a duty to use *all* technical means pos-

'As a lab student I could afford to make mistakes; now the stakes are higher'

sible to provide children. In my view, it is illogical and unnecessary to invoke this argument. When we speak of justification for medical practice, we are talking simply about a universal obligation to relieve suffering. And childlessness is a particularly acute form of such suffering. There is a deep and pervasive felt need for family lineage and continuity of generations common to all peoples. I believe that human compassion dictates a response to individual couples who strongly sense that need, including the provision of in vitro fertilization. Moreover, this need is in no way diminished, as some have insisted, by the fact that most causes of female infertility stem from venereal infections. Indeed the need is enhanced by this fact. Rather the key question is whether or not these parents' urgent need for their own child obliges others to assume the unknown risks that experimental procedures on the unborn now entail.

Does the need justify the risks? According to one of the physicians approached by childless couples, the mere risk of a deformity produced during in vitro procedures does *not* dissuade many of them from a willingness to undertake this process if it is the sole means of their bearing children. Their needs are so deeply felt that they are willing to assume responsibility for their child and to provide whatever care it might need were it handicapped. Yet, no one is or will be able to define for them just what risks are involved. Can the parents rightfully assume this responsibility for their unborn child? Admitting but a few conditions, I believe they can. Once such childless couples have been appraised of all of the *foreseeable* hazards in in vitro procedures, there can be no objection to allowing them to make the decision to have a child by this means.

Assuming responsibility for the risks to the unborn. If, in dissuading this kind of childbearing, one raises the specter of "hidden dangers" and "unforeseeable consequences," he is using a specious moral argument. While it is imperative to weigh the extent and degree of foreseeable damage in vitro manipulations may produce, I recognize that we will only be able to pass judgment on the likely risks. Nevertheless, such an estimation can and must be made. What is necessary is to bring the evidence to bear on possible damage, to assess the risks and then to determine if at some point they fall to an *acceptable* level. In the case of human babies produced by in vitro procedures, presumably this level would be one which was equivalent to the risks normally undertaken in a "natural" pregnancy.

The current weight of public opinion and common standards of medical practice regarding the restoration of fertility to childless couples greatly reduces the cogency of any argument which would protect the in vitro embryo from any and all potential risks of damage. Fertility drugs which induce super-ovulation are used without regard to the likelihood of multiple births and resulting stunting of fetal growth, prematurity, and higher risk of respiratory disease and death. Artificial insemination with husband or donor semen is practiced on an ever more regular basis without knowledge of the possible increased incidence of mutations as the result of sperm storage or other uncertainties entailed in the insemination procedure. Moreover, this society has sanctioned the use of sex steroids like diethylstilbestrol to help women who are habitual aborters to have their own children, even when the safety of this artificial steroid was incompletely known.

Even in the face of current evidence that this latter steroid procedure probably caused vaginal tumors in girls born of diethylstilbestrol treated mothers, it is difficult to say that this procedure was unwarranted. Would such girls and their as yet unaffected siblings be better off unborn? At least one parent living with the uncertainty of whether or not her daughter will be affected has told me that she feels it was worth the risk. Certainly her daughter does. But this does not resolve the moral issue of parental responsibility, any more than does the forgiveness of a child with cleft lip. In either instance, the morality of parental choice could only be dictated by the knowledge of likely risk at the time. One might hope that with the increased availability of genetic counseling *responsible* choice may be enhanced, but that the moral right of parents to decide to bring their children into the world when they believe there is a reasonable probability of normalcy remains unsullied. This assumption is the moral basis of all genetic counseling.

Likely risks of in vitro procedures. What might be the real risks of manipulating human embryos in vitro? Recent evidence of the resiliency of the early mammalian embryo certainly indicates that fears of gross monstrosities are probably unfounded. It has proven possible in mouse embryos, for example, to introduce living cells from unrelated embryos in vitro, and then implant them in the uteri of surrogate mothers. The observable incidence of abnormalities in these and other artificially implanted mouse embryos (of which there are now many hundreds) has proven to be no greater than that occurring naturally—and perhaps even less. This has even proven true when the embryos have been subjected to the extreme manipulation of stripping off their protective outer cover and actually fusing them with a second embryo. This is not to say that human embryos would prove comparably resilient, but certainly there is no evidence to date to indicate that the physical procedures involved in these manipulations provide any discernible teratogenic (monster-producing) stimulation.

What about the combined procedure of in vitro fertilization coupled with implantation? Here the data is less complete, although a recent study has shown that of the successfully fertilized mouse ova which became blastocysts, nearly half implanted and went on to develop normally. The rest were never recovered.

The loss of this seemingly high proportion of embryos underscores a basic feature of embryonic development: a significant proportion of fertilized eggs in nature do not go to term. (As many as 10% to 20% of all human pregnancies may undergo spontaneous abortion.) The loss of these early embryos appears to be a selective process whereby abnormal embryos die in greater numbers than do normal ones. Although the exact proportion is incompletely known, as many as 80% of all chromosomally abnormal embryos may be lost during the first and second trimester of pregnancy. Thus, there is reason to believe that potentially abnormal human embryos developed in vitro would be subject to a winnowing process which would help reduce (but not necessarily eliminate) abnormal embryos. Other techniques, such as ensuring that overripe ova are not used and monitoring the early pregnancy by amniocentesis for possible genetic and chromosomal abnormalities, could further reduce the risks of developmental anomalies by permitting abortion of affected fetuses. These arguments reduce, but do not eliminate, the question of more subtle damage.

Throughout this discussion I have acknowledged that no one will be able to say when and if in vitro fertilization in man will become a risk-free procedure. But I have emphasized that traditionally no one has insisted that "natural" reproduction be completely safe for the fetus before it is undertaken. Even in the most extreme cases, for example among women with phenylketonuria, whose offspring are virtually certain of receiving some damage during gestation, no one has enjoined them for procreating except by moral suasion. Bentley Glass has stated that the preeminent right of the fetus is that it have a sound physical and genetic constitution—a lofty, but impractical, ideal. Would we constrain all couples who are carriers for the same deleterious recessive disease (such as sickle cell trait carriers) from childbearing simply because there is a tangible risk—here one in four—of having a child with the disease? If we accept the morality of couples making this childbearing decision, can we deny the needs of a couple childless because of the woman's blocked oviducts? Here the risk to the fetus in utero is probably also small but unknowable. What are our ethical obligations to these childless couples and their as yet unborn children?

Sanctioning in vitro experimentation. I would first urge that all possible areas of knowable risk be exhaustively studied before the first human implantation experiment is performed. This would certainly entail experiments in higher primates or monkeys. Secondly, I would urge that the national and perhaps the international scientific community be involved in the decision-making. The moral issue of human embryo manipulation is so great and of such importance to the course of the history of man, that nothing short of a consensus of the scientific communities involved would be needed before proceeding. One has only to envision those tiny groups of men with whom Oppenheimer caucused in closed rooms on the desirability of unleashing a nuclear holocaust on Japan, to recognize that we need large scale involvement in decision-making of this kind.

Admittedly, the process of reaching this consensus is virtually unprecedented, but the stakes are so high and the symbolic impact of failing to act in this way so great, that the effort would be justified. The first step would be a moratorium on experiments leading directly to human egg implantation. The second would be the establishment of an international body to study systematically the scientific basis of in vitro manipulation in man. Finally, one can only hope that the first baby fertilized in vitro would be produced as the endpoint of a collective and public effort of responsible scientists, and not as the premature experiment of a single physician or scientist.

The Moral Uses of 'Spare' Embryos
by CLIFFORD GROBSTEIN

With the birth of Elizabeth Jordan Carr on December 28, 1981, the United States had its first baby conceived through external (in vitro) fertilization techniques.* About twenty such births have been confirmed around the world. But the increasing frequency of the procedure has not dispelled all ethical questions. The latest uproar .occurred in Great Britain and involves the use of "spare" embryos.

On a British television program, "Test-Tube Explosion," broadcast on February 2, Patrick Steptoe and Robert Edwards, the British team that first produced a baby by external fertilization three and a half years ago, referred to plans to freeze human eggs or embryos for possible later use.

This technical possibility, which was foreseen earlier, has become reality. Several groups around the world who are conducting clinical trials on external fertilization are now reporting success rates when women are given hormones prior to the relatively minor surgical procedure of removing eggs from their ovaries. Hormonal stimulation early in the menstrual cycle causes more than one egg to mature.

The chances for obtaining a healthy embryo after external fertilization of the eggs are expected to increase if the most normal-looking egg is selected, or if more than one is implanted, or if "extra" eggs can be used for a second try in a later cycle. The last possibility raises the question of freezing, as well as the question of the moral status of eggs at this stage. This was discussed earlier in relation to the procedure in general but the question is now intensified by the possibility of additional manipulation and intervention.

If it is moral to remove a human egg from a woman and fertilize it (some believe it to be immoral), is it any less moral to do anything more to the subsequent early embryo other than to reinsert it into the uterus of its donor? To avoid this issue some clinics (including the Norfolk Clinic) remove only eggs that they expect to fertilize and reinsert all eggs (usually not more than two) that they judge to be normal.

But Edwards and Steptoe suggest that extra eggs can have other uses, for example, as reserves for a second try. Such an effort might occur some twenty-eight days after the first, when the uterus should again be at its most receptive state. But if a surviving egg were externally incubated for that long, it might reach a stage of development well beyond the optimal one for implanting. In animals, however, freezing stops egg development with minimal damage. When thawed, a very high percentage of such eggs still undergo normal development. In fact, in a number of species early embryos naturally stop developing temporarily before becoming implanted in the uterine wall. Therefore, freezing is technically promising as a way to increase the efficacy of the procedure.

Alan Trounson and Carl Wood at Monash University in Melbourne, Australia, already freeze spare embryos in liquid nitrogen so that they can be thawed and replaced in the patient "if, and when, she wants another child by in vitro fertilization." Or, if the patient does not want them, they can be offered to other women. So far no embryo has been successfully stored and reimplanted, but Trounson is quoted as saying, "We're concentrating on freezing the two-, four-, and eight-cell stage of development and . . . in the order of 50 percent of the embryos are looking perfectly good and developing on a short-term culture, after thawing. The earlier stage embryos are proving far more difficult to freeze—down to 20 percent" (New Scientist, Feb. 4, 1982, p. 315).

Edwards and Steptoe also suggested that if frozen eggs were not needed for the donor (because success was achieved by the first insertion) the "extra" eggs might be made available to another woman who could not produce fertilizable eggs. This would expand the range of external human fertilization in the treatment of sterility, making it an analogue to artificial insemination by donor (AID), which is widely used to compensate for male sterility. Edwards and Steptoe went still further, suggesting that extra eggs might be studied as an aid to better understanding the effects of external fertilization and necessary measures to limit untoward results.

Edwards says, in defending his research with spare embryos, "[They] can be very very useful. They can teach us things about early human life which will help that patient and other patients. It is very important to know that the types and patterns of growth that we get in our cultures are normal—as normal as we can ensure—and I believe it is absolutely essential to examine the speed of growth of these embryos . . . . [and] to examine the chromosomes . . . . which involves flattening them on a tiny piece of glass and looking at the number of chromosomes they have. This is terribly important because we want to make sure that we're not getting conditions which would lead to anomalies . . ." (New Scientist, Feb. 4, 1982, p. 314). Edwards' remarks were similar to those he had earlier published in Nature (Sept. 24, 1981).

Rumblings of concern have been reported in Australia about the embryos that lie in cold storage in Melbourne; and the British medical establishment has also expressed its worry about the possibility of embryo storage banks. Michael Thomas, a hematologist who is chairman of the British Medical Association's ethics committee, warned, "Medical technology is running ahead of morality" (New York Times, Jan. 29, 1982). He called for a moratorium on the work while his committee reviews the implications. Anti-abortion groups have also protested. For example, an organizer of an antiabortion group, Life, said that the idea "raises horrendous legal and ethical implications," and asked "What is the legal status of a child conceived in this way?"

The debate in Britain emphasizes the contentious issue of the status of pre-

CLIFFORD GROBSTEIN is professor of biological science and public policy in the Program in Science, Technology and Public Affairs, University of California, San Diego.

*I shall refer to this process as "external human fertilization." It has also been called "in vitro fertilization," where the Latin version of in glass is a euphemism for "technologically assisted." The term "test-tube babies" has also been used.

The Hastings Center Report, June 1982

implantation embryos outside the maternal body. In the United States, the issue was not addressed in this form by the Supreme Court abortion decision in *Roe* v. *Wade*. That decision concerned the embryo within the maternal body and explicitly avoided a general ruling on "when life begins." Legislation pending in Congress would resolve the matter by defining conception as the beginning of human life. If the legislation passes (and is judged to be constitutional) any manipulation of fertilized eggs might be construed as invasion of the privacy of a person. Such an interpretation would legally challenge not only external human fertilization but contraceptive techniques that act on fertilized eggs or directly or indirectly block their implantation.

Edwards has addressed these issues repeatedly over the last decade. The problem grows in difficulty, he believes, as gestation advances. Concerning the early stages under discussion, he says, however, "I would not myself have any doubt about using [them]." Although no purely scientific argument is likely to be totally convincing, particularly for individuals committed to a religious view of the matter, it is worth noting what developmental scientists have discovered about the properties of these early stages.

Following fertilization the egg undergoes a series of cell divisions (mitosis) without intervening growth of the division products. Such divisions are called cleavage and they produce a packet of cells of diminishing size. The first three divisions produce eight such cells. Observation and manipulation of these cells in mice and other nonhuman mammals demonstrate: first, that these cells are not yet tightly adherent, nor do they seem to be significantly interdependent developmentally. To all intents and purposes they behave as individual cells rather than as cell-parts of a multicellular individual. Second, in conformity with this interpretation, each cell, if isolated from the others, can form a complete embryo. Third, again in conformity, if two four-celled stages are fused, they form a single embryo whose cells give rise to a mosaic adult, that is, one made up of cells recognizably derived from both of the fused embryos.

These observations strongly suggest that up to the eight-cell stage, despite the establishment of *genetic* individuality at fertilization, a multicellular individual is still not present. Since persons, as usually defined, are multicellular individuals, it is difficult to maintain scientifically that a person has come into existence prior to the eight-cell stage. Indeed, since twinning in human development is believed to be possible as much as two weeks after fertilization—about when implantation is occurring—the entire preimplantation period can be regarded scientifically as one of preindividuality in a developmental sense. Moreover, developmental individuality appears to be prerequisite to personhood, though the two terms are not equivalent.

What does this line of argument do to the ethical and legal doubts expressed in England? Clearly, that depends in part upon the presumed relationship among science, ethics, and the law. Science is not the fountainhead of ethics and the law; much that ethics and law encompass relates to matters beyond scientific competence at a given time or possibly even relevance for all time. But some of what they address is also addressed by science. To the degree that science has achieved reasonable certainty by its technique of common verification, ethics and the law will certainly be in question, and will conceivably be judged unsound, if they ignore or contravene scientific findings. Medical practice and abortion policy are properly subject to ethical and legal constraints—but the rationale for these constraints should not involve assertions contrary to our best scientific knowledge.

In reaching a judgment about extending external human fertilization procedures to include freezing and thawing of embryos, the safety of the procedure clearly is a first consideration. Previous experience with animal embryos is relevant but not necessarily fully convincing, since human eggs and embryos may differ in sensitivity. Moreover, some individual instances of untoward effects in agricultural or laboratory animals can be tolerated, whereas even a single instance of induced defect in humans poses moral difficulties. Finally, animal observation, even on primates, does not readily dispel concern over possible subtle effects on brain function. Therefore, the first attempts to reinsert frozen-thawed human eggs or embryos must necessarily involve significant uncertainty.

On the other side, there are legitimate scientific grounds to argue that major abnormalities resulting from freezing and thawing can be observed microscopically. Moreover, any invisible damage is unlikely to affect born offspring since in the natural process abnormal embryos generally fail to implant or are spontaneously aborted. Finally, antenatal diagnosis is increasingly effective in detecting abnormality and abnormal pregnancies can be terminated by induced abortion.

Of course, some consider resorting to abortion immoral. Moreover, just as in the natural reproductive process, we can never be completely sure that all subtly abnormal embryos will be detected before birth. Scientific facts can thus provide reasonable estimates of the risk of reinserting frozen and thawed human embryos but no assurance that the risk will be zero or even no greater than in the natural process. On the ethical and legal side, however, scientific facts suggest that freezing of preimplantation stages does not constitute intervention in a multicellular *individual*.

If the safety of the procedure can be more fully established, or if the currently estimated risks are acceptable under a suitable procedure for informed consent, then the use of frozen-thawed embryos does not raise issues very different from those already discussed for the basic external human fertilization process. Freezing does, however, constitute another step on what many perceive as a slippery slope. Is this step-by-step determination of policy appropriate or is some effort needed to construct a more comprehensive policy framework?

So far no clear policy has been developed, either in the United States or abroad. The British Medical Association is drawing up a code of ethics for scientists involved in research on test-tube babies that it hopes to have ready by July. In the United States, external human fertilization has maintained a low profile; and the Secretary of Health & Human Services has not acted on the Ethics Advisory Board's 1979 recommendation to permit research funding under certain circumstances. Pierre Soupart, the Vanderbilt University researcher whose proposal was the specific subject of the Board's deliberations, died in June 1981 without an answer from the government.

But the issue of moral uses of spare eggs and embryos has been raised in this country too—for example, in testimony presented to the Ethics Advisory Board. Despite the scientific interest, any use of spare embryos for research or banking is likely to raise controversy here. Developments in each country are likely to be watched with interest by the other.

21

The Rios case made headlines last year. A millionaire couple from the United States, Mario and Elsa Rios wanted to have children. Though each had had children by former marriages, they were unable to conceive together. In 1981 they sought the help of researchers at Queen Victoria Medical Center in Melbourne, Australia. Three of Mrs. Rios's egg cells were removed and successfully fertilized in the laboratory with sperm from an anonymous donor. One of the resulting live embryos was then implanted in Mrs. Rios's womb; the two remaining embryos were frozen to preserve them for future implantation if the first implanted embryo should abort.

The implanted embryo did spontaneously abort after about ten days but Mrs. Rios said she was not emotionally ready then to have a second embryo implanted. Some time later the Rioses went to South America to adopt a child. In the spring of 1983, Mr. and Mrs. Rios and their adopted child were killed in a crash of their private airplane (*New York Times*, October 24, 1984).

The legal question was: Who should inherit the considerable assets of their estate? The common law tradition, including both United States and Australian law, has long permitted those who have been conceived but not yet been born to inherit. But their inheriting is contingent on their being born alive. "There is nothing in law," says William Salmond, "to prevent a man from owning property before he is born. His ownership is contingent, for he may never be born at all; but it is nonetheless a real and present ownership....A posthumous child, for example, may inherit; but if he died in the womb, or is stillborn, his inheritance fails to take effect, and *no one can claim through him*, though it would be otherwise if he lived for an hour after his birth."[1]

A will, of course, identifies the heirs, regardless of their parentage.

David T. Ozar, Ph.D., is associate professor of philosophy, adjunct associate professor of medicine, and director of the M.A. Program in Health Care Ethics, Loyola University of Chicago.

The Case Against Thawing Unused Frozen Embryos

by David T. Ozar

Whether one believes that the embryo has rights from the instant of conception, or that the embryo has no moral rights at all, the conclusion about the fate of unused frozen embryos is the same: they ought to be preserved in their frozen state until they are implanted in a woman's womb or are no longer able to survive implantation.

But when there is no will, as in the Rios case, is the embryo to be considered the child of the woman who bears it (and must she be bearing it when the deceased dies) or of the woman from whose ovum it has grown? And is the embryo the child of the man whose sperm fertilized that ovum or of some other? These are fascinating legal questions; but I shall not discuss them further here.[2]

Another question was: Who should decide the fate of the remaining frozen embryos? If the Rioses were still alive, it would be natural to conclude, both in law and from an ethical perspective, that they, together with the doctors and researchers involved, are the responsible parties.[3] With the Rioses now dead, should the executors appointed for the Rioses' estate or the Rioses' heirs or possibly the state take over the Rioses' role in these decisions?

A committee convened for the purpose later recommended that the embryos be destroyed. The legislators of the state of Victoria then rejected the committee's advice and passed an amendment to another bill, calling for an attempt to have the embryos implanted in surrogate mothers and then, if they came to term, placed for adoption. There has been no further word on whether they were actually implanted. Regardless of how this aspect of the matter is resolved, the doctors and researchers, who brought the sperm and ova together and who have preserved the embryos in their frozen state, will still have a role to play. I shall assume that, for our purposes, they bear the chief ethical responsibility for unused frozen embryos.

Is the fact that the Rioses are deceased of importance in determining what is the right thing to do with the remaining embryos? The answer is clearly, no. If it were determined that the embryos ought to be dealt with as pieces of property, organic goods duly owned by someone, then the fact that the Rioses are deceased means only that someone else owns them. By the same token, if it were determined that the embryos ought to be treated differently from pieces of property, then they ought to be so treated regardless of who has or has not died.

Suppose that the Rioses had lived, that the first implanted embryo had prospered and had been born a healthy baby, and that the Rioses had chosen to have only one child. The future of the two remaining embryos would still need to be decided. On this scenario the matter would probably have been decided privately between the Rioses and the hospital-laboratory team. A number of such decisions have undoubtedly been made in just this way, between the team and other couples. But the question is the same whether we as a community reflect on it or it is asked privately by doctors and researchers and the couples who are their patients; and its answer does not depend on the fate of Mr. and Mrs. Rios. How ought people to act, what ought people to do, in regard to unused frozen embryos?

Some might argue that this question misses the point, that the real issue concerns the morality of artificial reproductive techniques themselves, of which freezing live embryos is simply one example. From this perspective all forms of fertilization other than intercourse are profoundly unnatural and immoral.[4] The real point would be that these embryos should not have been fertilized and frozen in the first place. We are uncertain about how to proceed rightly from this point because the parties acted immorally at the outset.

This approach raises important questions about the reproductive technology that was offered to the Rioses. But this response is of little help to those who must now determine what to do about existing frozen embryos. Even if the acts that brought us to this pass were profoundly immoral, what we do next is still not a morally indifferent matter.

Obligation Toward Fetuses

In trying to answer this question, it is natural to examine the lines of thought that have been developed regarding our obligations toward fetuses. Unfortunately, many of these lines tell us little about a frozen eight- or sixteen-celled embryo. For example, any obligations that we might have toward a fetus by reason of its possession of neurological functions, and hence its possession of the beginnings of the most distinctive functions of the human species,[5] would not apply to an embryo whose cells have not yet begun to differentiate in terms of function. Even less could an embryo pass the test of actually engaging in acts of thinking, planning, choosing, or of being conscious and experiencing emotion, which some authors have made the key to a being's having rights and the rest of us having corresponding obligations.[6]

One approach that might seem helpful here focuses on viability outside the womb. The frozen embryo is obviously outside the womb and it is not dead or dying. Indeed it is being preserved in its frozen state precisely because of its potential for continued life.

Viability is one of the criteria employed by the United States Supreme Court in the ethical justification of the legal rulings in its landmark abortion decisions.[7] In *Roe* v. *Wade*, the Court held that the fetus is not a legal person, a bearer of legal rights, including the legal right not to be killed, at any point from conception until the moment of live birth. But the Court held that the state does have an "interest" in "protecting the potentiality of human life," and that this interest grows "in substantiality as the woman approaches term." Moreover, at some point in the pregnancy, the Court held, this interest may be considered "compelling," that is, sufficiently important that it may outweigh other fundamental values, in this case the mother's constitutional right to control her own body and thus to seek an abortion if she chooses.

The point at which the state's interest in protecting the potentiality of human life becomes "compelling," said the *Roe* Court, is "viability." Viability is in turn described as "the capability of meaningful life outside the womb"; but the term "meaningful" is not further defined by the *Roe* Court, so the Court's understanding of viability was still unclear. In *Danforth*, however, the Court upheld a Missouri statute containing this definition of viability: "that stage of fetal development when the life of the unborn child may be continued indefinitely outside of the womb by natural or artificial life-support systems."

But as Justice Sandra Day O'Connor has argued, there is still ambiguity here. In a dissent to the Court's 1983 *Akron* decision,[8] Justice O'Connor argues that "neither sound constitutional theory nor our need to decide cases based on the application of neutral principles can accommodate an analytic framework that varies according to the 'stages' of pregnancy, where those stages, and their concomitant standards of re-

view, differ according to the level of medical technology at a particular time....The *Roe* framework is clearly on a collision course with itself. As the medical risks of various abortion procedures decrease, the point at which the state may regulate for reasons of maternal health is moved further forward to actual childbirth. As medical science becomes better able to provide for the separate existence of the fetus, the point of viability is moved further back toward conception...." Thus if medical science had developed an artificial womb, in which embryos could develop until they could live independently, the Rioses' frozen embryos would be viable under the *Danforth* definition.

But lacking an artificial womb, what are we to say? The most likely interpretation is that "life" in these definitions means not only that the organism under consideration is not dying, but also that it is able to continue to perform life functions (with or without mechanical assistance) outside of a womb. On this interpretation, the frozen embryo is not viable. For, while capable in their frozen state of not dying, these embryos cannot continue to perform life functions, even simple cell divisions, independent of the nutritive and protective environment of a woman's womb.

Consequently, to return to *Roe* v. *Wade*, the state would not have a "compelling" interest in protecting the potential life of frozen embryos. That is, the state's interest in protecting their potential life could not outweigh the fundamental constitutional right of a woman to control her own body. But in the case of frozen embryos, no woman is involved, and thus no woman's right to control her body. Might the state's interest then be strong enough to protect frozen embryos' lives? Here the competing rights would have to be the property rights of those who own the equipment that preserves the embryos' lives. Is the state's interest in protecting the potential life of the embryo great enough to outweigh the equipment owners' rights to control their property? Or are the frozen embryos to be considered property themselves, so that their owners may dispose of them more or less as they wish, and their lives would not have any special weight in relation to the property rights of the owners of the equipment? Obviously we are now asking questions that cannot be resolved in terms of the criterion of viability. So it turns out that this criterion, like the others mentioned above, cannot resolve our question about how to act rightly toward unused frozen embryos.

The "Instant of Conception" View

But there are two approaches to our obligations toward fetuses that are informative regarding frozen embryos as well. First is the most inclusive moral position regarding obligations toward the unborn—the position that holds that the conceptus has a moral right not to be killed, and the rest of us have a moral obligation not to kill the conceptus or to intend to kill it, from the first instant of its conception.[9] (This right, stated more completely, is a right not to be *directly* killed, and the obligation is an obligation not to *directly* kill or to intend to *directly* kill the conceptus. The added term, "directly," is very important in other contexts; but it is not important in the present discussion, and therefore I shall use the more simplified statement.)

This position is commonly called the "right to life" position; but I shall call it the "instant of conception" position. Many other positions on these matters affirm life-related rights, including rights not to be killed under various sets of circumstances. In calling it the "instant of conception" position, I am focusing on what is truly distinctive about it and on its substantive claims in the present discussion.

According to this position, a frozen embryo, as the fruit of human conception, has a moral right not to be killed. Therefore the doctors and researchers responsible for the care of such an embryo could not morally place it in an environment known to be lethal to it. This would preclude deliberately permitting a frozen embryo to be thawed without placing it in the only environment in which it could survive thawing, namely, a woman's womb. Nor could the parents (by any definition) or anyone

else morally choose that a frozen embryo be dealt with in this way.

At the same time, the "instant of conception" position provides no basis for saying that an embryo has a moral right to be implanted in a womb. The moral right not to be killed does not automatically imply a right to the use of a womb. For an embryo may be implanted in a womb only by the free choice of the woman whose womb it is. Thus the obligation not to kill an embryo does not necessarily imply an obligation on anyone's part to offer her womb for its survival.

One possible exception is the genetic mother, the donor of the ovum whence the embryo has grown. It may be that, in bringing the embryo into being, she has undertaken an obligation to assist it in realizing its full potential for human life. But this obligation, if it exists, does not derive from a moral right of the embryo as the kind of being that it is, but rather from the mother's freely undertaking to bring it into being. (The genetic father might have a similar obligation, but since he cannot provide the womb that the embryo needs, I shall not consider his obligations further.)

I shall not attempt to resolve here the complicated questions about the degree of responsibility of genetic parents for their offspring.[10] The point is that, if the genetic mother does have such an obligation to the embryo, then she may be obligated to accept the unused embryo into her womb. If the genetic mother refuses to do so, however, or if she dies as Mrs. Rios did, so that responsibility for the frozen embryos now falls upon the hospital-laboratory team, no one would have an *obligation* to accept the embryo into her womb. If anyone did accept it, this would be an act of charity toward the embryo, not an act of obligation or an act to which the embryo had a right.

There are then two possibilities. If no one volunteers her womb for the implantation of the unused frozen embryo, those responsible for its care will fulfill their obligations simply by not killing it, that is, by keeping it frozen. If, on the other hand, someone does volunteer for its implantation, the responsible parties

would need to determine whether implantation in the womb of this particular volunteer would give the embryo a reasonable chance of survival and further development, as compared with continued freezing and the possibility of implantation in a future volunteer with more likelihood of success. It would be appropriate, also, for the responsible parties to seek out women who might desire to volunteer for implantation of unused embryos.

Since frozen embryos may deteriorate over time, let us assume that there is a point at which the hospital-laboratory team can accurately say that a particular embryo is no longer able to survive implantation. Such an embryo no longer has any potential for continued life. Because it is still frozen, it is not yet dead; yet death is its only conceivable prospect. I believe that the "instant of conception" position would conclude that such an embryo no longer has any moral right that would require its continued maintenance in the frozen state. Its condition is now analogous to that of someone who is irreversibly in the process of dying. The embryo may morally be thawed at this point, and the irreversible process of its death permitted to proceed to its conclusion.

The View that the Embryo Has No Moral Rights

The obligations that I have just outlined, based as they are on the most inclusive position regarding our obligations to the unborn, constitute the most extensive set of obligations toward unused frozen embryos that can reasonably be defended. Next we must ask: Is any lesser set of obligations toward unused frozen embryos more reasonable? In order to respond, I shall look at a position that accords no moral rights at all to the unborn.

If a frozen embryo has no moral rights of its own, if it is more like a piece of property (or is just like a piece of property) rather than a bearer of rights, still those who are responsible for it will have obligations regarding its use and the consequences of its use. If certain ways of dealing with it would lead to significantly more good than other ways, at relatively little cost in human effort, in monetary resources, and so on, then the responsible parties would be obligated to choose those ways of acting. If certain ways of acting would involve risk of significant harm, which could be avoided at relatively little cost in human effort, in monetary resources, and so on, then the responsible parties would be obligated to avoid them.

These straightforward moral principles point to the same conclusion as is defended by the "instant of conception" position, even if the embryo has no moral rights at all. My argument follows a pattern developed by Mary Anne Warren in a famous postscript to "On the Moral and Legal Status of Abortion." In response to criticisms that her criteria for having moral rights were so strict as to deny moral rights to infants, Warren argued that even when no moral rights are relevant, morality may require that human life be preserved and protected because of the negative consequences of doing otherwise.

Once the original outlay of expense and effort for freezing embryos has been made, embryos can be maintained in their frozen state at very little cost, in dollars or in human effort. Therefore if there are women who desire to bear a child and who might be successfully implanted with embryos unused by others, the moral principles just articulated argue strongly for maintaining unused embryos in their frozen state until they can be implanted. The costs of doing this are very small and the benefits to the mothers concerned (as well as to their spouses and other affected parties) are very great. In fact, if the good of enabling women to bear children can justify the sizable expense of developing or purchasing this technology in the first place, then it surely can justify the far smaller expense of maintaining unused embryos until other women who desire to bear a child have volunteered. It would also be reasonable for the doctors and researchers to seek out such women, especially if the frozen embryo does deteriorate over time, in the interests of maximizing the benefits and minimizing the costs of the process.

This same conclusion—that unused frozen embryos ought to be maintained in their frozen state for as long as they are able to survive implantation—can be reached in another way, which takes account of other consequences of the process. For even if frozen embryos do not have moral rights, they are still members of the human species with a potential for a full human life. Indeed it is precisely because of that potential that they were frozen in the first place. Consequently if hospital-laboratory teams, parents, or other responsible parties routinely followed a policy of simply disposing of unused frozen embryos, such a policy, if widely known, could have a negative impact on the ways in which we as individuals and as a community value and deal with human life generally, especially in other members of our species whose lives are in some way compromised.

Two questions need to be addressed here. One is a subtle question of social psychology. It asks how various policies concerning human life that are accepted within a community have an impact on individuals' values and future actions and on future policies within the community. The second is a normative question: What values, actions, and future policies regarding human life should we support and reinforce in our present policy making?

We are woefully short on answers to the first question. Some have argued that a community that values many other things over the life of a fetus will experience a gradual but significant lessening in the value of human life generally, so that previously unacceptable trade-offs between human life and other values will come to be accepted. Others have claimed that there is no such linkage in human feelings or in other parts of the human psyche between our valuation of human life in the unborn and the born.

I have no expert opinion to offer on the first question, but I believe that we do have some sense of the proper answer to the second, for it is clear that a great deal is at stake here. The value that we, as individuals and as a community, attach to human life is the most fundamental element of

the social morality that makes it possible for us to live together in some measure of security. Such valuing of human life is nurtured in many subtle ways in our habits and mores, and in our institutions. Such valuing is probably vulnerable as well, at least over the long run; it may even be subject to significant change as habits, mores, and institutions change.

Thus it is not beyond the realm of possibility that widespread public acceptance of a practice in which human embryos are made when it is efficient and economical to make them and disposed of when it is efficient and economical to dispose of them would have an impact on the community's valuing of human life in other contexts, an impact that would put the lives of those already born at risk when trade-offs of efficiency and economics did not favor them. We know far too little to predict that something like this will certainly occur. But we also know far too little to predict that it certainly will not. Certainly enough is at stake that we would be foolish not to acknowledge the risk.

Only reasons of economy and efficiency support a policy of disposal. But a policy of maintaining the lives of frozen embryos for as long as they could survive implantation and of actively seeking out women who might desire to bear them would be far less expensive than the setup costs of the technology that enabled us to freeze embryos in the first place. Thus, given the possible negative impact of disposing of human embryos for reasons of efficiency and economics, clearly the far better course of action is to maintain the frozen embryos until they can no longer survive implantation and to actively support their implantation when women desiring to bear them volunteer. This course of action avoids risk of significant harm at relatively little cost.

From this it is clear that those who would accord to frozen embryos no moral rights whatsoever, but who would still be guided in their obligations by consideration of the outcomes of their actions, would reach the same conclusion regarding unused frozen embryos as those who affirm the embryos' moral rights from the instant of conception. From both perspectives, as well as each of the intermediate moral positions, the responsible parties have an obligation to preserve the frozen embryos in their frozen state until such time as they can no longer survive implantation. In addition, they should support implantation of unused embryos in women who volunteer to bear them and should make reasonable efforts to locate such women when there are implantable embryos.

Freezing Multiple Embryos

The issues discussed so far presuppose the value of fertilizing multiple ova and freezing the resulting embryos on the chance that an implanted embryo will subsequently abort. Since the risk of spontaneous abortion of implanted embryos is considerable, the fertilization and freezing of multiple embryos seem a reasonable efficiency. But the previous arguments suggest that the production of embryos is not something to be undertaken lightly. So we need to reflect on the ethical appropriateness of the multiple frozen embryo procedure itself.

Some authors have argued that in vitro fertilization and the implantation of the resulting embryo are, without exception, profoundly unnatural and immoral. Obviously if this view is correct, nearly every aspect of the procedure of freezing multiple embryos is immoral; but I do not find the arguments offered in support of this view to be persuasive. Putting considerations of the just allocation of health care resources aside for the moment, I consider it a reasonable and therapeutic intervention to assist a woman who desires to bear a child by fertilizing her ovum in vitro and implanting the resulting embryo in her womb. If freezing the embryo at some point in its development will give it a better chance of surviving implantation, without harming its development in other ways, this too seems reasonable to me.

The ethical issue that has not been adequately addressed is precisely the procedure of fertilizing and freezing *multiple* embryos. The most obvious reason for this procedure is that it is easier and cheaper to fertilize several ova at the same time and to have the resulting embryos available for a second or third implantation whenever they are needed, rather than go back to fertilizing an ovum from the beginning if the first (second, third) implantation fails.

The problem is, as before, that the organisms being used to make the procedure cheaper and easier are genetically complete human organisms. It is, again, their very potential for full human life that prompts the hospital-laboratory team to fertilize and preserve them in the first place. Therefore the same considerations that argue for thoughtful caution in our dealings with unused embryos argue for a similar caution in our making and freezing of embryos at all.

If it becomes common knowledge that human embryos are fertilized and frozen in quantity in order to make a particular medical procedure easier and less expensive, could this not have a significant negative impact on individuals' and communities' values and future actions, at least over the long run? Are the benefits of such a procedure valuable enough to run the risks that the procedure involves?

In response, it could be argued that it is precisely in the interests of human life that human life is being used in this way. Everyone involved in this technology is striving to enable children to be born who otherwise could not have been born. The chances of a particular child's being born are multiplied by two or three or whatever the number, it would be argued, if we are able to fertilize and freeze two or three or more embryos at the start. Does not this goal of extending human life to those who would otherwise not have it justify the multiple frozen embryo procedure?

When we are dealing with those already born, we do not permit anyone's life to be used to improve another person's chances unless the helper undertakes the task voluntarily. If we are dealing with children or others who cannot choose on their own, we would permit one's life to be used in the interests of another in only the rarest of circumstances, if ever. Still, "using a life" usually does not mean giving a new life, as it does when multiple embryos are fertilized and frozen. On the other hand, the frozen embryo procedure is not the only way to obtain a second, third, or fourth living embryo if the first implantation should fail. So we are left with a question: If it was certain that every embryo fertilized and frozen in this procedure would have a chance for implantation, as in the policy argued for in the preceding section, then would the way in which the embryos' lives are "used" in this technology be morally acceptable? Or would manipulating the lives of human embryos in this way still pose a risk of negatively affecting the ways in which individuals and communities value and deal with human life? Considerations of efficiency and laboratory economy alone would not seem worth this risk.

But what about the value to the mothers involved, the value of bearing a child? To be sure, the good of childbearing is a great good; and the future of our species, itself a considerable good, depends on it. But a particular woman's ability to bear a child is not an absolute good; it can be outweighed by a variety of other considerations, singly or in combination. Nor is childbearing the only possible basis of parenting, which is the good that at least some candidates for this procedure seek. We must at least inquire whether adoption would not fulfill the most important needs of many who seek the assistance of reproductive technologies without the risks and costs of such technologies.

A single-minded commitment on the part of the physicians and researchers involved in reproductive technologies to enable women to bear children who would otherwise be unable to do so is understandable and perhaps even commendable. But in making policy the larger community must take more into account than the ability of patients to bear children and the ability of doctors and researchers to develop efficient procedures to this end.

The issue can be posed in a different way. Ought every woman who has healthy ova but who cannot bear children without such a procedure receive the benefits of multiple frozen embryo technology? As soon as we ask the question in this way, recognizing that many thousands of women might be candidates for the procedure (by some current estimates, 15 percent of all married couples are infertile),[11] we realize that we must consider the costs. Making the procedure available to every woman who might benefit would almost certainly draw significant resources away from other pressing health care needs or from other uses of resources within the larger community.

Is this procedure so valuable that we would be willing to close immunization programs or blood banks or a significant number of medical schools, or reduce the resources devoted to arthritis research or the like, in order to make it available to all who might benefit? Is it more valuable than efforts to provide better education to our disadvantaged young or decent survival to our elderly poor or basic foodstuffs and fresh water to the millions in the world community who cannot obtain them without assistance? We recognize immediately that the good that this technology pursues is a relative good; it must be weighed against other goods before we can know if pursuing it is worth the cost in resources, in human effort, and, as I have argued, in the risk of future harm.

At present the benefits of the multiple frozen embryo procedure are available only to the wealthy and to those who have been selected as research subjects. The latter pattern of allocating this therapy may be justified as long as the therapy is still experimental. But there is a clear injustice in giving the wealthy privileged access to an accepted therapeutic procedure. Admittedly some instances of "pure" research justify themselves only long afterwards by leading to benefits for many that could not have been foreseen. But we must ask who will benefit and how much, and how these benefits compare not only with the cost in resources and human effort, but also with the risk of future harm within the larger community.

An Unusual Opportunity

In the case of freezing multiple embryos we have an unusual opportunity for agreement on a question of reproductive morality. Richard McCormick, David Thomasma, and many others, have stressed that we cannot resolve by law and public policy a set of issues on which there is not, within the community at large, a consensus on the underlying values.[12] On the issue of the legality of abortion, and of the constitutionality of laws prohibiting or regulating it, our community appears to be profoundly divided; and this division has been deepened and entrenched by strident rhetoric on both sides.

But if I am correct in claiming that the two most frequently opposed moral positions about reproductive morality must reach the same conclusion regarding our obligations toward unused frozen embryos, then here is a possible starting point from which respectful conversation and the search for a broader consensus can begin. To be sure, different patterns of reasoning are involved in the two positions. But on this issue at least, the two sides need not begin their conversation at odds, committed to showing first of all that the other's position is without substance. On this issue there is a basis for agreement, and therefore for respect and for further conversation.

References

[1] William Salmond, *Jurisprudence*, twelfth edition, edited by P.J. Fitzgerald (London: Sweet and Maxwell, 1966), p. 303, emphasis in the original.

[2] See George Annas, "Redefining Parenthood and Protecting Embryos: Why We Need Laws," *Hastings Center Report*, October 1984, pp. 50-51. See also Steven R. Fersz, "The Contract in Surrogate Motherhood: A Review of the Issues," *Law, Medicine, and Health Care*, June 1984, pp. 107-14; Flannery, et. al., "Test Tube Babies: Legal Issues Raised by In Vitro Fertilization," *Georgetown Law Journal*, August 1979, pp. 129 ff.; "Note: Surrogate Mothers: The Legal Issues," *American Journal of Law and Medicine*, Fall 1981, pp. 323 ff.

[3] See Mark E. Cohen, "The 'Brave New Baby,' and the Law: Fashioning Remedies for the Victims of In Vitro Fertilization," *American Journal of Law and Medicine*, 4:3(1978), 319-36.

[4] A classic statement of this position appears in Pope Pius XXI's 1956 address to the Second World Congress on Fertility and Sterility, *Proceedings of the Second World Congress on Fertility and Sterility*, 2 vols. (Naples, Italy: University of Naples, 1957-1958), vol. I, p. 40. See also Leon Kass, "Making Babies—The New Biology and the 'Old' Morality," *Public Interest*, Winter 1972, pp. 23-49, and "'Making Babies' Revisited," *Public Interest*, Winter 1979, pp. 44-60. But also see Anthony Kosnik, et. al., *Human Sexuality: New Directions in American Catholic Thought* (New York: Paulist Press, 1977), pp. 137-40, and Margot Joan Fromer, *Ethical Issues in Sexuality and Reproduction* (St. Louis: Mosby, 1983), pp. 271-77. For a broad survey of ethical literature on in vitro fertilization, see LeRoy Walters, "Human In Vitro Fertilization: A Review of the Ethical Literature," *Hastings Center Report*, August 1979, pp. 23-43, and *Bioethics Reporter*, "Rights of Fetuses: Issues, Commentary, Literature, Court Cases, Legislation, and Bibliography," 1984.

[5] See, for example, Baruch Brody, *Abortion and the Sanctity of Human Life: A Philosophical View* (Cambridge: MIT Press, 1975).

[6] See, for example, Mary Anne Warren, "On the Moral and Legal Status of Abortion," *The Monist*, vol. 57 (1973) 43-61.

[7] *Roe v. Wade*, 410 U.S. 113 (1973); *Doe v. Bolton*, 410 U.S. 179 (1973); *Planned Parenthood v. Danforth*, 428 U.S. 52 (1979).

[8] *City of Akron v. Akron Center for Reproductive Health*, 103 U.S. 2481 (1983).

[9] For examples of this position, see John T. Noonan, Jr., "An Almost Absolute Value in History," in his *The Morality of Abortion: Legal and Historical Perspectives* (Cambridge: Harvard University Press, 1970) and Teresa Iglesias, "*In Vitro* Fertilization: The Major Issues," *Journal of Medical Ethics* vol. 10 (1984).

[10] This topic has not been carefully discussed in the literature. For a thoughtful discussion of voluntariness and responsibility in regard to a fetus conceived through intercourse, see Joel Feinberg, "Abortion," in Tom Regan, ed., *Matters of Life and Death*, (New York: Random House, 1980), pp. 209-14.

[11] Lori Andrews, *New Conceptions. A Consumer's Guide to the Newest Infertility Treatments, Including In Vitro Fertilization, Artificial Insemination, and Surrogate Motherhood* (New York: St. Martins Press, 1984).

[12] See Richard A. McCormick, S.J., "The Abortion Dossier," "Rules for Abortion Debate," and "Public Policy on Abortion," in his *How Brave a New World?* (Garden City, N.Y.; Doubleday, 1981), and David Thomasma, *An Apology for the Value of Human Life* (St. Louis: Catholic Health Association, 1983).

Only four years ago, embryo freezing (cryopreservation) was considered a technique raising "disturbing," "extremely difficult," "incredibly complex," and even "nightmarish" ethical issues. Currently, however, at least 41 of the 169 infertility clinics in the United States have added freezing to in vitro fertilization (IVF) protocols.[1] The number of frozen embryos in this country nearly tripled from 289 to 824 between 1985 and 1986.[2] An estimated ten infants in the U.S. and sixty in the world were born as of 1988 after having been frozen as embryos.[3]

Some physicians have concluded that freezing eliminates ethical dilemmas by allowing embryos to be stored rather than discarded, and researchers have contended that freezing poses few unique dilemmas.[4] It is true that if we look for evidence of public ethical controversy, predictions of perplexing quandaries have not, apart from the case of the Rios's "orphaned" frozen embryos in Australia, been realized. In the clinical setting, however, unanswered questions suggest the need to keep alive the ethical debate about the benefits to patients and society of embryo freezing.

Questionable Benefits

During a woman's initial IVF cycle, three or four of the embryos created are transferred to her uterus, while the rest are frozen for storage, to be thawed and transferred at a later date. Practitioners of IVF justify freezing as enhancing their ability to act in the patient's best interest.[5] In general, they presume freezing will benefit the patient physically, emotionally, and financially.

In theory, because not all embryos need be transferred in the first IVF cycle, freezing physically benefits a woman undergoing IVF by reducing the odds that a multiple pregnancy will occur—letting the patient recover from the stress of IVF before a second transfer of embryos, and sparing her

Andrea L. Bonnicksen is a professor of political science at Eastern Illinois University, Charleston, IL.

Embryo Freezing: Ethical Issues in the Clinical Setting

by Andrea L. Bonnicksen

As increasing numbers of infertility clinics in the U.S. offer embryo freezing as part of their IVF protocols, public debate on its ethical implications has calmed. Yet in clinical settings, unanswered questions suggest the need to keep alive the ethical debate about the benefits to patients and society of embryo freezing.

repeated ovarian hyperstimulation and egg retrieval surgeries (laparoscopies).[6] It furthers the patient's emotional needs by reducing anxiety when she knows she has succeeded in one part of IVF and has tangible evidence, in the form of stored embryos, of that success. Finally, the patient benefits financially in that freezing avoids repeated start-up IVF expenses of hormonal monitoring, laparoscopy, and time lost from work during the two-week IVF cycle.

There is a real distance between theory and practice, however. Clinics report freezing an average of fewer than three embryos per patient. From one-quarter to one-half of these embryos do not survive freezing and thawing in established centers, and the attrition rate is undoubtedly higher in newer centers. Thus an optimal scenario of freezing, in which around six embryos are stored for leisurely transfer over a period of months, has yet to be realized.[7]

Does freezing actually benefit the patient physically? No injuries such as uterine infections from the transfer of thawed embryos have been reported, but neither does the evidence demonstrate that freezing significantly reduces the physical stresses from IVF for patients. There are insufficient data to conclude whether the use of thawed embryos is correlated with fewer miscarriages or multiple pregnancies. Moreover, the reduction of hormonal stimulation and laparoscopy may be less than expected, since mild medication may be needed to prepare the uterus for embryo transfer with thawed embryos.[8] And due to the attrition rate of frozen embryos, the patient may have to undergo the rigorous initial IVF cycle only to be spared, at most, one repeat cycle.

Does freezing benefit patients emotionally? Physicians presume that patients build defenses against disappointment when embryos are stored, but some women do just the opposite and "enhance" the embryos by

Hastings Center Report, December 1988

coming to see them as babies. Patients may develop attachments to their embryos during regular IVF, as indicated by their naming the embryos, asking for the petri dishes in which the embryos were fertilized as mementoes, acting and feeling pregnant after the embryos are transferred to their uteruses, and mourning the embryos' loss if they do not implant. Freezing has the capacity to enhance rather than diminish such bonding.

Bonding poses problems if clients need to stop embryo freezing prematurely. Couples in freezing programs are warned that they may divorce or lose a spouse and therefore need to agree about what should be done with their embryos in such an event. They are also asked to accept the consequences of failure of freezing equipment, which would result in loss of the embryos. They are not, however, necessarily prepared for unexpected reasons for discontinuing freezing, as when the wife has a hysterectomy, is prematurely menopausal, or develops other medical problems precluding a pregnancy. Additionally, the costs of freezing might become excessive for the couple or they may have a multiple birth after the initial IVF cycle, adopt a child, or decide the strain of trying to circumvent infertility is too great and stop the process.

Anecdotal evidence suggests that the presence of frozen embryos is not necessarily like money in the bank, with more being better, for clients who find they must decide what to do with spare or unneeded embryos. Will the couple experience remorse or guilt by ordering the destruction of their embryos? If donation is an option, will they later regret donating their embryos to other couples? It is not clear whether couples easily affirm this anticipatory decision when the need to discontinue freezing is at hand.

Freezing also increases the patient's dependence on IVF as the answer to infertility in a way that can be emotionally unhealthy. Nurse coordinators have written of the need to counsel patients about resolutions to infertility treatment other than a pregnancy and birth, such as adoption or acceptance of infertility.[9] Freezing interferes with closure on

infertility for women who want to adopt or move on to other life goals but who find they cannot terminate the effort because of stored embryos. It also locks patients into treatment at the clinic where their embryos are stored even if they lose confidence in the program or feel pressured, either by clinic staff or by their own desires for pregnancy, to continue to try IVF.

Embryo freezing places women and men in the role of pioneers in uncharted psychological waters. By bidding technicians to judge embryos for their "freezability," it opens embryos to evaluation and encourages patients to evaluate their own self-worth (already assaulted by the legacy of infertility) by the number and quality of embryos they have stored. The embryo's appearance (regular or irregular? favorable or unfavorable?[10]) is a strong predictor of its ability to survive the freeze and thaw. Self-recrimination, which is already underway during IVF when women evaluate themselves on the basis of the number of follicles or eggs they produce, can be extended and broadened by embryo cryopreservation.

Embryo freezing also prolongs the experience of being a "patient" inasmuch as a genetic part of the couple is in the hands of an infertility clinic. This can add to couples' feelings of vulnerability and dependence by causing them to worry about embryos stored in a laboratory (fearing damage to the embryos or a mix-up of ampules).

The financial benefits of freezing are also questionable. Freezing can save couples thousands of dollars in start-up costs if a sizable number of embryos are frozen and survive the freeze/thaw, and if the couple is paying out-of-pocket for IVF. However, as noted, these conditions are usually only imperfectly met. Not only are few embryos frozen, but pregnancy rates appear slightly lower (or at least not demonstrably higher) for thawed than fresh embryos.[11]

Even if survival and implantation rates were high, freezing would save couples money only if it put them one step ahead of insurance coverage. If, however, the couple has access to insurance coverage that pays most of

the estimated $5,000 for each cycle, but refuses reimbursement for the still-experimental procedure of freezing embryos, then the couple will pay out-of-pocket for the preparation, storage, and thawing of embryos.

Thus, although freezing may save couples money in the long run, in the short term it perpetuates a traditional problem of IVF in which, with the absence of federal funds for research involving human embryos and the inhospitable political climate for such research, the clinical application of IVF and its innovations precedes controlled studies using human embryos.[12] Freezing will place couples one step behind insurance coverage unless, as in Arkansas, cryopreservation is explicitly included as part of an IVF protocol or couples are given a maximum benefit level for IVF to be spent at their discretion.[13] Moreover, couples are billed for freezing irrespective of the outcome. If the machinery malfunctions, or the couple donates the frozen embryos to other clients or to the hospital for study, or asks that they be discarded, the couple will still have paid for preparation and storage costs, which can run over time to hundreds or thousands of dollars.

Reservations about the physical, emotional, and financial benefits of embryo freezing raise questions about whether it is always in the best interests of patients and couples and how, if it poses harms as well as benefits, freezing can be practiced in a way that truly serves their needs. Should not their interests be an integral part of the criteria used to set up and administer freezing programs? What ethical obligations do practitioners have to their patients and to couples in deciding how to administer such programs?

Clinical Policies

Expediency, medical hunches, and the need to guarantee the program's future play a large role in how policies are made in pioneering freezing programs. Policies of innovative centers are passed to other centers in a lateral modeling through discussions among colleagues or through contracts with or workshops sponsored by well-known embryologists who pass on their programs' consent forms and policies. In lateral modeling, however, careful weighing of the physician's obligation to patients becomes lost in the effort to do what is expedient, efficient, and effective in other centers. A global notion of presumed beneficence replaces an individualized search for demonstrated beneficence.

Despite this modeling method, clinical policies exhibit a variety of approaches on a range of issues. Will a limit be placed on the number of years embryos are frozen? One center, for example, freezes embryos for a maximum of five years as a compromise measure between the two years proposed by some members of the hospital's ethics committee and the reproductive life cut-off favored by others. Others limit freezing time to avoid being in the "long-term storage business" or because they fear couples will move and abandon their embryos, leaving the program in an awkward legal position. Still others do not impose time limits to "keep our options open."

Most centers require couples to sign detailed consent forms stipulating the disposition of the embryo; others do not, arguing that such consent would be legally unenforceable in any event.

Should clinics charge for the procedure before they achieve their first success? Some centers do not charge for freezing or charge only a nominal amount until a clinical pregnancy results. Others charge up to $1,000 when setting up the program.

Should patients have the option of donating extra embryos for research or to other infertile couples? Some centers do not allow donation of extra frozen embryos; others require it as an alternative to discarding the embryos.

The physician's obligation in administering embryo freezing programs is to identify the patient's interests and integrate those interests into decisionmaking. This requires modesty about freezing's benefits for individual patients. It also requires a recognition of the pressure of unresolved societal dilemmas about working with human embryos that have implications for the needs of patients.

Freezing: Routine or Optional

Is it ever in the patient's interest to present freezing as a normal part of the IVF protocol rather than as an option? Directors report that over 90 percent of patients with spare embryos elect freezing, which indicates that freezing is presented in a way that encourages patients' participation in the protocol (for example, by stating "our policy is to freeze embryos in excess of four"). Yet this leads to concern about how detailed the information given to patients about the risks and uncertainties of the procedure actually is. An examination of consent forms confirms that, at least in writing, patients are given the most general information (for example, the risks are unknown, freezing has worked for animal models, the benefits "we hope" are to increase the chance of pregnancy).

It could be argued that generalized information (which in effect presumes the goodness of freezing) is more helpful than specific data that are too premature or sketchy, given the newness of embryo cryopreservation, to give accurate guidance. Some practitioners also contend that presenting freezing as an accepted part of IVF will save clients from the responsibility of making yet another decision in the already stressful IVF cycle.

The often-expressed presumption in IVF that the infertile patient is "desperate," "willing to try anything," and in need of urgent action due to her "ticking biological clock," seems to negate providing detailed information to her. Such views do not, however, justify withholding from clients detailed information about choices with respect to embryo freezing. The couple is not, in fact, in an emergency medical situation, and decisions need not be made under pressure if patients express their choices at the start of the IVF cycle. Moreover, the data are not so complex as to overwhelm most patients. While the legacy of infertility may indeed leave women in psychological distress with feelings of diminished self-worth, depression, and anxiety, others exhibit high ego-strength and a need to accumulate

information about the procedures in which they participate.[14] Where patients do perceive themselves as desperate, this ought to signal caution, not permission, about freezing and the desirability of conveying full information to the patient about the experimental nature of the procedure.

Another reason for full disclosure of information, even if that information is sketchy or seemingly not desired by the patient, is to check on unseemly incentives for offering freezing. There are many motives for freezing—enhancing a program's prestige, setting the stage for research, bringing in fees to be funneled back into the IVF program—and patients are needed to meet these goals. Hence, the exploitive dissembling that has occurred in regular IVF and ambiguity over pregnancy rates[15] is repeated in freezing when directors give global success rates only and do not itemize success rates at each stage of the freezing procedure.

Physicians, then, must integrate into their protocols avenues for enhancing the patient's choice about whether or not to freeze spare embryos. The information on freezing should be given at the beginning of the cycle (not after the laparoscopy, when there are time constraints on decisionmaking). It should include full information about costs, including whether the storage fee is for each embryo or for all embryos, indefinite or subject to periodic renewals, constant or subject to cost-of-living adjustments, and inclusive of thawing and transfer fees. Most importantly, it should contain written information about risks and success rates at that particular center, including the average number of embryos frozen at the center per patient; the number surviving the freeze/thaw; the number of thawed embryos transferred to patients; the number of clinical pregnancies and births with thawed embryos; and comparisons of pregnancy, birth, and pregnancy and birth complications for fresh and thawed embryos.

If the center is too new to have such data, the director should provide global data and data from one or two middle level centers (not just from the most successful centers). The patient should also be informed about freezing outcomes for women with situations similar to hers. Are embryos more likely to survive the freeze/thaw if the woman is stimulated with certain combinations of hormones? Are some couples more likely to produce morphologically sound embryos than others? Where data are not available, patients should be advised that many questions about freezing remain unanswered.

The Meaning of the Embryo

Lingering questions about the nature of the human embryo affect communication within the IVF/freezing program, and suggest that the physician recognize the broader societal context when making decisions about embryo freezing programs and respect the differing perceptions of the embryo that intermix in the clinical setting. To clients, the embryo symbolizes hope and potential parenthood. It affirms the wife's femininity, the husband's masculinity, and the couple's potency. It is a powerful symbol with which clients establish emotional connections. It may be the closest thing to parenthood the wife and husband experience.

To physicians and scientists, the embryo is a collection of cells with distinct properties relating to its stage of development.[16] Its morphology is evaluated on its predicted ability to cleave, grow, and survive the freeze/thaw, and evaluations are made on this basis. An ongoing question, for example, is whether technicians should transfer the strongest embryos while they are fresh and freeze the weaker ones (this makes sense if most embryos do not survive the freeze/thaw), or transfer the weak embryos and freeze the strong ones (which makes sense if the strong embryos will survive and can be transferred to the woman at a later, presumably more receptive cycle when she has not been hormonally stimulated).[17] The importance of an embryo's appearance in predicting success rates places technicians in the position of identifying the criteria of an embryo that "looks good" or "looks odd," and this adds another qualification to the embryo's "worth."

> To see in new techniques a way of reducing dilemmas is to fail to question the virtue of the model already being built. Where dissembling, ambiguous language, untested presumptions, and narrow medical criteria combine in the clinical setting, there is diminished opportunity for enlightened debate about the value of freezing and its technological successors for society as a whole.

Freezing creates an ironic situation in which clients tend to personalize their embryos over time and physicians tend to depersonalize them as they evaluate the embryo's freezability. These different perspectives may reduce meaningful communication between patient and doctor because one is using subjective criteria for making decisions and the other objective criteria. In deciding the disposition of unwanted frozen embryos, for example, couples who develop attachments to their embryos (especially if they have had a child through an earlier IVF cycle) may "see" donation of embryos to other couples as akin to giving a child for adoption, or "see" discarding the embryo as akin to abortion. A physician unaware of these perceptions may decide what choices to offer couples on the basis of expediency and with diminished sensitivity to their emotional attachments.

The legal dimensions of embryo freezing add another "personality" to the embryo. In 1984 the American Fertility Society advised that concepti are the property of the donors.[18] Following the Rios's case of ownerless embryos, IVF programs integrated language about ownership and property into consent forms, stating, for example, that "each embryo shall be the joint property of both of you, as the wife and the husband, who are deemed to be the legal owners." Couples who freeze embryos are asked to provide for the disposition of their embryo-as-property in the event of death or divorce. On the one hand, this personalizes the embryo

as a potential child by bidding the couple to take responsibility for it. On the other, it commercializes this responsibility by defining it as one between owners and property.

The varied meanings of the embryo and the amalgam of language used to describe embryos (clients naming them "twins" or "preemie," doctors calling them "sets of tissues" or "pre-zygotes," and consent forms referring to "property" and "owners") reveal the moral uncertainty still underlying activities involving embryos. This uncertainty is heightened by language referring to the embryo's destruction. Some centers are euphemistic (for example, "You should be aware that the embryo that is thawed and not transferred will not undergo further development") and others are blunt (embryos will be "destroyed" or "disposed of"). Some centers refer to "ethical methods" of embryo disposal, without specifying what these methods are. Others give the clients the option of overseeing embryo disposal, as if in a ritual of death. All this conveys confused messages that hinder communication. If, for example, the embryo is a "mere" set of cells or property, why do program personnel hedge when talking about its destruction? If this is done to avoid arousing public attention, what is the effect on communication within the IVF center?

The implication is that much uncertainty continues to underlie cryopreservation in IVF centers: Ethical dilemmas remain unresolved and misunderstandings arise from faulty communication. The patients will bear the brunt of techniques used before the moral meanings are understood in the public debate. It may be in the patient's interest for physicians to depersonalize the embryo and use scientific language to prevent unfruitful and probably disappointing bonding. However, this runs the danger of closing communication between physician and patient that would reveal the subjective but morally significant perspectives of patients.

Open and frank discussion among ethics committees, patients, nurse coordinators, and physicians is required to resolve the question of the many meanings of the embryo. A pragmatic, honest language is essential, one that does not disguise the embryo (in itself an acceptable term) either by personalizing it (for example, calling it "little one") or depersonalizing it (by calling it "the pre-zygote"). Honesty is also served by forthright communication about what will be done with embryos no longer needed. False propriety does little good, as when consent forms state that embryos will be "disposed of ethically," but the method is unstated and staff members cannot articulate what an ethical method of disposition is. If it means a passive act (exposing the embryo to the air so it will disintegrate) rather than an active move (washing it down the sink), this should clearly be included in the consent form by stating, for example, that unwanted frozen embryos will be exposed to light and will disintegrate in a given amount of time.

Beneficent Embryo Freezing

The growing field of alternative conception owes its energy to mixed forces, including the demands of patients, scientists' yearning for discovery, physicians' interest in satisfying patients' needs, lucrative possibilities, and public fascination with technology. At a basic level, however, it is the physician operating in the infertility clinic who makes everyday decisions that affect whether the techniques will serve or detract from societal interests.[19] Where physicians adhere to traditional notions of virtue in presenting freezing in the clinical setting, they take an important step toward integrating it into society in a way that will promote its promise. However, when they make ad hoc decisions with the clinic's interests primarily in mind, overlook the emotional side-effects of the technique, and presume the benefit of freezing, patient and societal interests are ill-served.

With normalcy and routine comes a diminished will and inclination to question the ethical dimensions of embryo freezing. The subtle ethical quandaries that arise in freezing programs are in danger of being overlooked in the absence of highly visible crises. Already ovum freezing is being presented as an innovation that raises no ethical issues and negates the need for the more problematic embryo freezing.[20] To see in new techniques a way of reducing dilemmas is to fail to question the virtue of the model already being built. Where dissembling, ambiguous language, untested presumptions, and narrow medical criteria combine in the clinical setting, there is diminished opportunity for enlightened debate about the value of freezing and its technological successors for society as a whole. Clinical interactions are gatekeeping interactions. They ought to be developed and refined on the basis of ethically defensible criteria in which the observed needs of patients play a central part.

References

The author wishes to acknowledge the financial help of The American Philosophical Society and The National Endowment for the Humanities in gathering interview material for this article.

1 Andrea L. Bonnicksen and Robert H. Blank, "The Government and In Vitro Fertilization (IVF): Views of IVF Directors," *Fertility and Sterility* 49:3 (March 1988), 396-98. Of the 88 directors who responded to the survey in early 1987, 41 already offered embryo cryopreservation and most others planned to offer it within two years.

2 Medical Research International, The American Fertility Society Special Interest Group, "In Vitro Fertilization/Embryo Transfer in the United States: 1985 and 1986 Results from the National IVF/ET Registry," *Fertility and Sterility* 49:2 (February 1988), 212-15.

3 U.S. Congress, Office of Technology Assessment, *Infertility: Medical and Social Choices* (Washington, DC: U.S. Government Printing Office, 1988), 298.

4 Alan Trounson, "Preservation of Human Eggs and Embryos," *Fertility and Sterility* 46:1 (July 1986), 1-12; John A. Robertson, "Ethical and Legal Issues in Cryopreservation of Human Embryos," *Fertility and Sterility* 47:3 (March 1987), 371-81.

5 Although technically the "patient" in IVF is the husband and wife as a couple, for clarity in the following pages attention is directed to the female partner as the patient.

6 Jacques Testart et al., "Factors Influencing the Success Rate of Human Embryo Freezing in an In Vitro Fertilization and Embryo Transfer Program," *Fertility and Sterility* 48:1 (July 1987), 107-12; Robertson, "Ethical and Legal Issues," 371.

7 Medical Research International, "In Vitro Fertilization/Embryo Transfer in the United States," 213; Testart et al., "Factors," 109.

8 Testart, et al., "Factors," 108.

9 See, for example, C.H. Garner, "Psychological Aspects of IVF and the Infertile Couple," in *Foundations of In Vitro Fertilization*, Christopher M. Fredericks et al., eds. (Washington, DC: Hemisphere Publishing Corporation, 1987), 305-11.

10 Trounson, "Preservation," 6; Testart et al., "Factors," 111.

11 Trounson, "Preservation," 5; Testart et al., "Factors," 111.

12 Susan Abramowitz, "A Stalemate on Test-Tube Baby Research," *Hastings Center Report* 14:1 (February 1984), 5-9.

13 Office of Technology Assessment, *Infertility*, 151.

14 Garner, "Psychological Aspects"; Ellen W. Freeman et al., "Psychological Evaluation and Support in a Program of In Vitro Fertilization and Embryo Transfer," *Fertility and Sterility* 43:1 (January 1985), 48-53.

15 Michael R. Soules, "The In Vitro Fertilization Pregnancy Rate: Let's Be Honest with One Another," *Fertility and Sterility* 43:4 (April 1985), 511-13.

16 Rafael I. Tejada and William G. Karow, "Semantics Used in the Nomenclature of In Vitro Fertilization, or Let's All Be More Proper," *Journal of In Vitro Fertilization and Embryo Transfer* 3 (1986), 341-42.

17 Testart et al., "Factors."

18 American Fertility Society, "Ethical Statement on In Vitro Fertilization," *Fertility and Sterility* 41:1 (January 1984), 12-13.

19 Eugene B. Brody, "Reproduction without Sex—But with the Doctor," *Law, Medicine and Health Care* 15:3 (Fall 1987), 152-55.

20 Trounson, "Preservation," 11.

LAW AND THE LIFE SCIENCES

Redefining Parenthood and Protecting Embryos: Why We Need New Laws
by GEORGE J. ANNAS

Dependable birth control made sex without reproduction possible. Some saw the separation of procreation from sex as an affirmation of pleasure and love; others saw it as a sin against nature. One consequence was a relaxation of the inhibition against sex with multiple partners; venereal disease replaced pregnancy as the worst physical consequence. Nonetheless, venereal disease in women has its own potential side effect—sterility. Other factors, such as postponing pregnancy until the late 30s, also increased the incidence of infertility.

Now medicine is closing the circle opened with the advent of sex without reproduction by offering methods of reproduction without sex; including artificial insemination by donor (AID), in vitro fertilization (IVF), and surrogate embryo transfer (SET). As with birth control, artificial reproduction is defended as life-affirming and loving by its proponents, and denounced as unnatural by its detractors. How concerned should society be about artificial reproduction?

In England, working groups have produced three reports on artificial insemination over the past three decades. In July, the Warnock Commission issued the latest and most comprehensive report on "human assisted reproduction." In Australia, working groups have reported on IVF and are looking at frozen embryos. In the United States, the Ethics Advisory Board of the then-Department of Health, Education and Welfare issued the most re-

cent national report in 1979. Lately it has been suggested that a new National Commission study and monitor developments in this area. The reason for all these panels and commissions is that artificial reproduction raises profound social and ethical issues touching the nature of family relationships, and the nature and value of the human embryo.

"To allay public fear" concerning the consequences of new developments, the Warnock Commission developed sixty-three recommendations: thirty-three involving a proposed licensing board to regulate clinical services and research, seven involving the National Health Service's infertility program, and twenty-three for new British laws, including proposals to create seven new crimes involving human reproduction and embryo research.

The Warnock approach is legal overkill, since it seems premature to outlaw as criminal so many aspects of artificial reproduction. Nonetheless, just because we cannot answer all the questions raised by these new techniques does not mean that we should remain silent about those areas in which action is imperative to protect important societal interests. Protecting the child and family, and protecting the real and symbolic value of the human embryo are cases in point. Two areas merit quick and decisive legal action: defining maternity and paternity at the moment of birth, and protecting the human embryo from commercial exploitation.

Identification of the Mother and Father

Artificial insemination by donor for the first time separated the genetic father of a child from the act of sexual intercourse in its conception. The procedure has become recognized as a standard "treatment" for infertility of a married couple when the husband is sterile. Customarily the sperm comes from an anonymous vendor who (so long as the husband of the woman consents) is not considered the *legal* father of

the child. Thus we have developed a technique in which the mother's husband replaces the genetic father as the legal father of the child.

This model places personal agreements or contracts among the parties ahead of genetic or "blood line" considerations, and has been suggested as the model to apply to embryo transfer. The question is: Does it fit? The Warnock Commission, for example, recommended that

> In order to achieve some certainty in this situation [egg donation] . . . legislation should provide that when a child is born to a woman following donation of another's egg the woman giving birth should, for all purposes, be regarded in law as the mother of that child, and that the egg donor should have no rights or obligations in respect of the child.

This treats the donation of sperm and egg on an equal footing and seems reasonable as far as it goes; but it does not go far enough. We need a rule that applies equally to *all* births. The reason we require legislation to guarantee the obligations of the social or rearing father and extinguish the rights and obligations of the genetic father is that society has always assumed that the genetic father is *the* father of the child for all purposes.

Nonetheless, to protect children and foster families, children born during the course of a marriage are legally *presumed* to be the legitimate offspring of the couple. To challenge this legal presumption successfully, state laws commonly require the husband to disown the child affirmatively and present evidence in court proving beyond a reasonable doubt that he is not the genetic father. This is a reasonable rule because it protects the child and helps ensure that it has another parent (in addition to its mother) who is identifiable as financially responsible for its well-being, and who is likely to help rear the child.

In dealing with the mother, however, an additional biological consideration makes the identification issue more complicated.

GEORGE J. ANNAS J.D., M.P.H., *is Utley Professor of Health Law, Boston University School of Medicine; and chief, health law section, Boston University School of Public Health. Portions of this article are adapted from testimony before Rep. Albert Gore's Subcommittee on Investigations & Oversight of the Committee on Science and Technology, U.S. House of Representatives, August 8, 1984.*

In males one need only distinguish the genetic from the social or rearing father. But, as John Robertson has noted, in females we might have to distinguish among the genetic mother, the gestational mother, and the rearing mother. The question is: When these three are different women, which one should the law presume is the legal mother with the obligation to support and nurture the child?

This is a completely novel question. Previously, at birth there was *never* any question who the mother was since she was *always* both the genetic and the gestational mother (only the identity of the father was uncertain, and this uncertainty was clarified by a social decision to presume paternity in the mother's husband). Now, in cases of surrogate embryo transfer, and embryo transfer to a woman other than the egg donor, the identity of the genetic and gestational mother will be different. Which of these two women has a greater claim to be identified in law as the child's "mother," and is her claim superior to any claim a rearing mother might have who is neither genetically nor gestationally connected to the child?

The current legal presumption that the gestational (or birth) mother is the legal mother should remain. This gives the child and society certainty of identification at the time of birth (a protection for both mother and child), and also recognizes the biological fact that the gestational mother has contributed more of herself to the child than the genetic mother, and therefore has a greater biological investment and interest in it. If any agreements regarding transfer, relinquishing of parental rights, or adoption are to be made, they should be made only by the gestational mother, and only after she has had a reasonable time after the birth to consider all her and her child's options.

To protect both the integrity of the family and the interests of the children involved, the current legal presumptions should remain and be codified so they cannot be modified by private contract: the child's father should be presumed to be the husband of the child's mother, and the child's mother should be presumed to be the woman who gave birth to the child. We can permit the husband to overcome this presumption by presenting proof of nonpaternity beyond a reasonable doubt (so long as he did not consent to the procedure that resulted in the birth), but the maternal presumption should be conclusive and irrebuttable.

Protection of the Extracorporeal Embryo

Whether and how we should protect the extracorporeal embryo depends upon how we view it. We need not, of course, consider it a person to afford it legally recognized protection, any more than we need consider a dog a person to protect it against cruelty, or a dolphin a person to protect it against destruction, or a national park a person to protect it against loggers. Nor need we grant the embryo any legal rights of its own to afford it legal *recognition*.

With in vitro fertilization in which all fertilized eggs are replaced in the uterus of the ovum donor (embryo replacement) the issue of embryo protection concerns mainly care of it for the short time it is in vitro. Protection becomes a much more important issue if some of the embryos are not replaced, but are frozen for future implantation or research.

The human embryo is equal to more than the sum of its constituent parts. It not only has the complete genetic complement of a human being, but it also is a powerful symbol of human regeneration. We can thus value it and afford it legal recognition even though we do not so value or legally recognize either the egg or the sperm. On the other hand, we do recognize and accept a significant loss of embryos in nature, and make no efforts to recover and freeze them. We also permit destruction of and research on fetuses under certain circumstances. Thus what we seem to be dealing with are the added obligations that we incur by actively intervening in the natural process of human reproduction by using freezing techniques as a method of embryo storage.

To protect the gamete donors, and the interests of society in protecting the integrity of assisted reproduction techniques, embryos should only be frozen with the informed consent of both gamete donors, and only for a specific and specified purpose (usually use in subsequent cycles when a pregnancy is not obtained). When the purpose is fulfilled, the frozen embryo should be destroyed.

Likewise, when something other than the original use of the embryo is contemplated, the informed consent of both gamete contributors should be required. If only one is alive, that one should have the decision-making authority, since that person has the most interest in and is thus likely to be most protective of the embryo.

When they both die, the embryo should be destroyed. Recommendations like that of the Warnock Commission—to permit the frozen embryo to pass to the storage facility, which may dispose of the embryo as it sees fit (subject to certain licensing laws)—treat the embryo too much like unclaimed luggage, and give insufficient weight to its origins and symbolic value.

Sales of Frozen Embryos

In this country there is an almost universal consensus that kidneys should not be bought and sold, and the arguments against the sale of human embryos are even more compelling. In this case the specter of a coercive offer that exploits the bodies of the poor is replaced by the potential of a commercial market in prefabricated, selected embryos, which encourages us to view embryos as things or commodities that are simply means to whatever ends we design, rather than as human entities without a market price. Ian Kennedy has argued that we know intuitively that a human embryo is more valuable than a hamster or other experimental animal, and that is why we have trouble permitting experiments on human embryos. Likewise, we know intuitively that a human embryo is more "valuable" than a kidney and of much more symbolic importance regarding human life: that is why we feel that embryos should not be the subject of commerce. The reason is not so much the embryo itself (although many will find its intrinsic value sufficient justification to outlaw sales), but the implications for the children that will result following the sale and implantation of a frozen embryo.

Embryos will be bought and sold, if at all, on the belief that they will produce a healthy child, and possibly one of a certain physical type, IQ, stature, and so on. When the child is not born as warrantied or guaranteed, what remedies will the buyer have against the seller? Even a brief glance at the sales provisions in the Uniform Commercial Code (UCC) informs us that this is not an area in which we can permit sales or if we do permit them, it is an area in which we need a new set of sales statutes.

The UCC provides, for example, that "if the goods or the tender of delivery fail in any respect to conform to the contract, the buyer may (a) reject the whole; or (b) accept the whole; or (c) accept any commercial unit or units and reject the rest" (sec.

34

2-601). Section (c) might be read to apply to twins or triplets, and section (a) leaves us wondering who is responsible for the child. Likewise, "if the seller gives no instructions within a reasonable time after notification of rejection the buyer may *store* the rejected goods for the seller's account or *reship* them to him or *resell* them for the seller's account . . ." (sec. 2-604) This could be read as applying more directly to the frozen embryo itself, but its potential application to the child produced as a result of the embryo transfer process simply illustrates the inappropriateness of sales in this area at all, and the ease with which *sale of human embryos can quickly become confused with sale of human children.* In this regard the Warnock Commission is correct in recommending legislation to ensure that "there is no right of ownership in a human embryo," but the commission is simplistic in lumping "gametes and embryos" together in their discussion of a policy on sales.

Aladdin's Lesson

The lesson of Aladdin is not only that we must be cautious with genies, but also that we should not exchange "new lamps for old" until we know the value of each. Ideally, the state and federal government should stay out of the arena of human reproduction. Unfortunately, if the children resulting from new techniques such as surrogate embryo transfer and the use of frozen embryos are to be adequately protected, this is no longer possible. Private contractual agreements tend to favor the interests of the infertile couple over those of the potential child.

Action on three levels is warranted: (1) a model state law designed to clearly define the identity of the legal mother and father of all children, including those born to other than their genetic parents, should be drafted and enacted; (2) professional organizations, with public participation, should develop and promulgate guidelines for sound clinical practice; and (3) a national body of experts in law, public policy, science, medicine, and ethics should be established to monitor developments in this area and report annually to Congress and the individual states on the desirability of specific regulation and legislation.

At all levels, the primary focus should be on protecting the interests of the children, even if their protection sometimes comes at the expense of some infertile couples. This general policy will also protect the integrity of artificial reproduction itself.

Embryo* freezing as an adjunct to in vitro fertilization (IVF) is an important step forward in the treatment of infertility and control of human reproduction. Yet many questions concerning frozen embryos must be answered if the promise of this novel technology is to be realized.[1]

An immediate practical concern is decisional authority over frozen embryos. A recent dispute between a divorcing couple over custody of stored embryos highlights many of the issues that couples and IVF programs face when they cryopreserve human embryos.

The Tennessee Dispute

Mary Sue Davis, a twenty-eight-year-old secretary, and Junior Lewis Davis, a thirty-year-old housing authority employee, married in 1980. Their efforts to have a family over the last six years have been unsuccessful. Because of damage to Ms. Davis's fallopian tubes from ectopic pregnancies, six unsuccessful attempts at IVF have occurred. The last attempt resulted in seven extra embryos that were cryopreserved for possible use during later cycles. No document or consent form specifying disposition of these embryos was executed.[2]

The dispute over the fate of the embryos arose when the couple filed for divorce. The husband has sought to enjoin the fertility clinic from releasing the embryos to Ms. Davis or others for purposes of thawing and implantation. With divorce imminent, his concern is that neither his wife nor anyone else bear a child with these embryos, so that he will not end up a parent. Ms. Davis, on the other hand, wants very much to have a child with these embryos even if she is divorced. She insists that the embryos are living and that as the mother she

*The term "embryo" rather than the technically more accurate term "preembryo" is used to refer to the postfertilization, preimplantation entities discussed in this paper.

John A. Robertson *is James Watt Gregory Professor in Law at the School of Law, University of Texas at Austin.*

Resolving Disputes over Frozen Embryos

by John A. Robertson

The relation between respect for family and reproductive choice and use of IVF technology is in dispute in recent legal cases on the disposition of frozen embryos. Couples in IVF programs should be encouraged to stipulate in advance binding instructions regarding the disposition of such embryos.

has the right to initiate a pregnancy with them. If unable to use them herself, she wants to donate them to an infertile couple who could bring them to term.

Alternative Resolutions

Since few laws deal explicitly with the status and disposition of preimplantation embryos, direct precedents for deciding this case do not exist. The resulting decision, however, should clarify rules for IVF and embryo freezing generally or show the need for legislation or other policy solutions.

Several possible bases for resolving this dispute will not work. For example, there is no explicit prior agree-

ment between the couple for disposition of embryos to which either could be bound. Nor can one imply an agreement to implant all embryos from the fact one has provided gametes for IVF, since so many contingencies could intervene to change original plans (death, divorce, illness, disability, financial reversal, etc.). Creation of embryos alone should not be taken as an irrevocable commitment to reproduction.

A presumption in favor of embryo transfer, to "protect" embryos by giving them the chance to implant and come to term, also is not persuasive in the absence of state law giving embryos such rights. Legally, extracorporeal embryos have no right to be implanted in Tennessee or most other states. Respected ethical advisory bodies in several countries have also concluded that embryos are not persons with rights.[3]

A policy of always discard in the case of dispute is also unsatisfactory. While postmortem anatomic gift laws and federal fetal research regulations require the consent of both parents, there is no inherent reason why one parent should have veto power in such matters.[4] Nor does the desirable goal of assuring every child two rearing parents justify such a rule, since the alternative for the child in question is never being born at all. Being raised by one parent does not amount to wrongful life, and other rearing parents may enter the picture later.

Equally unacceptable is a "sweat equity" position that always favors the woman's decision because she has put more effort into production of the embryo, having undergone ovarian stimulation and surgical retrieval of eggs. Great differences in physical burdens do not require that divorcing mothers always receive custody of children. Moreover, the difference in bodily burdens between the man and woman in IVF is not so great (especially with transvaginal aspiration of eggs) that it should automatically determine decisional authority over resulting embryos.

Finally, equal division of embryos, like division of other marital assets, will not do because embryos are a unique kind of marital "property." Equal division avoids the core conflict

Hastings Center Report, November/December 1989

between producing or avoiding offspring, while implicitly resolving that conflict in favor of the party desiring to reproduce by assuring him or her some embryos to use in that effort. At the same time, it may so reduce the chance of a successful pregnancy that it is ultimately unsatisfactory to the party seeking to reproduce.

With these alternatives not applicable to the Tennessee case, its resolution requires a close look at the competing interests of each party: the one in avoiding the financial and psychosocial burdens of parenthood, and the other in using the embryos in question to become a parent. This analysis shows that the party wishing to avoid reproduction should prevail whenever the other party has a reasonable possibility of having offspring through other means.

Burdens of Unwanted Reproduction

A person who objects to transfer to a uterus of embryos formed from his or her gametes may experience significant financial and psychosocial burdens if the embryos lead to offspring.

Risks of Financial Liability. If the embryo implants and a child is born, the unwilling genetic father or mother may have legal obligations of support until the offspring reaches majority. Unless a statute provides an exemption, the traditional rule is that a man providing sperm for insemination or conception is the legal father, with rearing rights and duties, including support requirements.[5]

Since this rule is clearly established where conception occurs coitally, even when the woman has deceived the man about her ability to conceive, the rule is likely to be applied to noncoital conception as well.[6] The policy interest of holding men responsible for the consequences of their behavior and assuring offspring a male rearing parent also arises with noncoital insemination when no consenting male partner of the egg provider exists. Although the male is not engaging in sex, he is engaging in a transaction that makes offspring possible, and thus on policy grounds could be held responsible for resulting offspring.

Relieving the sperm source of financial responsibility is least likely to happen when there is no rearing male involved, as might happen when the sperm is provided to an unmarried woman, when a frozen embryo is used by a divorced wife, or when the embryo is donated to an unmarried woman. Under current law the sperm source for an embryo donation would be at substantial risk for financial liability in such situations.

The possibility of imposing support obligations on a woman who objects to transfer of embryos produced by her eggs is much less clear but cannot be ruled out in all situations. Precedents making the egg provider legally liable do not exist, because the egg source and the gestational mother have, until IVF made egg and embryo donation possible, always been identical.[7] Moreover, since the gestational mother will most likely have full rearing rights and duties the need to assure a responsible female parent for the child will not exist as it does with males.

Still, situations can be imagined in which the egg source would be financially liable if the unconsented transfer of embryos occurred. Suppose the father employs a gestational surrogate to bring the embryo to term, making him a single parent. Reversal of fortune could so diminish his resources that the child and the courts look to the genetic mother for support. Or suppose that the embryo were donated to an infertile couple, and that couple became incapable of supporting the child. Until it is clearly established that embryo donation severs all rearing rights and duties in the providers of the embryo, equal application of the rules applied to male gamete sources could lead to the female gamete source also being held liable for child support in these situations.

Psychosocial Impact. Whether or not the gamete source who opposes embryo transfer incurs child support obligations, he or she will still face the potentially significant psychosocial impact of unwanted biologic offspring. A marriage that had failed would have produced biologic offspring, for which the unconsenting partner may have strong feelings of attachment, responsibility, guilt, etc.

Even if no rearing duties or even contact result, as might occur if the embryos are donated to another couple, the unconsenting partner may learn that biologic offspring exist, with the powerful attendant reverberations which that can ignite. The psychosocial burdens of unwanted parenthood are significant and should be given appropriate weight in deciding individual disputes.

The Burdens of Non-Transfer

Arrayed against the interest in avoiding the financial and psychosocial burdens of unwanted reproduction is the interest of the partner who wishes to use the embryos to reproduce. At stake for the woman wishing to use the embryos is gestation and rearing of her biologic offspring, while for the man there is the interest in rearing his biologic offspring. Let us assume that the interest of either the man or woman in reproducing is significant and ordinarily should be honored. The question, however, is whether it is of greater or lesser importance than the interest of the partner who wishes to avoid the financial and psychosocial burdens of reproduction. Since one person's loss is the other person's gain, it may appear that there is no objective way to arbitrate the dispute.

A way out of the dilemma exists if we consider the irreversibility of the respective losses at issue and the essential fungibility of the embryos. The party who wishes to avoid offspring is irreversibly harmed if embryo transfer and birth occur, for the burdens of unwanted parenthood cannot then be avoided. On the other hand, frustrating the ability of the willing partner to reproduce with these embryos will—in most instances—not prevent that partner from reproducing at a later time with other embryos. As long as the party wishing to reproduce could without undue burden create other embryos, the desire to avoid biologic offspring should take priority over the desire to reproduce with the embryos in question. If other embryos are reasonably available, there is no inherent reason to prefer already existing embryos over new ones that can be produced (given that the embryos

37

themselves have no rights to be transferred).

In most instances the partner wishing to save the embryos to reproduce will be able to create new embryos to achieve his or her reproductive goals. For example, the male partner would be able to reproduce with another woman by remarrying, by obtaining an egg donation and surrogate gestator, or by serving as a sperm donor if no rearing is sought.

The woman, in most instances, should also be able to reproduce either with a new partner or a sperm donor. As long as her ovaries still function and hyperstimulation and egg retrieval are not medically contraindicated, she will be able to produce new embryos. Of course, she will have to undergo the moderate physical burdens of IVF stimulation and egg retrieval, but it does not appear unreasonable to ask her to bear moderate additional physical burdens to prevent the irreparable loss to the party seeking to avoid genetic offspring.

This solution is not available, however, if later reproductive opportunities do not exist for medical, financial, or social reasons. At that point the conflict between the right to reproduce and the right to avoid reproduction must be directly faced, with the argument for using the embryos against the wishes of the objecting partner then being strongest. One might then reasonably argue that the equities favor the party who has no alternative opportunity to reproduce, because the pleasures of parenthood will be deeper and more intense than the discomfort of unwanted genetic offspring.

Opting for reproduction when there is no other alternative assumes that the party wishing to reproduce will, if female, gestate and rear, or rear if male. The claim to reproduce against the wishes of the other is much less compelling if the party merely wishes the embryos donated to an infertile couple in order to have but not rear biologic offspring. The strongest argument in their favor, when they have no other reasonable reproductive opportunities, exists when they will assume all financial and childrearing burdens so that the unwilling party will have only the burden of genetic offspring *tout court*.

On this analysis the Tennessee case should be resolved in favor of the husband, who wishes the embryos not transferred, and against the wife, who wishes that they be transferred to her uterus or the uterus of a willing recipient. Her interest in reproduction can be satisfied by having her undergo yet another IVF cycle with a new partner or donor. She appears healthy and responds well to ovarian stimulation. The fact that she has already submitted to six attempts at IVF is not determinative, since the burdens of any one additional retrieval cycle are moderate and acceptable, at least relative to the irreversible burdens of imposing fatherhood on the husband. Even if she ultimately prevails because of the many stimulation and retrieval cycles that she has undergone, cases in which the woman has undergone only one or two cycles should be decided in favor of the husband who now objects to reproduction with previously frozen embryos. (See page 11).

Whatever the balance struck by the Tennessee court, the Davis case is important for calling attention to the need for clear legal rules concerning disposition of frozen embryos. An essential starting point for such rules is recognition that the couple who provide the gametes jointly "own"— have dispositional authority over— the resulting embryos. Two legislative solutions to avoid future disputes should then be considered: embryo protection laws and prior directives.

The Couple's Ownership

Few persons would disagree that the gamete providers are the primary decisionmakers or "owners" of the resulting embryos, rather than the doctors or scientists who provide the technical skill to create the embryos, or the operators of the embryo bank where they are stored. They have provided the gametes, and the resulting embryos have great reproductive significance for them. In this context the terms "ownership" or "property" refer to the locus and not the scope of decisional authority over embryos.

The more interesting question is whether their decisional authority can be limited, so that their "property" or "ownership" in embryos is less than their ownership of other kinds of property. For example, limitations on buying or selling or use in research may be more appropriate with embryos than with other property. However, the couple might still retain the right to decide whether transfer of embryos to a uterus will occur, and to make advance binding commitments concerning future disposition of embryos. At a minimum, legislation and public policy should recognize the couple's authority to make those choices concerning embryos that are legally available.

It follows then that the couple retains dispositional authority or ownership over embryos until they relinquish it to others, or until the state has restricted their options. If so, IVF programs and embryo banks have no right to retain embryos against the couple's joint wishes or to make other dispositions unless the couple has specifically ceded that right to them.

An embryo bank thus has no right to refuse to release a stored embryo to a couple for thawing without transfer, or for transport to another location, unless the couple had specifically agreed to this limitation. Even then, one may question the reasonableness of the program or bank insisting on enforcing that condition, though there will be some situations in which legitimate interests of the IVF program would be harmed if the condition were not enforced.[8]

The *Jones v. York* case in Virginia should clarify the couple's dispositional authority over stored embryos when an IVF program or embryo bank refuses to follow their instructions.[9] An infertile couple had one frozen embryo remaining after three unsuccessful attempts at IVF pregnancy at a leading program in Norfolk. After the couple moved to California, they sought to transport their frozen embryo to a Los Angeles IVF program for thawing and placement in the wife's uterus. The Norfolk program refused, citing the signed consent form, lack of IRB approval, legal liability risks, and the demeaning effect of shipping human embryos by air "a la cattle embryos."

The court denied the Norfolk

clinic's attempts to dismiss the couple's suit seeking release of their embryo. The judge found that the cryopreservation agreement between the couple and the program had created a bailor-bailee relationship, which imposed on the bailee an absolute obligation to return the subject matter of the bailment to the bailor when the purpose of the bailment had been terminated. Neither the state's human subject research law nor the terms of the agreement undercut the couple's property interest in the frozen embryo. Therefore, they had a *prima facie* claim to have their embryo released to them.

Jones v. York is significant because it assumes without question that embryos are the "property" of the gamete providers, and finds that any limitation of their dispositional authority in favor of an IVF program or embryo bank will be strictly construed against the IVF program. While a program could still insist that the embryos it creates not be transferred to other locations, such a restriction will be binding only if the program explicitly informs the couple that they are ceding their right to transport their embryos to other locations.

Prohibiting Embryo Discard?

The Davis case would have been easily resolved if Tennessee had enacted a law requiring that embryos be placed in a uterus whenever possible, either that of the woman providing the egg or a willing recipient. Louisiana currently bans the "intentional destruction" of IVF embryos, and mandates their donation in certain cases.[10] Other states may follow suit. But would such laws be constitutional? If so, is the limitation they place on a couple's dispositional authority justified?

The constitutional argument against such a statute rests on a right claimed by the couple or gamete providers individually to avoid the financial and psychosocial burdens of unwanted genetic parenthood. Supreme Court cases recognizing the right to use contraceptives and have abortions may reasonably be taken as establishing a right to avoid reproduction because of the financial, social, and physical burdens that reproduction entails.[11] Even if parenthood entails only psychological burdens, as would occur with mandatory donation of unwanted embryos, the interest at stake is still of paramount importance to individual identity and therefore warrants protection as a fundamental right. If so, the state's desire to protect embryos and signify the importance of human life would not constitute the compelling interest necessary to justify infringement of the fundamental right to avoid reproduction.[12]

The counterargument appears stronger, even if *Roe v. Wade* remains intact. Since the right claimed is to be free of a purely psychological burden (no financial or other rearing burdens attach), it is unlikely that a Supreme Court disinclined to expand the menu of unwritten fundamental rights would give the interest in avoiding genetic offspring *tout court* fundamental right status. If not a fundamental right, the state's interest in protecting embryos by requiring donation of unwanted extras would easily meet the rational basis test by which such a statute would be judged.[13] *Roe v. Wade* presents no obstacle to such a law as long as the woman is not herself forced to accept the embryos.

A variant on embryo protection laws might be to limit the number of embryos produced to avoid the problem of discard raised by extra embryos, for example, a law that prohibited insemination of more than five eggs during any one retrieval cycle. Such laws might have greater constitutional problems than mandatory embryo donation statutes, because they directly impair the couple's ability to become pregnant through IVF.[14] They might also effectively ban embryo freezing, since few extra embryos might result.

But are embryo protection laws desirable, even if they may be within the constitutional authority of the state? They would be a significant limitation on the couple's "ownership" or dispositional authority over their embryos, and could lead to imposition of unwanted parenting burdens. While a minority believes that a new person exists at fertilization, most people would disagree that the earliest stages of postfertilized human life, which consist of four to eight undifferentiated cells that are not yet biologically individual, are themselves persons or entities with rights. The consensus emerging from the Ethics Advisory Board, the Warnock Committee, the American Fertility Society, and most other ethics commissions throughout the world that have studied the matter is that special respect for embryos does not require treating them as actual persons or prohibiting couples from opposing transfer.[15]

If preimplantation embryos are too rudimentary in development to have interests, much less rights, protecting them can be justified only on symbolic or religious grounds that are not uniformly shared in a highly pluralistic society. In my view the argument for preferring early embryos over the competing concerns of couples or individuals who wish to prevent their placement in a uterus is not persuasive. Persons wishing to avoid reproduction have more to lose than society has to gain from laws that limit their dispositional authority over the embryos formed from their egg or sperm.

Advance Agreements on Disposition

A better policy solution would be to require couples to declare at the time that embryos are created or stored their instructions concerning disposition if they are unavailable or unable to agree when death, divorce, passage of time, or other contingencies occur. As part of the consent procedure, the gamete providers will be informed of the dispositional alternatives available at that program or bank, and asked to designate which alternatives they choose if certain stated contingencies occur. In some cases it may be possible for the couple to reserve the right jointly to change their designated disposition at later times, but until they do, the options selected would be binding when the specified events occur.

The argument for recognizing the binding effect of joint advance instructions rests on several grounds. The right to use embryos to reproduce or to avoid reproduction should include the right to give binding advance instructions because certainty about future outcomes is necessary to exercise reproductive options. In addition, all parties gain from the ability to plan for certain outcomes when future contingencies occur. Finally, it minimizes the frequency and cost of resolving disputes that arise over disposition of embryos.

But arguments against binding oneself in advance also exist. Advance instructions may be issued at a time relatively early in the IVF process, when a person's needs and interests may not be as fully realized as they would be when later events occur. One's interests and preferences might change as future events unfold, in ways that cannot be foreseen when the instructions are given. Since preconception agreements to abort, not abort, or give up for adoption are not enforceable, neither should preconception or preimplantation agreements for the disposition of embryos.[16] Also, there may be no easy way to assure that the parties are fully informed and aware of the legally binding choices

they would be making.[17] Finally, IVF programs and embryo banks may have such monopoly power that the conditions they offer give couples little real choice.

To assess the desirability of having couples bind themselves in advance, consider two situations in which one party wishes to revise the original instruction and the other party is unavailable or disagrees.

Advance Agreements to Have Embryos Transferred. Suppose the couple has agreed that all embryos will be transferred to the uterus of the egg source, or to another woman if the former is unwilling or unable to have the embryos placed in her. Before transfer, however, divorce occurs, and the husband now objects to thawing of the embryos for implantation in the former wife or a willing recipient. May the embryo bank transfer stored embryos on the basis of the previously executed instructions?

Since agreeing to this disposition may be viewed as a material condition on which the other party and program relied in creating and storing embryos, the agreement should be

binding. Indeed, enforcement is essential to provide the certainty about outcomes necessary for couples and IVF programs to proceed with embryo freezing. It is true that the husband may not have realized when the embryos were created that he would have had such strong feelings against postdivorce parenthood. But it is also true that neither partner may have been willing to create and freeze embryos unless they could rely on the certainty that all resulting embyros would be given a chance to implant.

The general unenforceability of preconception agreements not to abort by spouses or surrogate mothers should not apply to the very different situation of external embryos.[18] Enforcing a woman's agreement not to abort forces her to continue an unwanted pregnancy, but no bodily or gestational burdens are involved in enforcing the gamete sources' preimplantation agreement to have all stored embryos thawed and transferred to the uterus of a willing recipient.

Providing gametes to create embryos in this situation should thus be taken as a binding commitment

---

Davis: An Unwarranted Conclusion

Judge W. Dale Young recently ruled in the *Davis* case that the seven frozen embryos were "human beings existing as embryos," and "children in vitro" whose best interests required "that they be available for implantation." He awarded the embryos to Ms. Davis for purposes of implantation, but reserved questions of child support, custody, and visitation until the time that children are actually born.

Judge Young's conclusion that four-celled preimplantation human embryos are "children" and "human beings" is unprecedented and unwarranted. It has no discernible basis in common law precedents nor in Tennessee law (which recognizes a separate legal interest in prenatal human life only at viability). It is a view rejected by highly respected ethical advisory bodies in the United States, Great Britain, Canada, France, and several other countries.

This remarkable conclusion appears to represent the judge's own personal view of the significance of the biologic fact that a new human genome exists at or shortly after fertilization. But genetic uniqueness and potential

to develop into a newborn infant does not mean that a human entity—the preimplantation embryo—is already a "child" or "human being" with rights and interests of its own.

The terms "life" or "human life" contain a central ambiguity that the judge ignored. While the preimplantation embryo is clearly human and living, it does not follow that it is also a "human life" or "human being" in the crucial sense of a person with rights or interests. Indeed, such a ruling could lead to a ban on embryo freezing and even superovulation because of ensuing damage to or nontransfer of "in vitro children."

A decision in favor of Ms. Davis based on the burdens of her undergoing yet another IVF cycle would have been a reasonable, if disputable, solution to this controversy. In ruling on the broader and much less defensible ground that embryos are already "children," the trial judge has undercut the authority of his ruling, and rendered it highly vulnerable to reversal on appeal.

John A. Robertson

to reproduce. The parties were informed of that consequence at the time of election, relied on the commitment to transfer, and knew that the spouse was relying on that commitment as well.

Advance Agreements Not to Transfer Embryos. Consider a second case in which the couple (and IVF program) have specifically agreed that in case of divorce, separation, death, inability to agree, or passage of time any stored embryos will be removed from storage and not tranferred, that is, they will be allowed to die or be discarded. Avoiding the financial and psychosocial burdens of unwanted offspring is something that the parties may reasonably choose at the time of creation and storage. Since they may not undertake IVF and cryopreservation if they cannot be protected against unwanted offspring in those future situations, the agreement should be enforced, despite one party's change of mind and desire now to have the embryos transferred to a uterus. A suit by that party to enjoin thawing and nontransfer or for damages against the embryo bank that has thawed the embryos should fail.

Again an appeal to the unenforceability of agreements to abort fails because of the dissimilarity in the situation. A wife's agreement to abort if she becomes pregnant, or a surrogate mother's to abort if amniocentesis reveals a genetic defect would not be specifically enforced because of the bodily intrusion that enforcement entails. Nor would the woman be legally liable for damages for continuing the pregnancy in violation of her agreement (though the opposite result could be justified).

But here the embryos are extracorporeal and not yet implanted. A woman's right to continue a pregnancy unwanted by the male partner is not implicated. Only her wish to become pregnant with extracorporeal embryos or have them donated to a willing recipient is at issue—an entirely different situation. The need for certainty in entering into embryo freezing and preventing the burdens of parenthood that one partner insisted on avoiding outweigh the interest of the party who has changed his or her mind and now

wishes reproduction to occur. The need for certainty and efficient resolution of disputes over embryos demands that the prior commitment for embryo discard be honored. In this situation providing gametes to create embryos should not be viewed as a commitment to reproduce, because both parties explicitly agreed that it was not such a commitment.

Note that advance instructions should be binding by one party against another, or by the embryo bank or IVF program against the couple. The latter situation is important because IVF programs may have institutional or physician constraints on disposition of embryos, and thus need some certainty that couples will be held to limits on transfer, time of storage, donation, and the like. However, program-imposed restrictions should be binding only if they have been clearly disclosed to the couple at the start and are not inherently unreasonable.

The Best Guidelines

Because early embryos represent their potential offspring yet are too rudimentary in development to have interests in themselves, the couple's dispositional authority or ownership over extracorporeal embryos should be respected. They should have wide leeway in their decisions to form families through creation, storage, thawing, and transfer of embryos, yet should also be free to avoid reproduction with IVF embryos when their needs or circumstances have changed. Any limitation on their "ownership" must give due regard to their procreative freedom to have or to avoid having offspring.

Until the law prescribes otherwise, disputes over frozen embryos should be resolved first by looking to the joint wishes of the couple, and if they are not available or are unable to agree, to prior instructions which they gave for disposition of those embryos. If no instructions exist, we must then compare the relative burdens on each party of using or not using the embryos in question to see which party should prevail. These principles are the best guide for assimilating IVF technology into social practice while respecting family and reproductive choice.

References

The author gratefully acknowledges the comments of Andrea Bonnicksen, Douglas Laycock, and several colleagues at the University of Texas School of Law on an earlier draft.

[1] John A. Robertson, "Ethical and Legal Issues in Cryopreservation of Human Embryos," *Fertility and Sterility* 47:3 (1987), 371-81.

[2] R. Smothers, "Embryos in a Divorce Case: Joint Property or Offspring?," *New York Times,* 21 April 1989, 1.

[3] Robertson, "Ethical and Legal Issues."

[4] Uniform Anatomical Gift Act #3, 8A U.L.A. 8-9 (West Supp. 1987); 45 C.F.R. 46.209 (d).

[5] John A. Robertson, *In the Beginning: The Legal Status of Early Embryos* (forthcoming).

[6] *Hughes v. Hutt,* 500 Pa. 209, 455 A.2d 623 (1982); *In re Pamela P.,* 443 N.Y.S. 2d 343 (1981).

[7] John A. Robertson, "Technology and Motherhood: Legal and Ethical Issues in Human Egg Donation," *Case Western Reserve Law Review* 39:1 (1988), 1-38.

[8] Robertson, *In the Beginning.*

[9] *Jones v. York,* No. 33455 (E.D. Va. 1989).

[10] R.S. La. 9:125 (La. Supp. 1987).

[11] John A. Robertson, "Procreative Liberty and the Control of Conception, Pregnancy and Childbirth," *Virginia Law Review* 69:3 (1983), 405-414.

[12] John A. Robertson, "Embryos, Families and Procreative Liberty: The Legal Structure of the New Reproduction," *Southern California Law Review* 59:5 (1986), 939-1041.

[13] Robertson, "Embryos, Families and Procreative Liberty."

[14] Robertson, *In the Beginning.*

[15] *Report of the Committee of Inquiry Into Human Fertilisation and Embryology,* (London: Her Majesty's Stationary Office, 1984), 53; Victoria Committee to Consider the Social, Ethical and Legal Issues Arising from In Vitro Fertilization, *Report on the Disposition of Embryos Produced by IVF,* 1984; Ontario Law Reform Commission, 1985; The Ethics Committee of The American Fertility Society, "Ethical Considerations of the New Reproductive Technology," *Fertility and Sterility* 46 Suppl. 1 (1986), 1S-94S; U.S. Department of Health, Education, and Welfare (HEW), Ethics Advisory Board, "HEW Support of Research Involving Human In Vitro Fertilization and Embryo Transfer," 44 *Federal Register* 35, 033, 1979.

[16] *In re Baby M,* 537 A.2d 1227 (N.J. 1988).

[17] John A. Robertson, "Taking Consent Seriously: IRB Interventions in the Consent Process," *IRB: A Journal of Human Subjects Research* 4:5 (1982), 1-5.

[18] Robertson, "Embryos, Families and Procreative Liberty."

The medieval theory of the homunculus, the fully formed miniature person once held to reside in every sperm, is making a comeback. Although the following description was written by Laurence Sterne in *Tristram Shandy* (1760), it bears a disquieting resemblance to expert scientific testimony recently offered in a Tennessee courtroom:

The Homunculus, Sir, in however low and ludicrous a light he may appear, in this age of levity, to the eye of folly or prejudice;—to the eye of reason in scientific research, he stands confessed—a Being guarded and circumscribed with rights.—The minutest philosophers...shew us incontestably, that the Homunculus is created by the same hand,—engendered in the same course of nature,—endowed with the same locomotive powers and faculties with us:—that he consists as we do, of skin, hair, fat, flesh, veins, arteries, ligaments, nerves, cartileges, bones, marrow, brains, glands, genitals, humours, and articulations;—is a being of as much activity, and, in all senses of the word, as much and as truly our fellow creature as my Lord Chancellor of England. He may be benefited,—he may obtain redress;—in a word he has all the claims and rights of humanity, which Tully, Puffendorf, or the best ethic writers allow to arise out of the state and relation. (Bk. 1, ch. 2)

The case of *Davis v. Davis*, concerning the disposition of seven frozen embryos,[1] provides a powerful example of what can go wrong when a trial court judge takes it upon himself to "solve" major bioethical issues.

Davis v. Davis

Junior L. Davis and Mary Sue Davis decided to divorce in February 1989 after nine years of marriage. After five tubal pregnancies, Mrs. Davis had her fallopian tubes severed to prevent further risk to her. She and her husband thereafter decided to resort to *in vitro* fertilization. The couple went through six attempts at IVF before deciding to try adoption. After

George J. Annas is Utley Professor of Health Law, and director, Law, Medicine, and Ethics Program, Boston University Schools of Medicine and Public Health, Boston, MA.

AT LAW

A French Homunculus in a Tennessee Court

by George J. Annas

their efforts to adopt also failed, they returned to IVF. In their seventh IVF cycle (December 1988), two embryos were transferred, and seven additional embryos that had been created were frozen for possible future cycles. The seventh attempt was also unsuccessful. Having ultimately decided to divorce, the couple agreed to all aspects of their divorce settlement with the exception of the disposition of the seven frozen embryos. Mrs. Davis wanted to use them to attempt to have a child after their divorce; Mr. Davis objected to this use. They therefore sought a judicial determination of what should be done with the seven frozen embryos.

The case almost immediately attracted the attention of the national press. In fact, it seems fair to say that the case attracted more national notoriety than any case in Tennessee history since the trial of Joseph Thomas Scopes for teaching evolution in defiance of Tennessee creationist law.[2] It also seems fair to say that the level of science professed by

the judge was as rudimentary as that espoused by the anti-evolutionary preachers of the 1920's.

To decide this case, the trial judge could simply have determined which of the litigants had a greater interest in the embryos, or which had the most reasonable expectation that their wishes regarding the disposition of the embryos would be followed. Accordingly, the judge could have awarded the embryos to Mrs. Davis either on the basis that she had contributed more to them than Mr. Davis (because she had to undergo a surgical procedure to have the ova removed); or on the basis that her reasonable expectation in agreeing to have the seven embryos created and frozen was that they would be used by her in future attempts to have a child should the immediate attempt fail. He could, alternatively, have decided that the case was nonjusticiable (and required the parties to reach agreement without his help), or that in absence of an agreement, the embryos should be destroyed and could not be used, donated, or experimented on without the consent of both parties.

For reasons he never explains, and that may be more related to the media value of the case than its fair resolution, the judge framed the central issue not as who should get the embryos, but rather whether the embryos were people or products. This, of course, is *not* an outcome-determining categorization (since either way, the question of who gets them remains). Moreover, stating the question this way is very misleading: embryos could just as easily be considered *neither* products nor people, but put in some other category altogether. There are many things, such as dogs, dolphins, and redwoods that are neither products nor people. We nonetheless legally protect these entities by limiting what their owners or custodians can do with them. Every national commission worldwide that has examined the status of the human embryo to date has placed it in this third category: neither people nor products, but nonetheless entities of unique symbolic value that deserve society's respect and protection. By setting up a false dichotomy, the trial judge doomed himself from the outset to write an unsound opinion. This structural mistake led to a more serious error.

The judge believed it was up to him to decide whether or not embryos were people. With a rare combination of hubris and ignorance the trial judge, interviewed after his decision was issued, said that the U.S. Supreme Court had "ducked" this issue in *Roe v. Wade*, but that he had to decide it. Nor did the method he chose to decide whether embryos were people bring much credit to the judiciary: he decided to rely exclusively on the testimony of one witness, French right-to-life physician Jerome Lejeune.

The Testimony of Dr. Jerome Lejeune

As summarized by the trial judge in his opinion, Dr. Lejeune, who discovered the genetic basis of Down syndrome, testified among other things, to the following "facts":

- That each human being has a unique begining at the moment of conception;

- that the information coded in DNA molecules that is reproduced and transmitted as a result of fertilization animates matter, and that no other cell will ever again have the same instructions in the life of the person being created;

- that in cryopreservation time is frozen, not embryos;

- that at the three-cell stage a "tiny human being" exists, who, it can be experimentally demonstrated, "is uniquely different from any other individual";

- that according to the Hippocratic Oath, whatever the patient's size, a patient is still a patient; and

- that no scientist has ever offered the opinion that an embryo is property.[3]

The judge did not quote other testimony of Dr. Lejeune's that, "Putting tiny human beings in a very cold space, deprived of liberty, deprived even of time, they are as it were in a concentration camp....It is not a hospitable place as the secret temple of a woman's womb."[4] Nor did he recall the cross examination by Mr. Davis's lawyer, Charles Clifford, who pulled a chicken egg from his pocket and asked, "Can you tell me, doctor, what this is?" Lejeune replied, "It looks to me like it's an egg." To which Clifford responded, "I thought you would have told me that it was an early chicken."[5]

The judge concluded that the seven frozen embryos "are human beings...not property" and that "human life begins at the moment of conception." Based on this assessment, he was left only to determine "the best interests of the children." The conclusion followed naturally: "The Court finds and concludes that it is to the manifest best interest of the children, in vitro, that they be made available for implantation to assure their opportunity for live birth; implantation is their sole and only hope for survival." Temporary custody of the "children" is awarded to Mrs. Davis for purposes of implantation, while "all matters concerning support, visitation, final custody and related issues" are reserved by the court until "such time as one or more of the seven cryogenically preserved human embryos are the product of live birth."

What Does it Mean?

The overwhelming attribute of this opinion is that it makes almost no attempt to deal with the law. It cites only a handful of cases, and makes no attempt to analyze any of them. The most remarkable aspect of the opinion is that its holding that embryos are children is a conclusion based exclusively on the unsubstantiated testimony of one witness. The testimony of the other expert witnesses was rejected primarily because they all termed the embryos "pre-embryos." The judge decided, correctly I believe, that the invention of this term was simply an attempt to avoid determining the status of the early human embryo by redefining it as not an embryo at all.

Yet though the judge spends all his time deciding that the embryos are people, not property, he ends up treating them like property.[6] Instead of deciding custody, visitation, and support issues (which he would have to do if the embryos *were* children), he awards them to Mrs. Davis in exactly the way he would award a dresser or a painting. Of course, were these embryos really children there would have been no public interest in which parent received custody of them.

The decision itself trivializes and devalues children by treating them no better than embryos. Dr. Lejeune suggested the Nazi concentration camp experience as the proper analogy for cryopreservation. Physicians were tried, convicted, and sentenced to death at Nuremberg for freezing experiments performed on human beings during World War II. If these embryos really were children, people, or human beings it would not be lawful to conduct deadly experiments on them, such as freezing, and the physician who did so would have engaged in criminal conduct. Nonetheless, the trial judge nowhere suggests that there is anything wrong with freezing embryos, and thus he cannot really believe that embryos are children (unless, of course, we are to believe that he thinks freezing children with a view to thawing them out at a later date when the parents might be better able to care for them is an acceptable activity).

It seems that the judge was dazzled with Dr. Lejeune's testimony even though its "science" is woefully unsophisticated. The embryos are frozen, not time—as is apparent from the assertion that they can only remain frozen for two years (a dubious assertion itself, but one that admits that time continues to run for the embryos). Focusing on the "three-cell" stage is wonderfully curious since there is nothing to distinguish three cells from two or four cells, and this "stage" exists only because the two cells do not split simultaneously. The term "specialized" seems to have been used by Dr. Lejeune entirely differently than other witnesses and this seems to have confused the judge. Lejeune says "specialized" means unique; the other witnesses used "specialized" to mean specific.

Finally, if the judge really believed that he had to decide this case based on the "best interests of the children" he would have had at least to determine if Mrs. Davis was a fit mother to gestate them. Given her past history of inability to carry a fetus to term, there is little probability of her successfully gestating any of the seven embryos. Requiring her to hire a surrogate mother to gestate them would almost certainly enhance their chances to be born.

The Homunculus

The judge bows to the wonders of modern DNA techniques, but his opinion harkens back to the middle ages when the theory of the homunculus, the "little man," was in vogue. In commenting on this case columnist Ellen Goodman was reminded of the movie, "Honey I Shrunk the Kids."[7] The image is apt. The trial judge and his favorite witness each see embryos as space capsules containing miniature astronauts. This is why Dr. Lejeune could testify that a patient is a patient "no matter what the size of the patient," and that embryos are "tiny human beings."

Many right-to-life activists have been quoted as applauding the judge's opinion that embryos are children. But those who equate embryos and children show little respect for children. To use a simple example suggested by Leonard Glantz, if a fire broke out in the laboratory where these seven embryos are stored, and a two-month-old child was in one corner of the laboratory, the seven embryos in another, and you could only save either the embryos or the child, I doubt you would have any hesitancy in saving the infant. Saving the infant, however, acknowledges that the child is *not* equated with the embryo. Likewise, if embryos are children, there have been many more children in the world than we have thus far acknowledged (approximately 35% of all human embryos either do not implant or abort spontaneously early in pregnancy), and if we valued children, we would have to do something about this.

To save children, we would have to consider requiring women to strain their menstrual blood every month that they either had intercourse or were artificially inseminated to try to "rescue" the children that would otherwise be lost. Those that could not be saved could nonetheless be named and mourned, and added to the list of "deceased" brothers and sisters. If you are either amused or horrified at this scenario, it can only be because you know both rationally and intuitively that embryos are *not* children, even though some embryos will become children. The fact that embryos possess the *information* that *may* be translated into a child at some future date does not make the embryo a child, any more than a fertilized chicken egg is a chicken.

Celebrity Judges

Why did a doctor from France travel to Tennessee to testify about embryos and why did a trial judge open his courtroom to such testimony? "Bioethics" cases sell newspapers. Law has become part of popular culture, and this is probably good. *L.A. Law*, properly described as one part L.A. and one part law, has been said to have had "a beneficial influence on popular conceptions of law and legal ethics."[8] To sustain audiences, *L.A. Law* has had to ignore the 95-percent-plus tedium of law practice, and concentrate instead on the spectacularly controversial cases that make the national press, such as "medical ethics" issues involving the termination of life support, a psychiatrist's duty to warn, and forcing a terminally ill pregnant woman to have a cesarean section. One can argue persuasively that all of these cases were dealt with ineptly from a legal perspective, but they were dealt with in an entertaining manner—and entertainment is what television is all about.[8]

Unfortunately, few lower court judges have had exposure to television's version of "bioethics" issues, and their record of resolving them has been mixed at best. In some of the best-known cases, including *Quinlan, Bouvia, Bartling,* and *Baby M,* lower court judges issued opinions that were very wide of the mark, and led to unanimous and vigorous reversals by appellate courts. The opinions of these trial court judges suggest that lower courts are institutionally incompetent to deal with bioethics issues. Professional standards, blue ribbon commissions, and legislative bodies may be more appropriate.

This case is only "law" in the courtroom in Maryville, Tennessee, and no other judge in the world is likely to take this opinion seriously. But it illustrates another point. It is problematic enough to have trial court judges making bioethical (rather than legal) decisions. It is totally predictable that if trial courts decide to take advantage of the case before them to become celebrities, the result will be bad law and bad bioethics.

The trial court judges in *Quinlan, Bouvia, Bartling,* and *Baby M* mostly stayed out of the press. The judge in *Davis,* on the other hand, seems to have done almost everything he could to insure that the media's spotlight was on him. He even had himself filmed for television when he presented his written opinion to the clerk, and then proceeded to give interviews to TV, radio, and the press on the opinion after it was filed, a virtually unprecedented performance by a judge, and injudicious behavior at best.

Perhaps he really thinks that the primary function of law is to entertain, and that it is his job to demonstrate that *TN Law* can be as entertaining as *L.A. Law*. But as amused as we may be, we are left with no guidance as to how to treat human embryos.

References

[1] *Davis v. Davis v. King.* Fifth Jud. Ct., Tennessee, E-14496, Sept. 21, 1989 (Young, J.); see also John Robertson, "Resolving Disputes over the Disposition of Frozen Embryos," at pp. 7-12 in this issue.

[2] *Scopes v. State,* 289 S.W. 362 (Tenn. 1927).

[3] Quotations are from Dr. Lejeune's testimony.

[4] "Trial on Couple's Frozen Embryos Left to Judge," *St. Cloud (Minn) Times,* 11 August 1989, 4A.

[5] Michael Fitzgerald, "Embryo Trial Goes to Judge," *USA Today,* 11 August 1989, 3A.

[6] I am indebted to Wendy Mariner for this point.

[7] Ellen Goodman, "A Ruling in the Realm of Scientific Fantasy," *Boston Globe,* 26 September 1989, 16.

[8] Stephen Gillers, "Taking *L.A. Law* More Seriously," *Yale Law Journal* 98 (1989), 1607-23.

[9] Charles B. Rosenberg, "An L.A. Lawyer Replies," *Yale Law Journal* 98 (1989), 1625-29 (arguing that *L.A. Law* is not primarily about law and lawyers, but about "interesting people, some of whom happen to be lawyers.")

LAW AND THE LIFE SCIENCES

Contracts to Bear a Child:
Compassion or Commercialism?
by GEORGE J. ANNAS

Many medical students (and others) supplement their income by selling their blood and sperm. But while this practice seems to have been reasonably well accepted, society does not permit individuals to sell their vital organs or their children. These policies are unlikely to change. Where on this spectrum do contracts to bear a child fall? Are they fundamentally the sale of an ovum with a nine-month womb rental thrown in, or are they really agreements to sell a baby? While this formulation may seem a strange way to phrase the issue, it is the way courts are likely to frame it when such contracts are challenged on the grounds that they violate public policy.

In a typical surrogate-mother arrangement, a woman agrees to be artificially inseminated with the sperm of the husband of an infertile woman. She also agrees that after the child is born she will either give it up for adoption to the couple or relinquish her parental rights, leaving the biological father as the sole legal parent. The current controversy centers on whether or not the surrogate can be paid for these services. Is she being compensated for inconvenience and out-of-pocket expenses, or is she being paid for her baby?

Two personal stories have received much media attention. The first involves Patricia Dickey, an unmarried twenty-year-old woman from Maryland who had never borne a child, and who agreed to be artificially inseminated and give up the child to a Delaware couple without any compensation. She was recruited by attorney Noel Keane of Michigan, known for his television appearances in which he has said that for a $5,000 fee he will put "host mothers" in touch with childless

---

GEORGE J. ANNAS, J.D., M.P.H., *is associate professor of law and medicine, Boston University School of Medicine, and chief, Health Law Section, Boston University School of Public Health.*

couples. Ms. Dickey explained her motivation in an interview with the *Washington Post:* "I had a close friend who couldn't have a baby, and I know how badly she wanted one. . . . It's just something I wanted to do" (Feb. 11, 1980, p. 1). The outcome of Dickey's pregnancy—if one occurred—has not been reported.

More famous is a woman who has borne a child and relinquished her parental rights. Elizabeth Kane (a pseudonym), married and the mother of three children, reportedly agreed to bear a child for $10,000. The arrangement was negotiated by Dr. Richard Levin of Kentucky who is believed to have about 100 surrogates willing to perform the same services for compensation. Levin says, "I clearly do not have any moral or ethical problems with what we are doing" (*American Medical News,* June 20, 1980, p. 13). Mrs. Kane describes her relationship to the baby by saying, "It's the father's child. I'm simply growing it for him" (*People,* Dec. 8, 1980, p. 53).

Even this brief sketch raises fundamental questions about the two approaches. Should the surrogate be married or single; have other children or have no children? Should the couple meet the surrogate (they were in the delivery room when Mrs. Kane gave birth to a boy)? Should the child know about the arrangement when he grows up (the couple plans to tell the child when he is eighteen)? Is monetary compensation the real issue (the sperm donor has agreed to give Ms. Dickey more sperm if she wants to have another child for her own—could this cause more problems for both him and her)? What kind of counseling should be done with all parties, and what records should be kept? And isn't this a strange thing to be doing in a country that records more than a million and a half abortions a year? Why not attempt to get women who are already pregnant to give birth instead of inducing those who are not to go through the "experience"?

These questions, and many others, merit serious consideration. So far legal debate

has focused primarily on just one: can surrogate parenting properly be labeled "baby selling"? Some have argued that it can be distinguished from baby selling because one of the parents (the father) is biologically related to the child, and the mother is not pregnant at the time the deal is struck and so is not under any compulsion to provide for her child. But the only two legal opinions rendered to date disagree. Both a lower court judge in Michigan and the attorney general of Kentucky view contracts to bear a child as baby selling.

Court Challenge in Michigan

In the mid-1970s most states passed statutes making it criminal to offer, give, or receive anything of value for placing a child for adoption. These statutes were aimed at curtailing a major black market in babies that had grown up in the United States, with children selling for as much as $20,000. Anticipating that Michigan's version of this statute might prohibit him from paying a surrogate for carrying a child and giving it up for adoption, attorney Keane sought a declaratory judgment. He argued that the statute was unconstitutional since it infringed upon the right to reproductive privacy of the parties involved. The court was not impressed, concluding that "the right to adopt a child based upon the payment of $5,000 is not a fundamental personal right and reasonable regulations controlling adoption proceedings that prohibit the exchange of money (other than charges and fees approved by the court) are not constitutionally infirm." The court characterized the state's interest as one "to prevent commercialism from affecting a mother's decision to execute a consent to the adoption of her child," and went on to argue that: "Mercenary considerations used to create a parent-child relationship and its impact upon the family unit strike at the very foundation of human society and is patently and necessarily injurious to the community" (*Doe v. Kelley,* reprinted in 6 FLR 3011 (1980)).

The case is on appeal, but is unlikely to be reversed. The judge's decision meant that Ms. Dickey, and others like her, could not charge a fee for carrying a child. It did not, however, forbid her from carrying it as a personal favor or for her own psychological reasons.

The Kentucky Statutes

One of the prime elements of surrogate mother folklore held that contracts to bear a child were "legal" in Kentucky. On January 26, 1981, Steven Beshear, the attorney general of the Commonwealth of Kentucky, announced at a Louisville news conference that contracts to bear a child were in fact illegal and unenforceable in the state. He based his advisory opinion on Kentucky statutes and "a strong public policy against 'baby buying.'"

Specifically, Kentucky law invalidates consent for adoption or the filing of a voluntary petition for termination of parental rights prior to the fifth day after the birth of a child. The purpose of these statutes, according to the attorney general, is to give the mother time to "think it over." Thus, any agreement or contract she entered into before the fifth day after the birth would be unenforceable. Moreover, Kentucky, like Michigan, prohibits the charging of a "fee" or "remuneration for the procurement of any child for adoption purposes." The attorney general argued that even though there is no similar statute prohibiting the payment of money for the termination of parental rights, "there is the same public policy issue" regarding monetary consideration for the procurement of a child: "The Commonwealth of Kentucky does not condone the purchase and sale of children" (Op. Atty. Gen., 81–18). The attorney general has since brought an action to enjoin Dr. Levin and his corporation from making any further surrogate-mother arrangements in the state.

Who Cares?

Surrogate parenting, open or behind a wall of secrecy, is unlikely ever to involve large numbers of people. Should we care about it; or should we simply declare our disapproval and let it go at that? I don't know, but it does seem to me that the answer to that question must be found in the answer to another: what is in the best interests of the children? Certainly they are more prone to psychological problems when they learn that their biological mother not only gave them up for adoption, but never had any intention of mothering them herself. On the other hand, one might argue that the child would never have existed had it not been for the surrogate arrangement, and so whatever existence the child has is better than nothing.

One of the major problems with speculating on the potential benefits of such an arrangement to the parties involved is that we have very little data. There is only anecdotal information available on artificial insemination by donor, for example. It does not seem to harm family life. But the role of the mother is far greater biologically than that of the father, and family disruption might be proportionally higher if the mother is the one who gives up the child. The sperm donor in the Patricia Dickey case is quoted as having said:

It may sound selfish, but I want to father a child on my own behalf, leave my own legacy. And I want a healthy baby. And there just aren't any available. They're either retarded or they're minorities, black, Hispanic. . . . That may be fine for some people, but we just don't think we could handle it.

Is this man really ready for parenthood? What if the child is born with a physical or mental defect—could he handle that? Or would the child be left abandoned, wanted neither by the surrogate nor by the adoptive couple? The sperm donor has made no biological commitment to the child, and cannot be expected to support it financially or psychologically if it is not what he expected and contracted for.

Perhaps the only major question in the entire surrogate mother debate that does have a clear legal answer is: Whose baby is it? On the maternal side, it is the biological mother's baby. And if she wants to keep it, she almost certainly can. Indeed, under the proper circumstances, she may even be able to keep the child and sue the sperm donor for child support. On the paternal side, it is also the biological child of the sperm donor. But in all states, children born in wedlock are presumed to be the legitimate children of the married couple. So if the surrogate is married, the child will be presumed (usually rebuttable only by proof beyond a reasonable doubt) to be the offspring of the couple and not of the sperm donor. The donor could bring a custody suit—if he could prove beyond a reasonable doubt that he was the real father—and then the court would have to decide which parent would serve the child's "best interests."

It is an interesting legal twist that in many states with laws relating to artificial insemination, the sperm donor would have no rights even to bring such a suit. For example, to protect donors the Uniform Parentage Act provides that "The donor of semen provided . . . for use in artificial insemination of a woman other than the donor's wife is treated in law as if he were not the natural father of a child thereby conceived" (*See* Note, *Contracts to Bear a Child*, 66 Cal. L. Rev. 611, May, 1978). The old adage, "Mama's baby, papa's maybe" aptly describes the current legal reaction to a surrogate who changes her mind and decides to keep the child.

Should There be a Law?

The Science and the Family Committee (which I chair) of the Family Law Section of the American Bar Association is currently studying the surrogate mother situation (and the broader issue of in vitro fertilization) in an attempt to determine what, if any, legislation is appropriate in this area. DHEW's Ethics Advisory Board's final recommendation on in vitro fertilization and embryo transfer was that a "uniform or model law" be developed to "clarify the legal status of children born as a result of *in vitro* fertilization and embryo transfer." This seems to make some sense—although it does seem to be premature. We need a set of agreed-on principles regarding artificial insemination by donor and surrogate mothers—both technologies currently in use—if legislation on in vitro fertilization and embryo transplant is to have a reasonable chance of doing more good than harm.

Surrogate Mothers:
Not So Novel After All
by JOHN A. ROBERTSON

All reproduction is collaborative, for no man or woman reproduces alone. Yet the provision of sperm, egg, or uterus through artificial insemination, embryo transfer, and surrogate mothering makes reproduction collaborative in another way. A third person provides a genetic or gestational factor not present in ordinary paired reproduction. As these practices grow, we must confront the ethical issues raised and their implications for public policy.

Collaborative reproduction allows some persons who otherwise might remain childless to produce healthy children. However, its deliberate separation of genetic, gestational, and social parentage is troublesome. The offspring and participants may be harmed, and there is a risk of confusing family lineage and personal identity. In addition, the techniques intentionally manipulate a natural process that many persons want free of technical intervention. Yet many well-accepted practices, including adoption, artificial insemination by donor (AID), and blended families (families where children of different marriages are raised together) intentionally separate biologic and social parenting, and have become an accepted thread in the social fabric. Should all collaborative techniques be similarly treated? When, if ever, are they ethical? Should the law prohibit, encourage, or regulate them, or should the practice be left to private actors? Surrogate motherhood—the controversial practice by which a woman agrees to bear a child conceived by artificial insemination and to relinquish it at birth to others for rearing—illustrates the legal and ethical issues arising in collaborative reproduction generally.

An Alternative to Agency Adoptions

Infertile couples who are seeking surrogates hire attorneys and sign contracts with women recruited through newspaper ads. The practice at present probably involves at most a few hundred persons. But repeated attention on *Sixty Minutes* and the *Phil Donahue Show* and in the popular press is likely to engender more demand, for thousands of infertile couples might find surrogate mothers the answer to their reproductive needs. What began as an enterprise involving a few lawyers and doctors in Michigan, Kentucky,

JOHN A. ROBERTSON *is Marrs McLean Professor of Law at the School of Law, University of Texas in Austin.*

and California is now a national phenomenon. There are surrogate mother centers in Maryland, Arizona, and several other states, and even a surrogate mother newsletter.

Surrogate mother arrangements occur within a tradition of family law that gives the gestational mother (and her spouse, if any) rearing rights and obligations. (However, the presumption that the husband is the father can be challenged, and a husband's obligations to his wife's child by AID will usually require his consent.)[1] Although no state has legislation directly on the subject of surrogate motherhood, independently arranged adoptions are lawful in most states. It is no crime to agree to bear a child for another, and then relinquish it for adoption. However, paying the mother a fee for adoption beyond medical expenses is a crime in some states, and in others will prevent the adoption from being approved.[2] Whether termination and transfer of parenting rights will be legally recognized depends on the state. Some states, like Hawaii and Florida, ask few questions and approve independent adoptions very quickly. Others, like Michigan and Kentucky, won't allow surrogate mothers to terminate and assign rearing rights to another if a fee has been paid, or even allow a paternity determination in favor of the sperm donor. The enforcibility of surrogate contracts has also not been tested, and it is safe to assume that some jurisdictions will not enforce them. Legislation clarifying many of these questions has been proposed in several states, but has not yet been enacted.

Even this brief discussion highlights an important fact about surrogate motherhood and other collaborative reproductive techniques. They operate as an alternative to the nonmarket, agency system of allocating children for adoption, which has contributed to long queues for distributing healthy white babies. This form of independent adoption is controlled by the parties, planned before conception, involves a genetic link with one parent, and enables both the father and mother of the adopted child to be selected in advance.

Understood in these terms, the term "surrogate mother," which means substitute mother, is a misnomer. The natural mother, who contributes egg and uterus, is not so much a substitute mother as a substitute spouse who carries a child for a man whose wife is infertile. Indeed, it is the adoptive mother who is the surrogate mother for the child, since she parents a child borne by another. What, if anything, is wrong with this arrangement? Let us look more closely at its benefits and harms before discussing public policy.

The Hastings Center Report, October 1983

How Surrogate Mothering Works

For a fee of $5,000-10,000 a broker (usually a lawyer) will put an infertile couple (or less often, a single man) in contact with women whom he has recruited and screened who are willing to serve as surrogates. If the parties strike a deal, they will sign a contract in which the surrogate agrees to be artificially inseminated (usually by a physician) with the husband's sperm, to bear the child, and then at or soon after birth to relinquish all parental rights and transfer physical custody of the child to the couple for adoption by the wife. Typically the contract has provisions dealing with prenatal screening, abortion, and other aspects of the surrogate's conduct during pregnancy, as well as her consent to relinquish the child at birth. The husband and wife agree to pay medical expenses related to the pregnancy, to take custody of the child, and to place approximately $10,000 in escrow to be paid to the surrogate when the child is transferred. The lawyer will also prepare papers establishing the husband's paternity, terminating the surrogate's rights, and legalizing the adoption.

-J.A.R.

All the Parties Can Benefit

Reproduction through surrogate mothering is a deviation from our cultural norms of reproduction, and to many persons it seems immoral or wrong. But surrogate mothering may be a good for the parties involved.

Surrogate contracts meet the desire of a husband and wife to rear a healthy child, and more particularly, a child with one partner's genes. The need could arise because the wife has an autosomal dominant or sex-linked genetic disorder, such as hemophilia. More likely, she is infertile and the couple feels a strong need to have children. For many infertile couples the inability to conceive is a major personal problem causing marital conflict and filling both partners with anguish and self-doubt. It may also involve multiple medical work-ups and possibly even surgery. If the husband and wife have sought to adopt a child, they may have been told either that they do not qualify or to join the queue of couples waiting several years for agency adoptions (the wait has grown longer due to birth control, abortion, and the greater willingness of unwed mothers to keep their children[3]). For couples exhausted and frustrated by these efforts, the surrogate arrangement seems a godsend. While the intense desire to have a child often appears selfish, we must not lose sight of the deep-seated psychosocial and biological roots of the desire to generate children.[4]

The arrangement may also benefit the surrogate. Usually women undergo pregnancy and childbirth because they want to rear children. But some women want to have the experience of bearing and birthing a child without the obligation to rear. Phillip Parker, a Michigan psychiatrist who has interviewed over 275 surrogate applicants, finds that the decision to be a surrogate springs from several motives.[5] Most women willing to be surrogates have already had children, and many are married. They choose the surrogate role primarily because the fee provides a better economic opportunity than alternative occupations, but also because they enjoy being pregnant and the respect and attention that it draws. The surrogate experience may also be a way to master, through reliving, guilt they feel from past pregnancies that ended in abortion or adoption. Some surrogates may also feel pleased, as organ donors do, that they have given the "gift of life" to another couple.[6]

The child born of a surrogate arrangement also benefits. Indeed, but for the surrogate contract, this child would not have been born at all. Unlike the ordinary agency or independent adoption, where a child is already conceived or brought to term, the conception of this child occurs solely as a result of the surrogate agreement. Thus even if the child does suffer identity problems, as adopted children often do because they are not able to know their mothers, this child has benefited, or at least has not been wronged, for without the surrogate arrangement, she would not have been born at all.[7]

But Problems Exist Too

Surrogate mothering is also troublesome. Many people think that it is wrong for a woman to conceive and bear a child that she does not intend to raise, particularly if she receives a fee for her services. There are potential costs to the surrogate and her family, the adoptive couple, the child, and even society at large from satisfying the generative needs of infertile couples in this way.

The couple must be willing to spend about $20,000-25,000, depending on lawyers' fees and the supply of and demand for surrogate mothers. (While this price tag makes the surrogate contract a consumption item for the middle classes, it is not unjust to poor couples, for it does not leave them worse off than they were.) The couple must also be prepared to experience, along with the adjustment and demands of becoming parents, the stress and anxiety of participating in a novel social relationship that many still consider immoral or deviant. What do they tell their friends or family? What do they tell the child? Will the child have contact with the mother? What is the couple's relationship with the surrogate and her family during the pregnancy and after? Without established patterns for handling these questions, the parties may experience confusion, frustration, and embarrassment.

A major source of uncertainty and stress is likely to be the surrogate herself. In most cases she will be a stranger, and may never even meet the couple. The lack of a preexisting relation between the couple and surrogate and the possibility that they live far apart enhance the possibility of mistrust. Is the surrogate taking care of herself? Is she having sex with others during her fertile period? Will she contact the child afterwards? What if she demands more money to relinquish the child? To allay these anxieties, the couple could try to establish a relationship of trust with the surrogate, yet such a relationship creates reciprocal rights and duties and might create demands for an undesired relationship after the birth. Even good lawyering that specifies every contingency in the contract is unlikely to allay uncertainty and anxiety about the surrogate's trustworthiness.

The surrogate may also find the experience less satisfying than she envisioned. Conceiving the child may require insemination efforts over several months at inconvenient locations. The pregnancy and birth may entail more pain, unpleasant side effects, and disruption than she expected. The couple may be more intrusive or more aloof than she wishes. As the pregnancy advances and the birth nears, the surrogate may find it increasingly difficult to remain detached by thinking of the child as "theirs" rather than "hers." Relinquishing the baby after birth may be considerably more disheartening and disappointing than she anticipated. Even if informed of this possibility in advance, she may be distressed for several weeks with feelings of loss, depression, and sleep disturbance.[8] She may feel angry at the couple for cutting off all contact with her once the baby is delivered, and guilty at giving up her child. Finally, she will have to face the loss of all contact with "her" child. As the reality of her situation dawns, she may regret not having bargained harder for access to "her baby."

As with the couple, the surrogate's experience will vary with the expectations, needs, and personalities of the parties, the course of the pregnancy, and an advance understanding of the problems that can arise. The surrogate should have a lawyer to protect her interests. Often, however, the couple's lawyer will end up advising the surrogate. Although he has recruited the surrogate, he is paid by and represents the couple. By disclosing his conflicting interest, he satisfies legal ethics, but he may not serve the interests of the surrogate as well as independent counsel.

Harms to the Child

Unlike embryo transfer, gene therapy, and other manipulative techniques (some of which are collaborative), surrogate arrangements do not pose the risk of physical harm to the offspring. But there is the risk of psychosocial harm. Surrogate mothering, like adoption and artificial insemination by donor (AID), deliberately separates genetic and gestational from social parentage. The mother who begets, bears, and births does not parent. This separation can pose a problem for the child who discovers it. Like adopted and AID children, the child may be strongly motivated to learn the absent parent's identity and to establish a relationship, in this case with the mother and her family. Inability to make

that connection, especially inability to learn who the mother is, may affect the child's self-esteem, create feelings of rootlessness, and leave the child thinking that he had been rejected due to some personal fault.[9] While this is a serious concern, the situation is tolerated when it arises with AID and adoptive children. Intentional conception for adoption—the essence of surrogate mothering—poses no different issue.

The child can also be harmed if the adoptive husband and wife are not fit parents. After all, a willingness to spend substantial money to fulfill a desire to rear children is no guarantee of good parenting. But then neither is reproduction by paired mates who wish intensely to have a child. The nonbiologic parent may resent or reject the child, but the same possibility exists with adoption, AID, or ordinary reproduction.

There is also the fear, articulated by such commentators as Leon Kass and Paul Ramsey,[10] that collaborative reproduction confuses the lineage of children and destroys the meaning of family as we know it. In surrogate mothering, as with ovum or womb donors, the genetic and gestational mother does not rear the child, though the biologic father does. What implications does this hold for the family and the child's lineage?

The separation of the child from the genetic or biologic parent in surrogate mothering is hardly unique. It arises with adoption, but surrogate arrangments are more closely akin to AID or blended families, where at least one parent has a blood-tie to the child and the child will know at least one genetic parent. He may, as adopted children often do, have intense desires to learn his biologic mother's identity and seek contact with her and her family. Failure to connect with biologic roots may cause suffering. But the fact that adoption through surrogate mother contracts is planned before conception does not increase the chance of identity confusion, lowered self-esteem, or the blurring of lineage that occurs with adoption or AID.

The greatest chance of confusing family lines arises if the child and couple establish relations with the surrogate and the surrogate's family. If that unlikely event occurs, questions about the child's relations with the surrogate's spouse, parents, and other children can arise. But these issues are not unique. Indeed, they are increasingly common with the growth of blended families. Surrogate mothering in a few instances may lead to a new variation on blended families, but its threat to the family is trivial compared to the rapid changes in family structure now occurring for social, economic, and demographic reasons.

In many cases surrogate motherhood and other forms of collaborative reproduction may shore up, rather than undermine, the traditional family by enabling couples who would otherwise be childless to have children. The practice of employing others to assist in child rearing—including wet-nurses, neonatal ICU nurses, day-care workers, and babysitters—is widely accepted. We also tolerate assistance in the form of sperm sales and donation of egg and gestation (adoption). Surrogate mothering is another method of assisting people to undertake child rearing, and thus serves the purposes of the marital union. It is hard to see how its planned nature obstructs that contribution.

Using Birth For Selfish Ends

A basic fear about the new reproductive technologies is that they manipulate a natural physiologic process involved in the creation of human life. When one considers the potential power that resides in our ability to manipulate the genes of embryos, the charges of playing God or arrogantly

Guidelines for Physicians

Recognizing the intense interest in surrogate motherhood and the complex questions surrounding it, in May 1983 the American College of Obstetricians and Gynecologists (ACOG) issued guidelines for physicians on "Ethical Issues in Surrogate Motherhood." The two-page document states that the ACOG "has significant reservations about this approach to parenthood."

The guidelines identify five areas of consultation that present ethical difficulties: providing obstetric care to the pregnant surrogate; participating in the process of inseminating the surrogate; recruiting or screening potential surrogate mothers; counseling or referring couples who could be candidates for the procedure; and working with an organization that provides such services.

The guidelines first summarize the ethical issues shared by surrogate parenting and the more commonly accepted procedure of artificial insemination by donor (AID): the depersonalization of reproduction to some extent, stress on the relationship of the infertile couple, the risk of psychological stress on the sperm donor and the surrogate mother, possible misuse for eugenic manipulation, concerns about adverse psychological effects on children, and the maintenance of donor and surrogate anonymity. The guidelines then identify the special ethical issues attached to the surrogate arrangement:

1. The surrogate mother faces all the physical risks of pregnancy, including its long-term health effects, any complications, and even the remote possibility of death. She also faces possible psychological harm when she is separated from the infant.

2. It is not clear whether surrogate mothers should make decisions that affect the welfare of the fetus on their own or in conjunction with the prospective parents. These would include choices about whether to smoke or drink alcohol during pregnancy and decisions about pre-natal diagnosis and treatment, labor, delivery, and the methods of treating complications.

3. Difficulties may arise if the surrogate mother decides to have an abortion or keep the baby.

tampering with nature and the resulting dark Huxleyian vision of genetically engineered babies decanted from bottles are not surprising. While *Brave New World* is the standard text for this fear, the 1982 film *Bladerunner* also evokes it. Trycorp., a genetic engineering corporation, manufactures "replicants," who resemble human beings in most respects, including their ability to remember their childhoods, but who are programmed to die in four years. In portraying the replicants' struggle for a long life and full human status, the film raises a host of ethical issues relevant to gene manipulation, from the meaning of personhood to the duties we have in "fabricating" people to make them as whole and healthy as possible.

4. Difficulties may arise if, for some reason, custody of the child reverts to the surrogate.

In a special section on financial transactions, the guidelines point out that the selling of infants is both illegal and morally objectionable, and that it is difficult to differentiate between payments for the service of carrying the child and for the child itself. The guidelines do not explain, whether or how payment to a surrogate mother differs from payment for private adoptions.

This section also warns the physician against accepting payment for recruiting or referring potential surrogates or parents; or investing in enterprises specializing in surrogate arrangements. And it cautions that payment to surrogates, other than for expenses, raises the potential for exploitation.

In a section on "Special Situations," physicians are cautioned that they will be dealing not only with infertile couples but also with couples who might want to use a surrogate because they prefer not to interrupt career plans or undergo the risks of pregnancy. The guidelines point out that the dedication of couples to parenthood comes into question when "a risk that could be borne personally is assigned to someone else."

In conclusion, the guidelines leave the decision about whether to participate in surrogate arrangements up to the individual physician. They caution, however, that such decisions should be made only after carefully weighing the ethical implications, as well as the legal, psychological, societal, and medical factors involved. Though physicians are assured that they should feel justified in declining to participate in such arrangements, the document also advises that "when a woman seeks medical care for an established pregnancy, regardless of the method of conception, she should be cared for as any other obstetric patient or referred to a qualified physician who will provide that care."

Finally, the guidelines state that the surrogate mother is "the source of consent" with respect to clinical intervention and management of the pregnancy and that adoptive parents should play a role in decision making only with her consent.—**J.B.**

Such fears, however, are not a sufficient reason to stop splicing genes or relieving infertility through external fertilization.[11] In any event they have no application to surrogate mothering, which does not alter genes or even manipulate the embryo. The only technological aid is a syringe to inseminate and a thermometer to determine when ovulation occurs. Although embryo manipulation would occur if the surrogate received the fertilized egg of another woman, the qualms about surrogate mothering stem less from its potential for technical manipulation, and more from its attitude toward the body and mother-child relations. Mothers bear and give up children for adoption rather frequently when the conception is unplanned. But here the mother conceives the child for that purpose, deliberately using her body for a fee to serve the needs of others. It is the cold willingness to use her body as a baby-making machine and deny the mother-child gestational bond that bothers. (Ironically, the natural bond may turn out to be deeper and stronger than the surrogate imagined.)

Since the transfer of rearing duties from the natural gestational mother to others is widely accepted, the unwillingness of the surrogate mother to rear her child cannot in itself be wrong. As long as she transfers rearing responsibility to capable parents, she is not acting irresponsibly. Still, some persons assert that it is wrong to use the reproductive process for ends other than the good of the child.[12] But the mere presence of selfish motives does not render reproduction immoral, as long as it is carried out in a way that respects the child's interests. Otherwise most pregnancies and births would be immoral, for people have children to serve individual ends as well as the good of the child. In terms of instrumentalism, surrogate mothering cannot be distinguished from most other reproductive situations, whether AID, adoption, or simply planning a child to experience the pleasures of parenthood.

In this vein the problems that can arise when a defective child is born are cited as proof of the immorality of surrogate mothering. The fear is that neither the contracting couple nor the surrogate will want the defective child. In one recent case (*New York Times*, January 28, 1983, p. 18) a dispute arose when none of the parties wanted to take a child born with microcephaly, a condition related to mental retardation. The contracting man claimed on the basis of blood typing that the baby was not his, and thus he was not obligated under the contract to take it, or to pay the surrogate's fee. It turned out that surrogate had borne her husband's child, for she had unwittingly become pregnant by him before being artificially inseminated by the contracting man. The surrogate and her husband eventually assumed responsibility for the child.

An excessively instrumental and callous approach to reproduction when a less than perfect baby is born is not unique to surrogate mothering. Similar reactions can occur whenever married couples have a defective child, as the Baby Doe controversy, which involved the passive eu-

thanasia of a child with Down syndrome, indicates. All surrogate mothering is not wrong because in some instances a handicapped child will be rejected. Nor is it clear that this reaction is more likely in surrogate mothering than in conventional births for it reflects common attitudes toward handicapped newborns as much as alienation in the surrogate arrangement.

As with most situations, "how" something is done is more important than the mere fact of doing it. The morality of surrogate mothering thus depends on how the duties and responsibilities of the role are carried out, rather than on the mere fact that a couple produces a child with the aid of a collaborator. Depending on the circumstances, a surrogate mother can be praised as a benefactor to a suffering couple (the money is hardly adequate compensation) or condemned as a callous user of offspring to further her selfish ends. The view that one takes of her actions will also influence the role one wants the law to play.

What Should the State's Role Be?

What stance should public policy and the law take toward surrogate mothering? As with all collaborative reproduction, a range of choices exists, from prohibition and regulation to active encouragement.

However, there may be constitutional limits to the state's power to restrict collaborative reproduction. The right not to procreate, through contraception and abortion, is now firmly established.[13] A likely implication of these cases, supported by rulings in other cases, is that married persons (and possibly single persons) have a right to bear, beget, birth, and parent children by natural coital means using such technological aids (microsurgery and in vitro fertilization, for example) as are medically available. It should follow that married persons also have a right to engage in noncoital, collaborative reproduction, at least where natural reproduction is not possible. The right of a couple to raise a child should not depend on their luck in the natural lottery, if they can obtain the missing factor of reproduction from others.[14]

If a married couple's right to procreative autonomy includes the right to contract with consenting collaborators, then the state will have a heavy burden of justification for infringing that right. The risks to surrogate, couple, and child do not seem sufficiently compelling to meet this burden, for they are no different from the harms of adoption and AID. Nor will it suffice to point to a communal feeling that such uses of the body are—aside from the consequences—immoral. Moral distaste alone does not justify interference with a fundamental right.

Although surrogate mothering is not now criminal, this discussion is not purely hypothetical. The ban in Michigan and several other states on paying fees for adoption beyond medical expenses has the same effect as an outright prohibition, for few surrogates will volunteer for altruistic reasons alone. A ban on fees is not necessary to protect the surrogate mother from coercion or exploitation, or to protect the child from abuse, the two objectives behind passage of those laws. Unlike the pregnant unmarried woman who "sells" her child, the surrogate has made a considered, knowing choice, often with the assistance of counsel, before becoming pregnant. She may of course choose to be a surrogate for financial reasons, but offering money to do unpleasant tasks is not in itself coercive.

Nor does the child's welfare support a ban on fees, for the risk is no greater than in natural paired reproduction that the parents will be unfit or abuse the child. The specter of slavery, which some opposed to surrogate mothering have raised, is unwarranted. It is quibbling to question whether the couple is "buying" a child or the mother's personal services. Quite clearly, the couple is buying the right to rear a child by paying the mother to beget and bear one for that very purpose. But the purchasers do not buy the right to treat the child or surrogate as a commodity or property. Child abuse and neglect laws still apply, with criminal and civil sanctions available for mistreatment.

The main concern with fees rests on moral and aesthetic grounds. An affront to moral sensibility arises over paying money for a traditionally noncommercial, intimate function. Even though blood and sperm are sold, and miners, professional athletes, and petrochemical workers sell some of their health and vitality, some persons think it wrong for women to bear children for money, in much the same way that paying money for sex or body organs is considered wrong. Every society excludes some exchanges from the marketplace on moral grounds. But the state's power to block exchanges that interfere with the exercise of a fundamental right is limited. Since blocking this exchange stops infertile couples from reproducing and rearing the husband's child, a harm greater than moral distaste is necessary to justify it.

Although the state cannot block collaborative reproductive exchanges on moral grounds, it need not subsidize or encourage surrogate contracts. One could argue that allowing the parties to a surrogate contract to use the courts to terminate parental rights, certify paternity, and legalize adoption is a subsidy and therefore not required of the state. Similarly, a state's refusal to enforce surrogate contracts as a matter of public policy could be taken as a refusal to subsidize rather than as interference with the right to reproduce. But given the state's monopoly of those functions and the impact its denial will have on the ability of infertile couples to find reproductive collaborators, it is more plausible to view the refusal to certify and effectuate surrogate contracts as an infringement of the right to procreate. Denying an adoption because it was agreed upon in advance for a fee interferes with the couple's procreative autonomy as much as any criminal penalty for paying a fee to or contracting with a collaborator. (The crucial distinction between interfering with and not encouraging the exercise of a right has

been overlooked by the Michigan and Kentucky courts that have held constitutional the refusal to allow adoptions or paternity determinations where a fee has been paid to the surrogate mother. This error makes these cases highly questionable precedents.[15])

A conclusion that surrogate contracts must be *enforced*, however, does not require that they be specifically carried out in all instances. As long as damage remedies remain, there is no constitutional right to specific performance. For example, a court need not enjoin the surrogate who changes her mind about abortion or relinquishing the child once it is born. A surrogate who wants to breach the contract by abortion should pay damages, but not be ordered to continue the pregnancy, because of the difficulty in enforcing or monitoring the order. (Whether damages are a practical alternative in such cases will depend on the surrogate's economic situation, or whether bonding or insurance to assure her contractual obligation is possible.) On the other hand, a court could reasonably order the surrogate after birth to relinquish the child. Whether such an order should issue will depend on whether the surrogate's interest in keeping the child is deemed greater than the couple's interest in rearing (assuming that both are fit parents). A commitment to freedom of contract and the rights of parties to arrange collaborative reproduction would favor the adoptive couple, while sympathy for the gestational bond between mother and child would favor the mother. If the mother prevailed, the couple should still have other remedies, including visitation rights for the father, restitution of the surrogate's fee and other expenses, and perhaps money damages as well.

The constitutional status of a married couple's procreative choice shields collaborative arrangements from interference on moral grounds alone, but not from all regulation. While the parties may assign the rearing rights according to contract, the state need not leave the entire transaction to the vagaries of the private sector. Regulation to minimize harm and assure knowing choices would be permissible, as long as the regulation is reasonably related to promoting these goals.

For example, the state could set minimum standards for surrogate brokers, set age and health qualifications for surrogates, and structure the transaction to assure voluntary, knowing choices. The state could also define and allocate responsibilities among the parties to protect the best interests of the offspring—for example, refusing to protect the surrogate's anonymity, requiring that the contracting couple assume responsibility for a defective child, or even transferring custody to another if threats to the child's welfare justify such a move.

Not What We Do—But How We Do It

The central issue with surrogate mothering, as with other collaborative reproduction, is not the deliberate separation of biologic and social parentage, but how the separation is effected and the resulting relationship with the third party. If the third party's involvement in the reproduction is discrete and limited, collaborative reproduction is easily tolerated. Thus few people question the anonymous sperm donor's lack of rights and duties toward the offspring, except in the case where the mother and donor have expressly agreed that he would have some access to the rearing of a child.[16] The donor's claim—and possibly the child's need to connect—is less strong in such cases. Egg donations, though involving more risk and burden for the donor, should be similarly treated, for they are also discrete and limited.

Collaborative reproduction involving gestational contributors poses more difficult problems, because the nine-month gestational period creates a unique and powerful bond for both donor and offspring that seems to justify a claim in its own right. Yet in adoption we allow those claims to be nullified by the gestational mother's choice. Surrogate motherhood presents the same issue. The difference is that it is planned before conception, but that hardly seems to matter once the child is born and the mother wishes to fulfill her commitment. The issue of whether the mother should be held to a promise on which others have relied is distinct from the question of whether mothers can relinquish children deliberately conceived for others outside the agency-controlled adoption process.

Surrogate mothering casts particular light on one other collaborative technique that may soon be widely available—the transfer of the externally (or internally) fertilized egg of one woman to another woman who gestates and births it.[17] The third party in this situation is a gestational surrogate for a genetic and rearing mother, who is unable or unwilling to bear and birth her child. At first glance the gestational mother's claim to the child seems less compelling than the claim of the surrogate mother because the child is not genetically hers. Yet concerns will arise, as with surrogate mothers, over the severing or denial of the gestational bond, the degree to which the contract should be honored, and the gestational mother's relationship (if any) with the child.

The moral issues surrounding surrogate mothering also cast light on the problems with manipulative techniques such as genetic alteration of the embryo and nonuterine gestation of the fertilized egg. Since those techniques will be used primarily for paired reproduction, the main concerns will be the safety of the offspring and the morality of genetic manipulation. However, when manipulation and collaborative reproduction are combined, the relationship of the offspring to the third party contributor will come into question.

Surrogate mothering for a fee is neither the evil nor the panacea that many have thought. It is barely distinguishable from the many current practices that separate biologic and social parentage and that seek parenthood for personal satisfaction. The differences do not appear to be great enough to justify prohibition, active discouragement, or for that matter, encouragement. Like many human endeavors, in the final analysis, what matters is not *whether* but *how* it is done. In that respect public scrutiny, through regulation of the process of drawing up the contract rather than its specific terms, could help to assure that it is done well.

REFERENCES

The author gratefully acknowledges the comments of Rebecca Dresser, Mark Frankel, Inga Markovits, Phillip Parker, Bruce Russell, John Sampson, and Ted Schneyer on earlier drafts.

[1] People v. Sorenson, 68 Cal. 2d 280, 437 P.2d 495; Walter Wadlington, "Artificial Insemination: The Dangers of a Poorly Kept Secret,"*Northwestern Law Review* 64 (1970), 777.

[2] See, for example, Michigan Statutes Annotated, 27.3178 (555.54)(555.69) (1980).

[3] William Landes and Eleanor Posner, "The Economics of the Baby Shortage," *Journal of Legal Studies* 7 (1978), 323.

[4] See Erik Erikson, *The Life Cycle Completed* (New York: Norton, 1980), pp. 122-124.

[5] Phillip Parker, "Surrogate Mother's Motivations: Initial Findings," *American Journal of Psychiatry* 140:1 (January 1983), 117-118; Phillip Parker, "The Psychology of Surrogate Motherhood: A Preliminary Report of a Longitudinal Pilot Study" (unpublished). See also Dava Sobel, "Surrogate Mothers: Why Women Volunteer," *New York Times*, June 25, 1981, p. 18.

[6] Mark Frankel, "Surrogate Motherhood: An Ethical Perspective," pp. 1-2. (Paper presented at Wayne State Symposium on Surrogate Motherhood, Nov. 20, 1982.)

[7] See John Robertson, "In Vitro Conception and Harm to the Unborn," *Hastings Center Report* 8 (October 1978), 13-14; Michael Bayles, "Harm to the Unconceived," *Philosophy and Public Affairs* 5 (1976), 295.

[8] A small, uncontrolled study found these effects to last some four to six weeks. Statement of Nancy Reame, R.N. at Wayne State University, Symposium on Surrogate Motherhood, Nov. 20, 1982.

[9] Betty Jane Lifton, *Twice Born: Memoirs of an Adopted Daughter* (New York: Penguin, 1977); L. Dusky, "Brave New Babies," *Newsweek*, Dec. 6, 1982, p. 30.

[10] Leon Kass, "Making Babies—the New Biology and the Old Morality," *The Public Interest* 26 (1972), 18; "Making Babies Revisited," *The Public Interest* 54 (1979), 32; Paul Ramsey, *Fabricated Man: The Ethics of Genetic Control* (New Haven: Yale University Press, 1970).

[11] The President's Commission for the Study of Ethical Problems in Medicine and Biomedical and Behavioral Research, *Splicing Life: The Social and Ethical Issues of Genetic Engineering with Human Beings* (Washington, D.C., 1982), pp. 53-60.

[12] Herbert Krimmel, Testimony before California Assembly Committee on Judiciary, Surrogate Parenting Contracts (November 14, 1982), pp. 89-96.

[13] Griswold v. Connecticut, 381 U.S. 479 (1964); Eisenstadt v. Baird, 405 U.S. 438 (1972); Roe v. Wade, 410 U.S. 113 (1973); Planned Parenthood v. Danforth, 428 U.S. 52 (1976); Bellotti v. Baird, 443 U.S. 622 (1979); Carey v. Population Services International, 431 U.S. 678 (1977).

[14] Although this article does not address the right of single persons to contract with others for reproductive purposes, it should be noted that the right of married persons to engage in collaborative reproduction does not entail a similar right for unmarried persons. For a more detailed exposition of the arguments for the reproductive rights of married and single persons, see John Robertson, "Procreative Liberty and the Control of Conception, Pregnancy and Childbirth," *Virginia Law Review* 69 (April 1983), 405, 418-420.

[15] See Doe v. Kelley, 106 Mich. App. 164, 307 N.W.2d 438 (1981). Syrkowski v. Appleyard, 9 Family Law Rptr. 2348 (April 5, 1983); In re Baby Girl, 9 Family Law Reptr. 2348 (March 8, 1983).

[16] See C.M. v. C.C., 152 N.J. 160, 377 A.2d 821 (man who provided sperm for artificial insemination held to have visitation rights because of express agreement with the mother).

[17] See Richard D. Lyons, "2 Women Become Pregnant With Transferred Embryos," *New York Times*, July 22, 1983, p. A1, B7.

The Case against Surrogate Parenting
by HERBERT T. KRIMMEL

Is it ethical for someone to create a human life with the intention of giving it up? This seems to be the primary question for both surrogate mother arrangements and artificial insemination by donor (AID), since in both situations a person who is providing germinal material does so only upon the assurance that someone else will assume full responsibility for the child he or she helps to create.

The Ethical Issue

In analyzing the ethics of surrogate mother arrangements, it is helpful to begin by examining the roles the surrogate mother performs. First, she acts as a procreator in providing an ovum to be fertilized. Second, after her ovum has been fertilized by the sperm of the man who wishes to parent the child, she acts as host to the fetus, providing nurture and protection while the newly conceived individual develops.

I see no insurmountable moral objections to the functions the mother performs in this second role as host. Her actions are analogous to those of a foster mother or of a wet-nurse who cares for a child when the natural mother cannot or does not do so. Using a surrogate mother as a host for the fetus when the biological mother cannot bear the child is no more morally objectionable than employing others to help educate, train, or otherwise care for a child. Except in extremes, where the parent relinquishes or delegates responsibilities for a child for trivial reasons, the practice would not seem to raise a serious moral issue.

I would argue, however, that the first role that the surrogate mother performs—providing germinal material to be fertilized—does pose a major ethical problem. The surrogate mother provides her ovum, and enters into a surrogate mother arrangement, with the clear understanding that she is to avoid responsibility for the life she creates. Surrogate mother arrangements are designed to separate in the mind of the surrogate mother the decision to create a child from the decision to have and raise that child. The cause of this dissociation is some other benefit she will receive, most often money.[1] In other words, her desire to create a child is born of some motive other than the desire to be a parent. This separation of the decision to create a child from the decision to parent it is ethically suspect. The child is conceived not because he is wanted by his biological mother, but because he can be useful to someone else. He is conceived in order to be given away.

At their deepest level, surrogate mother arrangements involve a change in motive for creating children: from a desire to have them for their own sake, to a desire to have them because they can provide some other benefit. The surrogate mother creates a child with the intention to abdicate parental responsibilities. Can we view this as ethical? My answer is no. I will explain why by analyzing various situations in which surrogate mother arrangements might be used.

Why Motive Matters

Let's begin with the single parent. A single woman might use AID, or a single man might use a surrogate mother arrangement, if she or he wanted a child but did not want to be burdened with a spouse.[2] Either practice would intentionally deprive the child of a mother or a father. This, I assert, is fundamentally unfair to the child.

Those who disagree might point to divorce or to the death of a parent as situations in which a child is deprived of one parent and must rely solely or primarily upon the other. The comparison, however, is inapt. After divorce or the death of a parent, a child may find herself with a single parent due to circumstances that were unfortunate, unintended, and undesired. But when surrogate mother arrangements are used by a single parent, depriving the child of a second parent is one of the intended and desired effects. It is one thing to ask how to make the best of a bad situation when it is thrust upon a person. It is different altogether to ask whether one may intentionally set out to achieve the same result. The morality of identical results (for example, killings) will oftentimes differ depending upon whether the situation is invited by, or involuntarily thrust upon, the actor. Legal distinctions following and based upon this ethical distinction are abundant. The law of self-defense provides a notable example.[3]

Since a woman can get pregnant if she wishes whether or not she is married, and since there is little that society can do to prevent women from creating children even if their intention is to deprive the children of a father, why should we be so concerned about single men using surrogate mother arrangements if they too want a child but not a spouse? To say that women can intentionally plan to be unwed mothers is not to condone the practice. Besides, society will hold the father liable in a paternity action if he can be found and identified, which indicates some social concern that people should not be able to abdicate the respon-

HERBERT T. KRIMMEL *is professor of law, Southwestern University School of Law, Los Angeles. This article is an edited version of his testimony before the California Assembly Committee on the Judiciary on November 19, 1982, at its hearings on the proposed "Surrogate Parent Act," Assembly Bill #3771.*

sibilities that they incur in generating children. Otherwise, why do we condemn the proverbial sailor with a pregnant girlfriend in every port?

In many surrogate mother arrangements, of course, the surrogate mother will not be transferring custody of the child to a single man, but to a couple: the child's biological father and a stepmother, his wife. What are the ethics of surrogate mother arrangements when the child is taken into a two-parent family? Again, surrogate mother arrangements and AID pose similar ethical questions: The surrogate mother transfers her parental responsibilities to the wife of the biological father, while with AID the sperm donor relinquishes his interest in the child to the husband of the biological mother. In both cases the child is created with the intention of transferring the responsibility for its care to a new set of parents. The surrogate mother situation is more dramatic than AID since the transfer occurs after the child is born, while in the case of AID the transfer takes place at the time of the insemination. Nevertheless, the ethical point is the same: creating children for the purpose of transferring them. For a surrogate mother the question remains: Is it ethical to create a child for the purpose of transferring it to the wife of the biological father?

At first blush this looks to be little different from the typical adoption, for what is an adoption other than a transfer of responsibility from one set of parents to another? The analogy is misleading, however, for two reasons. First, it is difficult to imagine anyone conceiving children for the purpose of putting them up for adoption. And, if such a bizarre event were to occur, I doubt that we would look upon it with moral approval. Most adoptions arise either because an undesired conception is brought to term, or because the parents wanted to have the child, but find that they are unable to provide for it because of some unfortunate circumstances that develop after conception.

Second, even if surrogate mother arrangements were to be classified as a type of adoption, not all offerings of children for adoption are necessarily moral. For example, would it be moral for parents to offer their three-year-old for adoption because they are bored with the child? Would it be moral for a couple to offer for adoption their newborn female baby because they wanted a boy?

Therefore, even though surrogate mother arrangements may in some superficial ways be likened to adoption, one must still ask whether it is ethical to separate the decision to create children from the desire to have them. I would answer no. The procreator should desire the child for its own sake, and not as a means to attaining some other end. Even though one of the ends may be stated altruistically as an attempt to bring happiness to an infertile couple, the child is still being used by the surrogate. She creates it not because she desires it, but because she desires something from it.

To sanction the use and treatment of human beings as means to the achievement of other goals instead of as ends in themselves is to accept an ethic with a tragic past, and to

Historical Parallels

Proponents of surrogate mother arrangements refer to biblical passages such as Genesis 16, which deals with Abram's having children by his handmaid, Hagar, and Deuteronomy 25:5-6, which deals with the duty of a man to raise up children to his dead brother by his sister-in-law. However, it is quite clear that when Abram conceived Ishmael by Hagar, he had done so only after his wife, Sarai, had given Hagar to him as a second *wife* (Genesis 16:3). Similarly, Deuteronomy 25:5-6 deals with a situation where the woman becomes a wife. In both cases the so-called surrogate mother is not a surrogate at all, but an extension (albeit polygamous) of the family unit. In the biblical tradition, the second wife in no way relinquishes control or responsibility for the children she creates; therefore, analogies between such biblical passages and present-day proposed surrogate mother arrangements are incorrect.

If the proponents of surrogate mother arrangements wish to take biblical authorities as analogies, they might well look to the end of the story of Hagar and Ishmael: how they were driven out by Sarah after Sarah gave birth to Isaac (Genesis 21). The family animosity of thousands of years ago is with us today as the sons of Ishmael (the Arabs) and the sons of Isaac (the Jews) still have some difficulties getting along.

-H.T.K.

establish a precedent with a dangerous future. Already the press has reported the decision of one couple to conceive a child for the purpose of using it as a bone marrow donor for its sibling (*Los Angeles Times*, April 17, 1979, p. I-2). And the bioethics literature contains articles seriously considering whether we should clone human beings to serve as an inventory of spare parts for organ transplants[4] and articles that foresee the use of comatose human beings as self-replenishing blood banks and manufacturing plants for human hormones.[5] How far our society is willing to proceed down this road is uncertain, but it is clear that the first step to all these practices is the acceptance of the same principle that the Nazis attempted to use to justify their medical experiments at the Nuremberg War Crimes Trials: that human beings may be used as means to the achievement of other goals, and need not be treated as ends in themselves.[6]

But why, it might be asked, is it so terrible if the surrogate mother does not desire the child for its own sake, when under the proposed surrogate mother arrangements there will be a couple eagerly desiring to have the child and to be its parents? That this argument may not be entirely accurate will be illustrated in the following section, but the basic reply is that creating a child without desiring it fundamentally changes the way we look at children—instead of viewing them as unique individual personalities to be desired in their own right, we may come to view them as commodities or items of manufacture to be desired because of their utility. A recent newspaper account describes the business of an agency that matches surrogate mothers with barren couples as follows:

> Its first product is due for delivery today. Twelve others are on the way and an additional 20 have been ordered. The "company" is Surrogate Mothering Ltd. and the "product" is babies.[7]

The dangers of this view are best illustrated by examining what might go wrong in a surrogate mother arrangement, and most important, by viewing how the various parties to the contract may react to the disappointment.

What Might Go Wrong

Ninety-nine percent of the surrogate mother arrangements may work out just fine; the child will be born normal, and the adopting parents (that is, the biological father and his wife) will want it. But, what happens when, unforeseeably, the child is born deformed? Since many defects cannot be discovered prenatally by amniocentesis or other means, the situation is bound to arise.[8] Similarly, consider what would happen if the biological father were to die before the birth of the child. Or if the "child" turns out to be twins or triplets. Each of these instances poses an inevitable situation where the adopting parents may be unhappy with the prospect of getting the child or children. Although legislation can mandate that the adopting parents take the child or children in whatever condition they come or whatever the situation, provided the surrogate mother has abided by all the contractual provisions of the surrogate mother arrangement, the important point for our discussion is the attitude that the surrogate mother or the adopting parent might have. Consider the example of the deformed child.

When I participated in the Surrogate Parent Foundation's inaugural symposium in November 1981, I was struck by the attitude of both the surrogate mothers and the adopting parents to these problems. The adopting parents worried, "Do we have to take such a child?" and the surrogate mothers said in response, "Well, we don't want to be stuck with it." Clearly, both groups were anxious not be responsible for the "undesirable child" born of the surrogate mother arrangement. What does this portend?

It is human nature that when one pays money, one expects value. Things that one pays for have a way of being seen as commodities. Unavoidable in surrogate mother arrangements are questions such as: "Did I get a good one?" We see similar behavior with respect to the adoption of children: comparatively speaking, there is no shortage of black, Mexican-American, mentally retarded, or older children seeking homes; the shortage is in attractive, intelligent-looking Caucasian babies.[9] Similarly, surrogate mother arrangements involve more than just the desire to have a child. The desire is for a certain type of child.

But, it may be objected, don't all parents voice these same concerns in the normal course of having children? Not exactly. No one doubts or minimizes the pain and disappointment parents feel when they learn that their child is born with some genetic or congenital birth defect. But this is different from the surrogate mother situation, where neither the surrogate mother nor the adopting parents may feel responsible, and both sides may feel that they have a legitimate excuse not to assume responsibility for the child. The surrogate mother might blame the biological father for having "defective sperm," as the adopting parents might blame the surrogate mother for a "defective ovum" or for improper care of the fetus during pregnancy. The adopting parents desire a normal child, not *this* child in any condition, and the surrogate mother doesn't want it in any event. So both sides will feel threatened by the birth of an "undesirable child." Like bruised fruit in the produce bin of a supermarket, this child is likely to become an object of avoidance.

Certainly, in the natural course of having children a mother may doubt whether she wants a child if the father has died before its birth; parents may shy away from a defective infant, or be distressed at the thought of multiple births. Nevertheless, I believe they are more likely to accept these contingencies as a matter of fate. I do not think this is the case with surrogate mother arrangements. After all, in the surrogate mother arrangement the adopting parents can blame someone outside the marital relationship. The surrogate mother has been hosting this child all along, and she is delivering it. It certainly *looks* far more like a commodity than the child that arrives in the natural course within the family unit.

A Dangerous Agenda

Another social problem, which arises out of the first, is the fear that surrogate mother arrangements will fall prey to eugenic concerns.[10] Surrogate mother contracts typically have clauses requiring genetic tests of the fetus and stating that the surrogate mother must have an abortion (or keep the child herself) if the child does not pass these tests.[11]

In the last decade we have witnessed a renaissance of interest in eugenics. This, coupled with advances in biomedical technology, has created a host of abuses and new moral problems. For example, genetic counseling clinics now face a dilemma: amniocentesis, the same procedure that identifies whether a fetus suffers from certain genetic defects, also discloses the sex of a fetus. Genetic counseling clinics have reported that even when the fetus is normal, a disproportionate number of mothers abort female children.[12] Aborting normal fetuses simply because the prospective parents desire children of a certain sex is one result of viewing children as commodities. The recent scandal at the Repository for Germinal Choice, the so-called "Nobel Sperm Bank," provides another chilling example. Their first "customer" was, unbeknownst to the staff, a woman who "had lost custody of two other children because they were abused in an effort to 'make them smart.'"[13] Of course, these and similar evils may occur whether or not surrogate mother arrangements are allowed by law. But to the extent that they promote the view of children as commodities, these arrangements contribute to these problems. There is nothing wrong with striving for betterment, as long as it does not result in intolerance to that which is not perfect. But I fear that the latter attitude will become prevalent.

Sanctioning surrogate mother arrangements can also exert pressures upon the family structure. First, as was noted earlier, there is nothing technically to prevent the use of surrogate mother arrangements by single males desiring to become parents. Indeed, single females can already do this with AID or even without it. But even if legislation were to limit the use of the surrogate mother arrangement to infertile couples, other pressures would occur: namely the intrusion of a third adult into the marital community.[14] I do not think that society is ready to accept either single parenting or quasi-adulterous arrangements as normal.

Another stress on the family structure arises within the family of the surrogate mother. When the child is surrendered to the adopting parents it is removed not only from the surrogate mother, but also from her family. They too have interests to be considered. Do not the siblings of that child have an interest in the fact that their little baby brother has been "given" away?[15] One woman, the mother of a medical student who had often donated sperm for artificial insemination, expressed her feelings to me eloquently. She asked, "I wonder how many grandchildren I have that I have never seen and never been able to hold or cuddle."

Intrafamily tensions can also be expected to result in the family of the adopting parents due to the asymmetry of relationship the adopting parents will have toward the child. The adopting mother has no biological relationship to the child, whereas the adopting father is also the child's biological father. Won't this unequal biological claim on the child be used as a wedge in child-rearing arguments? Can't we imagine the father saying, "Well, he is my son, not yours"? What if the couple eventually gets divorced? Should custody in a subsequent divorce between the adopting mother and the biological father be treated simply as a normal child custody dispute? Or should the biological relationship between father and child weigh more heavily? These questions do not arise in typical adoption situations since both parents are equally unrelated biologically to the child. Indeed, in adoption there is symmetry. The surrogate mother situation is more analogous to second marriages, where the children of one party by a prior marriage are adopted by the new spouse. Since asymmetry in second marriage situations causes problems, we can anticipate similar difficulties arising from surrogate mother arrangements.

There is also the worry that the offspring of a surrogate mother arrangement will be deprived of important information about his or her heritage. This also happens with adopted children or children conceived by AID,[16] who lack

On the Legislative Front

The first bill to cover surrogate mother arrangements was introduced in the Alaska House of Representatives in 1981, and since then at least five other states—California, Maryland, Michigan, Ohio, and South Carolina—have considered or are planning to debate legislation on this issue. However, so far no state has actually enacted any law. The Michigan bill, HB 5184, on which the South Carolina proposal is modeled, would regulate the process by spelling out the specifics of the Probate Court's "order of filiation" establishing paternity, of a consent to relinquish parental rights by the surrogate mother, and of the adoption of the child by the wife of the biologic father. Included in the bill is a list of criteria for the evaluation of the suitability of the couple for "surrogate adoption." The California bill, AB 3771, would "facilitate the inability of infertile couples to become parents through the employment of the services of a surrogate." —C.L.

information about their biological parents, which could be important to them medically. Another less popularly recognized problem is the danger of half-sibling marriages,[17] where the child of the surrogate mother unwittingly falls in love with a half sister or brother. The only way to avoid these problems is to dispense with the confidentiality of parental records; however, the natural parents may not always want their identity disclosed.

The legalization of surrogate mother arrangements may also put undue pressure upon poor women to use their bodies in this way to support themselves and their families. Analogous problems have arisen in the past with the use of paid blood donors.[18] And occasionally the press reports someone desperate enough to offer to sell an eye or some other organ.[19] I believe that certain things should be viewed as too important to be sold as commodities, and I hope that we have advanced from the time when parents raised children for profitable labor, or found themselves forced to sell their children.

While many of the social dilemmas I have outlined here have their analogies in other present-day occurrences such as divorced families or in adoption, every addition is hurtful. Legalizing surrogate mother arrangements will increase the frequency of these problems, and put more stress on our society's shared moral values.[20]

A Tale for Our Time

An infertile couple might prefer to raise a child with a biological relationship to the husband, rather than to raise an adopted child who has no biological relationship to either the husband or the wife. But does the marginal increase in joy that they might therefore experience outweigh the potential pain that they, or the child conceived in such arrangements, or others might suffer? Does their preference outweigh the social costs and problems that the legalization of surrogate mothering might well engender? I honestly do not know. I don't even know on what hypothetical scale such interests could be weighed and balanced. But even if we could weigh such interests, and even if personal preference outweighed the costs, I still would not be able to say that we could justify achieving those ends by these means; that ethically it would be permissible for a person to create a child, not because she desired it, but because it could be useful to her.

Edmond Cahn has termed this ignoring of means in the attainment of ends the "Pompey syndrome":[21]

I have taken the name from young Sextus Pompey, who appears in Shakespeare's *Antony and Cleopatra* in an incident drawn directly from Plutarch. Pompey, whose navy has won control of the seas around Italy, comes to negotiate peace with the Roman triumvirs Mark Antony, Octavius Caesar, and Lepidus, and they meet in a roistering party on Pompey's ship. As they carouse, one of Pompey's lieutenants draws him aside and whispers that he can become lord of all the world if he will only grant the lieutenant leave to cut first the mooring cable and then the throats of the triumvirs. Pompey pauses, then replies in these words:

Ah, this thou shouldst have done,
And not have spoke on't!
In me 'tis villainy;
In thee't had been good service.
Thou must know tis not my profit that does lend mine honour;
Mine honour, it. Repent that e'er thy tongue
Hath so betrayed thine act; being done unknown;
I should have found it afterwards well done,
But must condemn it now. Desist, and drink.

Here we have the most pervasive of moral syndromes, the one most characteristic of so-called respectable men in a civilized society. To possess the end and yet not be responsible for the means, to grasp the fruit while disavowing the tree, to escape being told the cost until someone else has paid it irrevocably; this is the Pompey syndrome and the chief hypocrisy of our time.

REFERENCES

[1]See Philip J. Parker, "Motivation of Surrogate Mothers: Initial Findings," *American Journal of Psychiatry* 140:1 (January 1983), 117-18; see also Doe v. Kelley, Circuit Court of Wayne County Michigan (1980) reported in 1980 Rep. on Human Reproduction and Law II-A-1.

[2]See, e.g., C.M. v. C.C., 152 N.J. Supp. 160, 377 A.2d 821 (1977); "Why She Went to 'Nobel Sperm Bank' for Child," *Los Angeles Herald Examiner*, Aug. 6, 1982, p. A9; "Womb for Rent," *Los Angeles Herald Examiner*, Sept. 21, 1981, p. A3.

[3]See also Richard McCormick, "Reproductive Technologies: Ethical Issues" in *Encyclopedia of Bioethics*, edited by Walter Reich, Vol. 4 (New York: The Free Press, 1978) pp. 1454, 1459; Robert Snowden and G. D. Mitchell, *The Artificial Family* (London: George Allen & Unwin, 1981), p. 71.

[4]See, e.g., Alexander Peters, "The Brave New World: Can the Law Bring Order Within Traditional Concepts of Due Process?" *Suffolk Law Review* 4 (1970), 894, 901-02; Roderic Gorney, "The New Biology and the Future of Man," *UCLA Law Review* 15 (1968), 273, 302; J. G. Castel, "Legal Implications of Biomedical Science and Technology in the Twenty-First Century," *Canadian Bar Review* 51 (1973), 119, 127.

[5]See Harry Nelson, "Maintaining Dead to Serve as Blood Makers Proposed: Logical, Sociologist Says," *Los Angeles Times*, February 26, 1974 p. II-1; Hans Jonas, "Against the Stream: Comments on the Definition and Redefinition of Death," in *Philosophical Essays: From Ancient Creed to Technological Man* (Chicago: University of Chicago Press, 1974), pp. 132-40.

[6]See Leo Alexander, "Medical Science under Dictatorship," *New England Journal of Medicine* 241:2 (1949), 39; United States v. Brandt, Trial of the Major War Criminals, International Military Tribunal: Nuremberg, 14 November 1945-1 October 1946.

[7]Bob Dvorchak, "Surrogate Mothers: Pregnant Idea Now a Pregnant Business," *Los Angeles Herald Examiner*, December 27, 1983, p. Al.

[8]"Surrogate's Baby Born with Deformities Rejected by All," *Los Angeles Times*, January 22, 1983, p. I-17; "Man Who Hired Surrogate Did Not Father Ailing Baby," *Los Angeles Herald Examiner*, February 3, 1983, p. A-6.

[9]See, e.g., Adoption in America, Hearing before the Subcommittee on Aging, Family and Human Services of the Senate Committee on Labor and Human Resources, 97th Congress. 1st Session (1981), p. 3 (comments of Senator Jeremiah Denton) and pp. 16-17 (statement of Warren Master, Acting Commissioner of Administration for Children, Youth and Families, HHS).

[10]Cf. "Discussion: Moral, Social and Ethical Issues," in *Law and Ethics of A.I.D. and Embryo Transfer* (1973) (comments of Himmelweit); reprinted in Michael Shapiro and Roy Spece, *Bioethics and Law* (St. Paul: West Publishing Company, 1981), p. 548.

[11]See, e.g., Lane (Newsday), "Womb for Rent," *Tucson Citizen* (Weekender), June 7, 1980, p. 3; Susan Lewis, "Baby Bartering? Surrogate Mothers Pose Issues for Lawyers, Courts," *The Los Angeles Daily Journal*, April 20, 1981; see also Elaine Markoutsas, "Women Who Have Babies for Other Women," *Good Housekeeping* 96 (April 1981), 104.

[12]See Morton A. Stenchever, "An Abuse of Prenatal Diagnosis," *Journal of the American Medical Association* 221 (1972), 408; Charles Westoff and Ronald R. Rindfus, "Sex Preselection in the United States: Some Implications," *Science* 184 (1974), 633, 636; see also Phyllis Battelle, "Is It a Boy or a Girl"? *Los Angeles Herald Examiner*, Oct. 8, 1981, p. A17.

[13]"2 Children Taken from Sperm Bank Mother," *Los Angeles Times*, July 14, 1982; p. I-3; "The Sperm-Bank Scandal," *Newsweek* 24 (July 26, 1982).

[14]See Helmut Thielicke, *The Ethics of Sex*, John W. Doberstein, trans. (New York: Harper & Row, 1964).

[15]According to one newspaper account, when a surrogate mother informed her nine-year-old daughter that the new baby would be given away, the daughter replied: "Oh, good. If it's a girl we can keep it and give Jeffrey [her two-year-old half brother] away." "Womb for Rent," *Los Angeles Herald Examiner*, Sept. 21, 1981, p. A3.

[16]See, e.g., Lorraine Dusky, "Brave New Babies"? *Newsweek* 30 (December 6, 1982). Also testimony of Suzanne Rubin before the California Assembly Committee on Judiciary, Surrogate Parenting Contracts, Assembly Publication No. 962, pp. 72-75 (November 19, 1982).

[17]This has posed an increasing problem for children conceived through AID. See, e.g., Martin Curie-Cohen, et al., "Current Practice of Artificial Insemination by Donor in the United States," *New England Journal of Medicine* 300 (1979), 585-89.

[18]See e.g., Richard M. Titmuss, *The Gift Relationship: From Human Blood to Social Policy* (New York: Random House, 1971).

[19]See, e.g., "Man Desperate for Funds: Eye for Sale at $35,000," *Los Angeles Times*, February 1, 1975, p. II-1; "100 Answer Man's Ad for New Kidney," *Los Angeles Times*, September 12, 1974, p. I-4.

[20]See generally Guido Calabresi, "Reflections on Medical Experimentation in Humans," *Daedalus* 98 (1969), 387-93; also see Michael Shapiro and Roy Spece, "On Being 'Unprincipled on Principle': The Limits of Decision Making 'On the Merits,'" in *Bioethics and Law*, pp. 67-71.

[21]Edmond Cahn, "Drug Experiments and the Public Conscience," in *Drugs in Our Society*, edited by Paul Talalay (Baltimore: The Johns Hopkins Press, 1964), pp. 255, 258-61.

Should babies be treated as commodities? Should reproduction be commercialized? Should motherhood be determined by contract? A few years ago these questions seemed absurd. But the hope that surrogate motherhood would wither of its own weirdness is now beginning to seem quaint. Indeed, two recent court decisions strongly support commercial surrogate mother agreements. If surrogate mother companies were listed on the New York Stock Exchange, these cases would have sent their stock soaring.

Almost since its inception, Surrogate Parenting Associates, Inc. (SPA) was in trouble in its home state of Kentucky. In 1981, the Attorney General instituted proceedings against the corporation to revoke its charter. He charged that by entering into commercial surrogate arrangements in which a woman would be paid to be artificially inseminated, and then to bear a child for whom she would relinquish parental rights (for later step-parent adoption by the father-sperm-donor's infertile wife), the corporation violated the state's prohibition against the "purchase of any child for the purpose of adoption." The statute was amended in 1984 to add the words, "or any other purpose, including termination of parental rights" (KRS 199.950[2]).

A trial court ruled against the Attorney General, an Appeals Court in his favor, and the Supreme Court of Kentucky has now sided with the corporation (*Surrogate Parenting Associates v. Kentucky*, 704 S.W.2d 209 [1986]). The court declared that the intention of the legislature in prohibiting baby selling was solely "to keep baby brokers from overwhelming an expectant mother or the parents of a child with financial inducements to part with the child." It therefore approved of baby sales if the price was agreed to *before* conception, and the surrogate mother retained the

AT LAW

The Baby Broker Boom

by George J. Annas

George J. Annas, J.D., M.P.H., is Utley Professor of Health Law, Boston University School of Medicine; and Chief, Health Law Section, Boston University School of Public Health.

right to cancel the contract up to the point of relinquishing her parental rights.

Surrogate motherhood is a non-technical application of artificial insemination that requires no sophisticated medical or scientific knowledge or medical intervention. But the court saw surrogate motherhood as modern science, and did not want to interfere with "a new era of genetics," "solutions offered by science," and "new medical services."

The majority's opinion thus misses the focus of the Attorney General's argument: surrogacy's essence is not science, but commerce. The only "new" development in surrogacy is the introduction of physicians and lawyers as baby brokers who, for a fee, locate women willing to bear children by AID and hand them over to the payor-sperm donor after birth. The novelty lies in treating children like commodities.

This Justice Vance, one of two dissenting justices, understood. He noted that the corporation's "primary

purpose is to locate women who will readily, for a price, allow themselves to be used as human incubators and who are willing to sell, for a price, all of their parental rights in a child thus born." His rationale was that payment is made to the surrogate in two parts. The first part "of the fee is paid in advance for the use of her body as an incubator." But the second portion of the fee is not paid unless and until "her living child is delivered to the purchaser, along with the equivalent of a bill of sale, or quit-claim deed, to wit—the judgment terminating her parental rights." As the judge persuasively argues, the last payment must be for the child, since if the child is not delivered, the last payment need not be made.

The majority probably thought it was approving very *limited* baby selling: permitting a father-sperm donor to purchase the gestational mother's interest in his genetic child if the gestational mother contracted to make such a sale prior to conception and still desires to sell her child after its birth.

But limiting baby buying to fathers does not make baby buying any more tolerable than permitting a father to kidnap his biological child from its mother would make kidnapping tolerable. If mothers are to give up their parental rights to fathers, it should be *voluntarily*, and without a monetary price that converts the child into a commodity. That is what the Kentucky legislature undoubtedly had in mind when it outlawed baby selling.

The Kentucky court did not address baby selling in the case of full surrogacy: a surrogate who "gestates" an embryo to which she has made no genetic contribution. But a lower Michigan court has. Twenty-three-year-old Shannon Boff was pregnant with a child genetically unrelated to her at the time the question of her motherhood came up (*Smith & Smith v. Jones & Jones*, 85-532014 DZ, Detroit, MI, 3d Jud. Dist., March 14, 1986, Battani, J.). For the first reported time in the U.S., in vitro fertilization (IVF) had been used to fertilize an ovum from an infertile woman (who lacked a uterus), and the resulting embryo was implanted into another woman, who agreed to act as a surrogate

Hastings Center Report. June 1986

mother by gestating the fetus.

This raised an undecided legal question: Should the genetic or the gestational mother be considered the "legal" mother? That is, which woman should have legal rearing rights and responsibilities? The genetic parents, who had paid $40,000 for this "project" ($10,000 of which went to Ms. Boff) wanted to have their own names listed on the child's birth certificate, not the names of Ms. Boff and her husband.

Unfortunately, the case was a set-up. Even though both "competing" sets of parents were represented by legal counsel, they all wanted the judge to rule the same way. Since she did, there will be no appeal and no further judicial analysis of the question. Nor did the judge appoint anyone to represent the interests of the potential child. Like the Kentucky court, the Michigan judge decided to let contracts and commerce rule the day, rather than deal with any wider social issues, or consider the best interests of any child.

In so doing, the judge consistently put form over substance. For example, in determining that Ms. Boff's husband should not be presumed to be the father of his wife's child, the judge accepted the argument of their attorney that he could not be presumed the father under the AID statute because he signed a "nonconsent to any type of artificial insemination of his wife." But given his active participation in the entire project (he said he rubbed and drew faces on his wife's enlarged stomach and treated the pregnancy as if his wife was carrying their own child), his signature is hardly the "clear and convincing evidence" the statute requires. Moreover, the entire Paternity Act under which the case was brought covers only children "born out of wedlock," so the court may have had no jurisdiction at all over this case (MCLA 722.711 et. seq.).

The discussion of maternity is taken even less seriously. Like the Kentucky court, the Detroit judge saw her primary task as trying to make the law conform with and comfort modern science. Promoting private contract and personal profit were also seen as appropriate judicial strategies. To get to this point, the judge found

it necessary to rule that the state's paternity statute must be applicable to women as well as men, to afford women "equal protection of laws."

This is, of course, true only if there are no significant differences between maternity and paternity. But if there are no significant differences, then the female gamete donor should logically be treated "equally" to a male gamete donor: the child would then have *two* genetic "fathers," but would have a [gestational] mother as well. Not to so recognize the gestational mother's status dehumanizes her (and all mothers?), turning her into mere breeder stock. Of course, had Ms. Boff asserted her rights and identity as the child's mother, the judge would almost certainly have upheld her claim.

In applying the paternity statute to maternity, the court concluded that the gestational mother (whom the court referred to as the "birthing mother"), is acting as a "human incubator for this embryo to develop." Where the incubator "contracted to do this" via IVF, and where subsequent tissue typing confirms the genetic links of the child to the gamete donors, then "the donor of the ovum, the biological mother, is to be deemed, in fact, the natural mother of this infant, as is the biological father to be deemed the natural father of this child."

Besides putting contract above biology, this conclusion begs the question of who the child's mother is during pregnancy, and also makes identification of the child's mother at birth impossible. It thus fails to protect either the child or its mother where decisions regarding the newborn infant's care need to be made quickly. The judge dealt with this by saying that her decree would depend upon HLA tissue-typing confirming the identity of the genetic parents, a procedure that would not resolve the issue until at least a few days after the birth.

Although commerce won out in court, Ms. Boff said she would leave the baby business herself: "I'm going into retirement; any more babies coming from me are going to be keepers."

The contrary conclusion—that the woman who gestates a child should

be considered the child's legal mother for all purposes—is not based on antiscience, anachronistic, or sentimental views of motherhood. Rather, it is a recognition of the gestational mother's greater biological contribution to the child, including risks and physical contributions of the nine months of pregnancy, and the need to protect the newborn by always providing it with at least one immediately identifiable parent.

The gestational mother, for example, contributes more to the child than the ovum donor does in the same way she contributes more to the child than a sperm donor does. Other considerations also argue for this traditional view of motherhood. What if there are three "competing" mothers, as happens if the genetic ovum donor is anonymous (as most sperm donors are), the gestational mother a surrogate, and the contracting rearing mother simply someone who wants to raise the child? In this scenario the only relationship the rearing mother has is monetary: she paid the surrogate a fee to gestate the embryo and give up the child. If we *really* believe money and contracts should rule, then the identity of the child's mother will depend upon contract and payment only, and both genetics and gestation (and therefore all biological ties) will be irrelevant.

Since neither of these results seems reasonable, and since the traditional presumption would always provide the child with an identifiable mother who would be the same woman who biologically contributed the most, the traditional assumption should continue to be utilized, even in this "brave new world," and whether or not any contracts have been signed or any money changes hands. The Kentucky court's ruling, of course, is consistent with this view. The gestational mother could honor her prior contract, but could also change her mind and retain *her* child anytime before formally relinquishing parental rights.

Commercial surrogacy promotes the exploitation of women and infertile couples, and the dehumanization of babies. If the courts think this is a small price to pay to promote the "baby business," then it's time for state legislatures to define motherhood by statute.

No recent case has provoked as strong reactions as the case of "Baby M." It evokes both the emotional and rational aspects of life; from the right to reproduce to severing the mother-child bond, from the right to contract to visions of slavery, from the greed of the baby-brokers to the love of parents for their children, from a view of traditional families to one of families defined by intentions rather than by genes or gestation. These issues deserve a competent, fair, and unbiased hearing.

Unfortunately, in deciding the case of Baby M, Judge Harvey R. Sorkow of the New Jersey Superior Court spent most of his effort trying to produce a reversible-proof record of fact-finding. He wound up rendering a sermon filled with contradictions, double-standards, inapt analogies, and unsupported conclusions (*In re Baby M*, 13 FLR 2001, April 7, 1987).

Judge Sorkow's opinion was not his first in the battle between William and Elizabeth Stern and Mary Beth Whitehead, a married mother of two who agreed to be inseminated with the sperm of William Stern and to give up the resulting child to him after birth for a fee of $10,000. The parties had been put in contact by the Infertility Center of New York, which brokers arrangements between infertile couples and women willing to bear children for them, and provides a standard contract. The contract was signed, the insemination took place, and on March 27, 1986, Mrs. Whitehead gave birth to a child (denoted as "Baby M" in the litigation), whom she named Sara and the Sterns named Melissa. She took the baby home three days after her birth, and there turned her over to the Sterns.

The next day, Mrs. Whitehead and her sister went to the home of the Sterns and, with their consent, took the child back—a move the Sterns believed would be temporary. The next week Mrs. Whitehead told the Sterns that she had decided to keep the child. She threatened to leave the country if court action was taken. On

---

George J. Annas is Utley Professor of Health Law, Boston University School of Medicine, and chief, Health Law Section, Boston University School of Public Health.

AT LAW

Baby M: Babies (and Justice) for Sale

by George J. Annas

April 20, the Whiteheads listed their home for sale, indicating that they were moving to Florida. On May 5, attorneys for the Sterns appeared in Judge Sorkow's court and, without notice to the Whiteheads, and without affording them any opportunity to respond, asked the court to grant Mr. Stern immediate custody of the child. The basis was that the Whiteheads "were considering moving to Florida," and that if notified of court proceedings, they would flee the jurisdiction. The judge ordered immediate surrender of the child to Mr. Stern's custody.

Later that same day, the Sterns arrived at the Whitehead residence with five policemen and the temporary custody order. During the ensuing confusion, Mrs. Whitehead managed to hand the child out a window to her husband. She was thereafter handcuffed and placed in a police cruiser, but was later released. The following morning, the Whiteheads fled the state with Baby M. For the next eighty-seven days they lived in Florida. During July Mrs. Whitehead made two phone calls to Mr. Stern to try to dissuade him from continuing the court action. In the first she said, "I'd rather see me and her dead before you get her....I gave her life, I can take her life away." In the second she said that throwing dirt in

a custody battle could go two ways, and threatened to accuse Mr. Stern of sexually molesting her ten-year-old daughter.

At the end of July, while Mrs. Whitehead was hospitalized with a kidney infection, Florida police raided the household of Mrs. Whitehead's parents, knocking down Baby M's grandmother, and seizing the child. The child was placed in the custody of Mr. Stern, and the Whiteheads returned to New Jersey. They had some difficulty obtaining legal counsel, but by September the Whiteheads were trying to regain custody of Baby M. Limited visitation was granted, but Judge Sorkow would not be moved. On October 31, for example, he justified his original May 5 *ex parte* order on the basis of "possible flight:" "It turns out that the fear of the plaintiff was justified because Mrs. Whitehead eloped for some period of time when confronted with the order for delivery of the child."

Mrs. Whitehead, of course, "eloped" primarily because of the order itself and the fact that police were attempting to take her baby away by force. She had no lawyer to represent her and no faith in a judicial system that would permit such violence.

Judge Sorkow surely knew that the temporary custody order almost always becomes the permanent order, and he structured his task as justifying his original May 5 temporary custody order. He apparently decided to attempt to dehumanize the Whiteheads, to lionize the Sterns, and to pontificate on the devastation of infertility and the joys of parenthood.

Whether one agrees with the ultimate custody order or not, one must marvel at the overt contempt Judge Sorkow shows for the lower-middle-class Whiteheads, and the obsequiousness he displays for the upper-middle-class Sterns. The Sterns, for example, "were married by a minister friend of the family." The Whiteheads "were married." While in high school, Mr. Stern "contributed to the support of his family by working at various after school jobs." Mrs. Whitehead, "while in school....held a part-time job primarily as a hand in a pizza-deli shop." "The Stern *home*

Hastings Center Report. June 1987

is located near parks, the library, and is a short walk to the shopping area" (emphasis added); whereas "the Whiteheads' *house* is described as having a living room, kitchen and a back porch with 3 bedrooms and a bath" (emphasis added). The Sterns appropriately seek professional help when confronted with life crises; Mrs. Whitehead acts impulsively without professional advice.

True, Mrs. Stern, a pediatrician, self-diagnosed the multiple sclerosis she alleged was a risk to childbearing, did not seek professional help as to its definitive diagnosis or implications for pregnancy, and misrepresented her infertility. But the judge found this understandable, and described the Sterns as "credible, sincere, and truthful people." Mrs. Whitehead, on the other hand, has a "fundamental inability to speak the truth."

The Contract

The internal inconsistencies in the opinion indicate an inability to bring reason or logic to this highly emotional case. For example, the judge exalts the contract, but never examines its terms. Indeed, the average judge would spend more time examining the terms of a door-to-door vacuum cleaner sale than Judge Sorkow spent looking at the totally one-sided contract Mrs. Whitehead signed. The contract, for example, required her to undergo amniocentesis, and in the event the fetus was "genetically or congenitally [sic] abnormal" to abort the fetus "upon the demand of William Stern." Refusal to abort would terminate Mr. Stern's obligations under the contract. An abortion at his demand, on the other hand, would result in a $1,000 payment to Mrs. Whitehead.

In the event of miscarriage prior to the fifth month of pregnancy, Mrs. Whitehead would receive *no* compensation; miscarriage or stillbirth thereafter would result in a $1,000 payment. In view of this payment schedule—$1,000 for a stillbirth, and $10,000 to deliver a live child to Mr. Stern—there is *no* reasonable doubt that what is being paid for is a child, *not* an egg, gestation, and childbirth "services."

This services/product dichotomy is

"Mary Beth Whitehead, Surrogate, Agrees....

that she will not abort the child once conceived except, if in the professional medical opinion of the inseminating physician, such action is necessary for the physical health of Mary Beth Whitehead or the child has been determined by said physician to be physiologically abnormal. Mary Beth Whitehead further agrees, upon the request of said physician to undergo amniocentesis (see Exhibit "D") or similar tests to detect genetic and congenital defects. In the event said test reveals that the fetus is genetically or congenitally abnormal, Mary Beth Whitehead, surrogate, agrees to abort the fetus upon demand of William Stern, Natural Father, in which event, the fee paid to the surrogate will be in accordance with paragraph 10 [$1,000.00]. If Mary Beth Whitehead refuses to abort the fetus upon demand of William Stern, his obligations as stated in this agreement shall cease forthwith, except as to obligations of paternity as imposed by statute. [Clause 13]"

"...to adhere to all medical instructions given to her by the inseminating physician as well as her independent obstetrician. Mary Beth Whitehead also agrees not to smoke cigarettes, drink alcoholic beverages, use illegal drugs, or take nonprescription medication or prescribed medications without written consent from her physician. Mary Beth Whitehead agrees to follow a prenatal medical examination schedule....[Clause 15]"

the essence of any principled discussion of "surrogate" contracts, yet the judge refuses to even acknowledge it. Instead he says simply, "At birth, the father does not purchase the child. It is his own biological genetically related child. He cannot purchase what is already his." But this is what the case is all about. The child would not have existed at all but for the promise of a $10,000 payment for it, and the judge knows it.

Moreover, the conclusion that the "child is already his" obliterates the mother completely. By refusing to acknowledge that the child is also hers, he treats her contribution of the genetic and gestational components as either nonexistent, or far less important than the male's sperm. Indeed, at one point the judge describes Mrs. Whitehead's role in purely mechanistic terms, a "viable vehicle" to provide the Sterns with a family. In carrying Baby M, he concludes, "she received her fulfillment."

The Constitution

The judge makes a feeble attempt to bring the U.S. Constitution to the aid of the sperm donor-father by arguing that if the state sought to prohibit such contracts, "The surrogate who voluntarily chooses to enter such a contract is deprived of a constitutionally protected right to perform services." There is no constitutionally protected right to sell your children, even to their fathers; nor is there a constitutionally protected right to be a breeder for paying customers any more than there is to be a slave, a kidnapper, or a baby broker. Likewise, the court's notion that if men are legally permitted to sell their sperm, women must be legally permitted to gestate children for pay, is constitutionally and biologically baseless. Equal protection *may* require that women be permitted to donate or sell their eggs but it surely does not require that gestation be for sale.

The "right to procreate" is determinative in this case only if we assume it is exclusively a male right, and not one that Mary Beth Whitehead herself retains. The judge assumed that Mrs. Whitehead somehow gave up her right to rear her child, so that only the child's father should have any rights to Baby M. But did she? This is the *real* constitutional issue.

Mary Beth Whitehead agreed to her husband's vasectomy after the birth of their first two children. She said at the time that they had a "perfect family." The judge used this statement against her. But is this a "waiver" of the right to procreate? What if she and her husband changed their minds about the optimal size of their family? Could she not have access to artificial insemination? And if she could so easily waive her right to have children, couldn't the Sterns equally easily waive theirs by refusing to risk a pregnancy of their own, or by postponing childbirth until after Mrs. Stern completed her medical training?

Mrs. Whitehead is alleged to have prospectively waived her rights to Baby M more directly by signing the contract. Will this do it? The judge grudgingly concedes that she could not prospectively give up her right to have an abortion during pregnancy, or assign to another the right to compel her to have an abortion. This would be an intolerable restriction on her liberty and under *Roe v. Wade*, the state has no constitutional authority to enforce a contract that prohibits her from terminating her pregnancy.

But why isn't the same logic applicable to the right to rear a child you have given birth to? Her constitutional rights to rear the child she has given birth to are even stronger since they involve even more intimately, and over a lifetime, her privacy rights to reproduce and rear a child in a family setting. Thus absent the showing of a compelling state interest (such as protecting a child from an unfit parent), the state should not be constitutionally able to prohibit Mrs. Whitehead from rearing Baby M.

Judge Sorkow says we cannot wait until the child is born (as is done in adoption) to give the mother a chance to bond with her baby and change her mind based on radically changed circumstances. His reasoning is rhetorical. If we held this contract and others like it "in limbo until the result of the intended agreement is available....how would one handle the marriage contract....?" How indeed. If Judge Sorkow is to be taken literally, he is arguing that when a couple enters into marriage "until death do us part" the contract should be specifically enforceable. Neither

husband nor wife should have the right to ask for a divorce when they discover that "the result of the intended agreement" is not what they thought it would be. If contract was the real issue, the judge would have had to deal with the customary remedy for breach of contract: money damages rather than specific performance.

With all these inconsistencies and failed analogies it should not be surprising that, having concluded that existing adoption and termination of parental rights laws are inapplicable to "surrogacy arrangements," he nonetheless uses his opinion specifically to terminate Mrs. Whitehead's parental rights. And immediately after reading his decision to the press, he called the Sterns into his chambers so that Mrs. Stern could legally adopt the child.

The Haves Win Out

Judge Sorkow's opinion implicitly counsels: hire a mother for your child whom a judge is likely to view as unfit to raise it. Why aren't we all outraged at this suggestion and the trashing of Baby M's mother? We can't really think that "a contract is a contract" and "a deal's a deal." Not when the father can walk out of the contract at any time, leaving the mother holding (or carrying) the child, with only financial support obligations. Can it really be acceptable to sell babies in a country in which we have outlawed the sale of kidneys and other human organs?

The Baby M opinion has been praised because it has been misrepresented. Infertile couples are portrayed as the real plaintiffs, even though the Sterns were not infertile, and even though few, if any, infertile couples would want a child whose price was the police literally snatching it from its mother's breast. And Mary Beth Whitehead, the mother who "tends to smother her child" with love, was successfully portrayed as an ogre for fleeing the police, and fighting the child's father with the only weapons she thought available to protect her daughter.

At the May 5, 1986, *ex parte* hearing the judge should have set a hearing date for temporary custody, giving the

Whiteheads notice and an opportunity to obtain legal representation. A restraining order prohibiting them from removing Baby M from the jurisdiction could have been entered as well. Had Baby M remained with the Whiteheads for the past year even Judge Sorkow would doubtless have concluded that it would be in her best interests to stay with the Whiteheads. The judge concludes, for example, that despite many moves, job problems, and financial and alcohol-related difficulties in the past, the Whiteheads "have a stable marriage now." Mrs. Whitehead loves the child (although the judge notes, "Too much love can smother a child's independence"), and "has been a good mother for and to her older children."

It was primarily the financial ability of the Sterns to hire an expert on family law and successfully obtain an *ex parte* order for temporary custody that determined the ultimate outcome of this case. In this sense, reinforced by the economic bias of the mental health experts and the judge, those critics who have labeled this custody decision a classist opinion favoring the haves over the have nots are correct. Justice seems to have been for sale along with Baby M. There is no "best interest" solution to this tragic custody case. Baby M should have one set of parents. Given the unfairness and bias of the court proceedings to date, however, justice requires that reasonable consideration be given to returning Baby M to the permanent custody of the Whiteheads.

The generic battle now moves to the state legislatures. They should act quickly to affirm that the birth (gestational) mother is to be considered the legal mother for all legal purposes, and cannot give up her parental rights or relinquish her child for adoption until a reasonable time after the birth of the child. The sale of children should be specifically outlawed, as should the sale of human embryos. Paying women to have children for other people is a bad idea; we should neither encourage it by law nor permit the power of the state, through the courts and the police, to be used to seize children from their mothers on the basis of preconception contracts.

Both advocates and opponents of "surrogate motherhood" have eagerly awaited the opinion of the New Jersey Supreme Court in the case of *Baby M*.[1] Because the opinion was unanimous and written by the Chief Justice, like the decision involving Karen Ann Quinlan,[2] its influence is likely to be even greater than originally anticipated. The decision in *Baby M* will set the legal agenda for future discussion of surrogate motherhood.

This highly publicized case involves a custody dispute between a father and a mother. The father, William Stern, had contracted with the mother, Mary Beth Whitehead, to bear him a child through artificial insemination. The contract, among other things, provided that she would receive a fee of $10,000 upon terminating her parental rights and giving up the child to him. A lower court held that the contract was enforceable; and that custody of the child, known as "Baby M," should be awarded to Mr. Stern on the basis of the child's best interests. In addition, the lower court terminated Mrs. Whitehead's parental rights, and granted Elizabeth Stern's request to adopt Baby M. Mrs. Whitehead appealed, asking the court to determine "surrogacy contracts" unenforceable and void, to reinstate her parental rights, and to grant her custody of Baby M. The opinion of the lower court reflected bias towards favoring the rich over the poor, and was "filled with contradictions, double-standards, inapt analogies and unsupported conclusions."[3] The Supreme Court's unanimous opinion remedies many of these flaws by invalidating surrogate contracts, applying existing law to determine custody, and restoring Mrs. Whitehead's parental rights.

Surrogacy Terminology

The most powerful and well-reasoned portions of the opinion deal with "surrogacy contracts." The court

---

George J. Annas is Utley Professor of Health Law, Boston University School of Medicine; and Chief, Health Law Section, Boston University School of Public Health

AT LAW

Death Without Dignity for Commercial Surrogacy: The Case of Baby M

by George J. Annas

is not impressed by attempts to sanitize the surrogacy procedure by mislabeling it. It notes simply, "the natural mother [is] inappropriately called the 'surrogate mother.'" Mary Beth Whitehead is not and was not a "surrogate mother"; she is Baby M's natural mother.

The opinion also highlights the deceptive nature of the claim by supporters of surrogacy that the practice is family building. The court clearly understands that this method of reproduction can help one family only at the expense of another. The dissolution of the marriage of the natural mother is not necessary to the success of the contract, but a severing of the mother-child bond is: the "surrogate mother" arrangement creates a family bond only by destroying a family bond.

The court also recognizes that the common assertion that surrogacy involves new science and medical technology is nonsense. The only technology involved is donor insemination, an already well-established procedure. The novelty in the method is *legal*: a contract drafted by lawyers to define the legal relationships between a mother, a father, and their child in an attempt to circumvent state laws regarding custody, adoption, termination of parental rights, and baby selling. Fooled by broker publicity touting the innovative and beneficial aspects of such arrangements, Superior Court judge Harvey R. Sorkow saw surrogacy as so modern and marvelous that it could not possibly be subsumed under any existing laws. The Supreme Court saw through surrogacy and focused on the contract's reality and the body of applicable existing law.

The Surrogacy Contract

The court determined surrogate contracts invalid because they conflict with (a) statutes that prohibit the payment of money to a woman to induce her to give her child up for adoption; (b) the state's adoption laws that permit irrevocable surrender of a child only *after* birth; and (c) laws requiring proof of abandonment or unfitness prior to termination of parental rights or adoption without consent.

Like most states, New Jersey law prohibits paying or accepting money in connection with any placement of a child for adoption (fees to an approved nonprofit entity and certain childbirth expenses are excepted). The contract attempted to make the surrogacy arrangement look like "payment for services" by the father rather than payment to obtain a child, but the court was not persuaded. It properly noted that payment was limited to $1,000 if the child was stillborn (even though all "services" would have been rendered), and all parties knew that Mrs. Stern planned to adopt the child. The court rightly observed: "It strains credulity to claim that these arrangements, touted by those in the surrogacy business as an attractive alternative to the usual route leading to an

Hastings Center Report, April/May 1988

adoption, really amount to something other than a private placement adoption for money."

What's wrong with using money to place a child for adoption? Why has New Jersey made this a "high misdemeanor" with a penalty of three to five years in prison? Why does the court consider payment "illegal [and] perhaps criminal"? The court provides several reasons for condemnation of "the evils inherent in baby bartering." First, there is no concern for the child, who "is sold without regard for whether the purchasers will be suitable parents." Second, the process fails to provide any counseling or guidance for the mother or to inhibit the coercive nature of payment to her. Finally, there is a potential for exploitation of all parties involved. The court could have added that commodification of children devalues them (and all children), treating them like products or pets for our own pleasure.

The profit motive is additionally suspect for it takes precedence over concerns for even predictable and devastating human suffering. For example, in this case the baby broker agency failed to make any further inquiry when a psychological evaluation of Mrs. Whitehead revealed that she might change her mind and want to keep the child. The court reasoned, "It is apparent that the profit motive got the better of the Infertility Center....To inquire further might have jeopardized the Infertility Center's fee." The broker's greed is the prime motivation behind "surrogacy"—not the pain of infertile couples or the ability of women to enter into binding contracts. As the court properly underlines, the originator of this scheme to circumvent the adoption laws by private contract is "a middle man, propelled by profit" who "promotes the sale....The profit motive predominates, permeates, and ultimately governs the transaction." The court assures us, however:

There are, in a civilized society, some things that money cannot buy....There are...values that society deems more important than granting to wealth whatever it can buy, be it labor, love, or life.

Even if money is removed from the transaction, two further condi-

---

Brokers need a dose of realism. They should not be permitted to hide behind the grief of infertile couples. They are not in business to help them; they are in business to make money....The primary screening brokers do is monetary: does the couple have the $25,000 fee?

---

tions must be satisfied before a "surrogate agreement" could be consistent with New Jersey law. The mother must retain the right to revoke the agreement at least until the child is formally given up for adoption *after* birth. And, if the father decides to contest her revocation by a custody suit, the mother's parental rights can only be terminated upon a showing of either unfitness to parent or abandonment. Parenting is more than a contractual statement of intentions.

The court also determined that surrogacy contracts violate public policy on two independent grounds. The first is that the best interests of the child (not monetary payment) should govern in a custody dispute. Secondly, surrogacy contracts violate the basic policy that "the rights of the natural parents are equal concerning their child, the father's no greater than the mother's."

Constitutional Issues

The court did not deeply examine the constitutional issues that might arise should the state enact a statute permitting surrogacy contracts. The constitutional argument favoring such contracts has been based on the legal content of a husband's "right to procreate." The court concluded that the constitutional "right to procreate" is limited to "the right to have natural children, whether through sexual intercourse or artificial insemination."

The issue of custody was properly treated separately from that of procreative rights, and decided in exactly the same way as in any out-of-wedlock birth. The court ruled that fathers have no constitutional right to custody when it is opposed by the mother,

and that the constitutional rights of the father to custody can in no way be greater than those of the mother. Although the analogy was not used by the court, it would also seem that the husband of an infertile wife would have no more constitutional right to purchase a child from its mother than he has to purchase a license for a second (fertile) wife.

Custody of Baby M

The court rejected a proposal that to deter future surrogate mother agreements, it should award custody to Mrs. Whitehead, regardless of the best interests of the child. Instead, the court maintained, "Our declaration that this surrogacy contract is unenforceable and illegal is sufficient to deter similar agreements. We need not sacrifice the child's interests in order to make that point sharper." Likewise, it was suggested by some that because the initial *ex parte* hearing, which resulted in a decision to give temporary custody of the child to Mr. Stern, was so unfair and outcome determinative, justice would be served only by returning the child to Mrs. Whitehead.[4] The court also rejected this suggestion, noting that the primary concern must be the best interests of the child under present circumstances, even if these circumstances resulted from legal error.

The court concluded that it would be in the child's best interests for her to remain with the Sterns, primarily because of the stability of their marriage and the fact that she has lived with them for so long. Because of the importance of the parent-child bond to the child, custody decisions almost always depend heavily on the length of time a child has lived with one of its parents. Although the court maintained several times that Mrs. Whitehead's recent divorce and remarriage did not affect the custody decision, it almost certainly made it easier.

Doesn't this conclusion, however, amount to an endorsement of surrogacy, and provide a practical way to persuade women not to attempt to retain custody of their children, since they will surely lose when their less affluent life-style is compared to that of the wealthy father and his wife?

This is certainly one possible reading of the opinion. But the court's disapproval of the initial decision awarding temporary custody to Mr. Stern, and of "surrogacy contracts" in general, is strong. Perhaps to forestall this possibility, the court insists that, in any future custody battles, physical custody of the newborn child remain with the mother during the hearing to determine permanent custody. The court's reason is that the bond between mother and newborn is more significant than that between father and newborn. Since Mrs. Whitehead's parental rights were restored and she was declared a fit mother by the court, there is little doubt that had Mrs. Whitehead retained custody during the hearing and appeal, she would have been awarded permanent custody of the child by this court.

This part of the opinion may be the most controversial, since it appears to contradict the court's assertion that the rights of the mother and father in custody cases must be equal. But, in order to avoid an immediate tug-of-war and an arbitrary judicial ruling prior to a full hearing (like the one in this case), we need a *rule* that states who will retain custody during the hearing. It must be one or the other, and it seems reasonable to choose the mother. Treating the mother's rights as superior immediately after birth simply recognizes the biological reality that the mother at this point has contributed more to the child's development, and that she will of necessity be present at birth and immediately thereafter to care for the child. In situations where the mother is poor, and the father is financially well off, support payments during the

hearing (rather than "custody to the rich") also seem reasonable.

Since Mrs. Whitehead's parental rights were unlawfully terminated initially, there was no basis to deny her visitation rights. Just what form they should take should be determined by the Sterns and Mrs. Whitehead, who, hopefully, will attempt to work out the details of visitation with Baby M's best interest foremost. If they cannot, however, yet another court hearing will, unfortunately, be required to decide this issue.

Responses

The responses to this sound opinion by the commercial baby brokers have been predictable. California's William Handel, for example, has said that the decision is "not going to affect surrogate parenting" at all. Handel has never thought that the contracts he drafts are enforceable; and in his practice no mother changes her mind, and "no one loses." In his words, "The surrogate mothers walk out fulfilled and satisfied...."[5] Michigan's Noel Keane, "the father of surrogate parenting," says, "The legal implication is simply that it's a New Jersey decision and it's limited to New Jersey."[6] And some "surrogate mothers" continue to use inaccurate rhetoric to justify their actions. In the words of Shannon Boff, "For us, giving someone a baby is as noble as giving a kidney to someone who needs it."[7] Ms. Boff failed to note that children are not organs, that if they were, it would be illegal to sell them everywhere, and that she does not "give" the baby away, she sells it.

Brokers need a dose of realism. They should not be permitted to hide behind the grief of infertile couples. They are not in business to help them; they are in business to make money. The sperm donor's wife is not screened for infertility, and in the *Baby M* case, Mrs. Stern herself was not infertile. The primary screening brokers do is monetary: does the couple have the $25,000 fee? Organizations that represent infertile couples, like RESOLVE, have always opposed baby selling and have been skeptical of surrogacy. No one is "giving" anyone anything in surrogacy: it is the sale of the mother's

interests in a child to its father.

The New Jersey Supreme Court might accept noncommercial or voluntary surrogacy where there is true "gift-giving" and no monetary exploitation. Others have argued that voluntarism is just as bad as commercialized surrogacy, because it still involves the planned destruction of a mother-child bond that may be contrary to the best interest of the child. I have some sympathy for this view, but one can distinguish between doing something out of love and doing it for money. As long as existing adoption laws are followed, voluntary relinquishment of a child to a close relative (such as an infertile sister) seems acceptable.

Legislation to "outlaw" surrogacy will be widely proposed, but as this opinion indicates, in states with laws like New Jersey's, such laws are probably unnecessary. Noel Keane and William Handel have been right all along: surrogacy contracts are not enforceable. Now that mothers know that they *can* legally change their minds and retain custody of their babies, many more are likely to do so, and fewer couples are likely to risk this possibility. In addition, now that there is a strong state supreme court opinion labelling commercial surrogacy "baby selling," state attorney generals, local district attorneys, and child protection agencies are likely to be much less tolerant of the practice, and the prosecution of at least some baby broker agencies should be anticipated. And it is time for licensing boards to ask attorneys who continue to act as brokers in surrogacy arrangements the question: Why isn't it legal malpractice and fraud to charge clients money to draft a contract you publicly describe as "unenforceable"?

It seems prudent to enact legislation now to head off the development of so-called full surrogacy, in which new science (in vitro fertilization and embryo transfer) is used to implant an embryo into a woman who is not genetically related to the embryo.[8] This could make "surrogacy" much more attractive, since the resulting child will be the genetic child of both members of the couple, and the gestational mother could simply be considered an incubator or container with no rights or interests in the child at all. For all the reasons the New Jersey court gives to favor the mother over the father for temporary custody immediately after birth, and in addition, because pregnancy and childbirth is much more psychologically and physically demanding than egg production, it seems reasonable to designate the gestational mother, rather than the genetic mother, the legal or "natural" mother of the child.[9] A statute that clearly and irrebuttably so designates the gestational mother would be protective of children, and make the exploitation of poor women by the rich through "full surrogacy" much more difficult.

The opinion in the *Baby M* case, coupled with its previous significant decisions on the right to refuse treatment, firmly establishes the New Jersey Supreme Court as the country's preeminent "bioethics court." The court has properly applied the laws related to custody, adoption and termination of treatment to enhance the welfare of children, rather than adults. In this context, commercial surrogacy deserves the death without dignity to which the court has condemned it. Efforts to resuscitate it would not be in the best interests of children, families or society.

References
[1] *In the Matter of Baby M*, A-39-87, Feb. 3, 1988.
[2] *In re Quinlan*, 355 A.2d 647 (NJ 1976).
[3] George J. Annas, "Baby M: Babies (and Justice) for Sale," *Hastings Center Report* 17:3 (June 1987), 13-15.
[4] Annas, "Baby M: Babies (and Justice) for Sale."
[5] "Court Ruling Won't Hold Surrogate Parenting Back," *USA Today*, Feb. 8, 1988 at 15A.
[6] M. McQueen, "Baby M: Debate Not Over Yet," *USA Today*, Feb. 8, 1988 at 10A.
[7] McQueen, "Baby M: Debate Not Over Yet."
[8] George J. Annas, "The Baby Broker Boom," *Hastings Center Report* 16:3 (June 1986), 30-31.
[9] Sherman Elias and George J. Annas, *Reproductive Genetics and the Law*, (Chicago: Yearbook, 1987), 238-42.

On January 4, 1985, amid massive media publicity, Britain's first commercial surrogate baby was born. The mood of the British public was so hostile and disapproving that the Government rushed to pass criminal legislation. Six months later, the Surrogacy Arrangements Act 1985 was in force. The Act makes it a criminal offense for third parties to benefit from commercial surrogacy. Fines of up to £2000 may be ordered by the courts.

Much pious sentiment has been directed at the practice of surrogacy, and most particularly at commercial surrogacy. But is it all justified? Should it be a criminal offense to pay a surrogate mother for her services? Or would other alternatives better serve the interests of all parties?

Baby Cotton

The issue of commercial surrogacy came to a head in Britain with a court case involving Britain's first commercial surrogate baby. Baby Cotton was born in North London on January 4, 1985. Her mother, Mrs. Kim Cotton, had been hired by a surrogate agency headquartered in the U.S. In addition to her fee of £6,500, she received £20,000 to tell her story to a morning newspaper.

Baby Cotton's "social parents" (her natural father and his wife) were a couple in their thirties who had been married for several years. The husband was fertile, but the wife had a congenital defect that prevented her from ever having a baby. Since the adoption process is slow, and children may be four or five by the time the papers come through, this couple turned to surrogacy.

The father first contacted an agency in the U.S. in 1983 and entered into a contract with them. Upon payment of a sum of money, the agency agreed to find a suitable surrogate mother to bear his child. She was also to receive payment. An associated agency was set up in England and in 1984 the father came to England to provide seminal fluid

Diana Brahams is a lawyer and the editor of the British quarterly, Medico-Legal Journal.

The Hasty British Ban on Commercial Surrogacy

by Diana Brahams

While commercial surrogate parenting arrangements continue to flourish in the U.S., Britain has made it a criminal offense for third parties to benefit from surrogacy. Voluntary surrogacy, however, is still within the law. Banning commercial surrogacy while leaving voluntary surrogacy lawful seems neither logical nor fair. A more equitable solution would be to license stringently and control both commercial and nonprofit agencies to provide these services.

for artificial insemination of the surrogate.

The father and surrogate did not meet at any point. The baby was to be handed to the father at birth. However, the local social services department intervened by making the baby the subject of a "place of safety" order under the jurisdiction of the juvenile court. This is a procedure used by local authorities to protect children thought to be at risk. Subsequently, full enquiries made by the social services staff revealed that the father and his wife were both materially and emotionally equipped to give the baby a good home. They were warm, caring, sensible, and highly intelligent. They had a nice home and would be able to cope with the kind of questions that might arise in the future.

On January 8, the baby's natural father applied to have Baby Cotton made a ward of court. On January 11 Mr. Justice Latey, an experienced judge sitting in the Family Division, gave the natural father and his wife care and control of Baby Cotton and granted them permission to take her out of Britain. Mr. Justice Latey explained that his decision to award control to the social parents was in the best interests of the baby. At the same time, he issued strict orders to the press and others that no efforts should be made to identify the natural father or to publish anything that might lead to identification of the baby and her father and his wife.

Mr. Justice Latey reasoned that although the circumstances of the baby's creation and birth raised complex and delicate ethical issues and problems, those matters were not for the court to consider after the child was born and was the subject of wardship proceedings. But in any future situation, the judge said, the best step would be for the child to be made a ward of the court immediately, since the High Court in its wardship jurisdiction had very wide powers and resources to deal with urgent cases, which the juvenile court did not have.

Though Baby Cotton has been taken out of British jurisdiction, she remains a ward of the court, and the restriction on publicity continues. "The reasons for this are self evident," the judge said. "Is this baby to grow into childhood, adolescence, and adulthood with the finger pointed at her as 'this is the girl who...?' It is unthinkable that this should be so. Were it otherwise the injury to her mental and emotional health might be grave indeed."

At the time of the Baby Cotton decision there were no laws in Britain concerning surrogacy. But the Warnock Committee had already pro-

Hastings Center Report, February 1987

posed that most surrogacy arrangements should be banned by criminal law. The Warnock Committee was established by the government in July 1982 to consider evidence and report its recommendations on surrogacy and other issues in human assisted reproduction, such as in vitro fertilization, the use of human embryos in research and the freezing and storage of germinal material. On June 25, 1984, the Warnock Committee recommended to the Government the criminalization of the creation or operation of profit-making and nonprofit-making surrogate agencies, as well as the actions of "professionals and others who knowingly assist in the establishment of a surrogate pregnancy."[1] And, while it stopped short of recommending that private surrogate arrangements should be criminalized (in order to avoid "children being born to mothers subject to the taint of criminality"), it suggested that "it be provided by statute that all surrogacy agreements are illegal contracts and therefore unenforceable in the courts."

The Surrogacy Arrangements Act

The Government was still debating the Warnock Committee's recommendations when Baby Cotton was born. But the mood of the public was so disapproving that the Government rushed to pass criminal legislation.

The Surrogacy Arrangements Act, which became law on July 16, 1985, attempts to prevent third parties from deriving financial benefit from surrogacy. Under the Act, a surrogate mother is defined as a woman who carries a child in pursuance of a prior arrangement, and with the intent of handing the child over to another person or other persons. In deciding whether it is the woman's intent to hand over the child, the court may consider all the circumstances and in particular any promise or understanding that she will receive payment. "Payment" means reimbursements in the form of money or money's worth; this definition seeks to prevent nonpecuniary rewards as a method of circumventing the act.

The Act prohibits, among other things: (a) initiating or taking part in negotiations with a view to the making of a surrogacy arrangement; (b) offering or agreeing to negotiate the making of surrogacy arrangements; and (c) compiling any information with a view to its use in making, or negotiating the making of, surrogacy arrangements.

However, as Susan Sloman has pointed out,[2] neither the payment of money by the commissioning couple to a surrogate mother, nor the receipt of money by the surrogate is illegal under the Act. Thus it is inaccurate to say that the Act outlaws commercial surrogacy. However, if a payment is made the parties may be guilty of an offense under the Adoption Act of 1958. Also, by allowing the commissioning couple to pay the surrogate mother without adequate safeguards, the Act (presumably intentionally) does not protect either party from financial exploitation by the other.

Mere contemplation of payment in connection with surrogacy is enough to bring the Act into play, and the Act describes a situation where payment is made not to the person who actually negotiates the agreement but to another, for example, a member of the family. The Act also prohibits advertising in connection with commercial surrogacy and, by implication, professional involvement. Convictions under the Act can result in fines of up to £2,000. So far, despite its obvious shortcomings, the Act has apparently ousted commercial surrogacy in Britain.

To date, however, voluntary surrogacy is not illegal in Britain, and no attempt has been made to define the status of babies born under such circumstances. Perhaps this issue has been avoided for fear of suggesting that such a contract is officially recognized as legal. Presumably, the courts will deal with each case on its merits, and though such cases are likely to be few, they can form future precedents.

The Drawbacks of a Ban

But is commercial surrogacy any worse than voluntary surrogacy from the child's point of view? I suggest that the opposite may be true. Although commercial surrogacy is illegal, a child may be better off born to a woman totally outside the family circle with no emotional claims on the baby. In the ideal surrogate arrangement, the child is biologically wholly the offspring of the adoptive parents and is simply being carried (or "hatched") for them by the surrogate mother. Morally and legally she should have no claim to the child at its birth. But in order for this to happen medical help is required in the form of such procedures as in vitro fertilization, egg donation, embryo transfer, and most cases of artificial insemination by donor. But it would be a brave pioneer of a doctor who would risk the wrath of his peers in Britain today by undertaking such procedures with a commercial surrogate mother arrangement.

Concern has also been expressed about the exploitation and potential harm inflicted on the surrogate mother who hands over the baby at birth. Yet is this concern a reasonable basis for criminalizing commercial but not voluntary surrogacy? After all, dangerous sports and leisure pursuits (which may involve risking the lives not only of participants but also those called on to rescue them), are not criminal per se (though attempts to control, limit, or ban prize-fighting, or the consumption of drugs, alcohol, and cigarettes may be interpreted in this light).

Is this moralistic attack on the practice of commercial surrogacy fair or logical? Should not the respect for the rights and freedom of the individual be the supreme aim of a liberal civilized society? Even if the actions of a few offend the majority?

The Roots of British Disquiet

At the same time that policies were being formulated to outlaw commercial surrogacy, Britons were treated to displays of quite different American attitudes on nightly news programs. Here they could see American couples, with their surrogate babies and surrogate mothers, presented as one extended, albeit rather confusing, family. While the American Fertility Society[3] and the Judicial Council of the AMA[4] have noted many serious ethical questions raised by surrogacy, and while isolated cases of contested custody have come to the courts, both voluntary and commercial arrangements are still legal in the U.S. Why have the British moved so quickly and decisively to criminalize commercial surrogacy, while Americans have taken a far more permissive stance?

To put contemporary anxious British attitudes toward surrogacy into perspective, we need to see them against the very significant liberalizing shifts in attitudes, aspirations, and the law that have occurred over the past twenty-five years—shifts that some regard as the dismal slide into today's rudderless society.

● Suicide, traditionally regarded as self-murder, ceased to be a crime in Britain in 1961, though aiding and abetting suicide remains an offense and so does euthanasia.

● In 1967, homosexuality was legalized and "indecency" between consenting men over the age of twenty-one and committed in private ceased to be a crime.

● Also in 1967, subject to certain provisos, abortion was legalized for immature fetuses that were incapable of being born alive. Maximum gestation is twenty-eight weeks, but abortions are not normally performed over twenty-three or twenty-four weeks.

● In the late 1960s, the age of majority was reduced from twenty-one to eighteen.

● In 1970 the divorce laws underwent radical changes with the abolition of the need to prove marital fault. Since then divorce rates have risen rapidly; it is far easier to become divorced than formerly, and divorce (unlike illegitimacy) now carries little or no social stigma.

What are the consequences of all this liberalization? The spread of sexually transmitted diseases throughout the community? The breakdown of the family, which harms the young and our society generally on a broad scale? It has also been argued that the suspension of the death penalty and birching has increased the likelihood of violent crime against the young, the elderly, and the helpless. Against this background of liberalization we now have 47,000 people in prison in the UK—the highest number on record ever. Perhaps we are seeing the beginnings of a reversal—an "Enough is Enough" syndrome in Britain.

Few would challenge the benefit of in vitro fertilization when the woman's eggs are fertilized by her husband's sperm. It is merely a technical helping hand to bring about for a few what nature has done for the majority. However, once a woman agrees to bear a child for another couple, anxieties arise. When a child is artificially created without love between the parents, particularly if a financial reward is involved, English sensibilities are offended.

Some argue that such arrangements diminish our society's values and so must diminish us all. Yet is it true that the creation of a child through the medium of a surrogate is procreation without love? While it is morally abhorrent (and against public policy) to deal in children for money, the consequences need to be considered. An adopted child may bring enormous happiness to the desperate adoptive couple and enjoy a far better home than if it had remained with its natural parents or in a children's home. Similar arguments might be made on behalf of surrogate children and their social parents. After all, there has been little criticism of AID, even where sperm donors are paid small sums for their services.

Physicians' Responses

In general, British doctors consider the act of aiding commercial surrogacy to be unethical and unacceptable. I share their disapproval of the practice though I would not recommend making commercial surrogacy a criminal offense at this stage. While I see widescale development of surrogacy as undesirable in British society, it is conceivable that in some situations it could be beneficial; it is also too early to assess the long-term effects on all the parties concerned with the arrangements. Therefore, if the parties are willing to proceed, I believe it is not for me to judge in advance that they should not. For example, there may be cases when a desperate couple, ideally suited to becoming responsible and loving parents, have the chance to rear a child either 50 percent or even wholly biologically their own, only through

surrogacy and in vitro fertilization. Is it for me to say that this couple should be denied, on pain of the criminal law, the joy that most of us take for granted?

We do not place such controls on "natural" parents, who are often predictably wholly unfit to shoulder parental responsibilities. A convicted murderer or sex offender or child abuser (out on parole or released from prison) may procreate naturally without constraint. Parents who have starved, abandoned, beaten, neglected or even killed their offspring often create more progeny. Who can prevent them if they are free in society? True, the children may be taken from their custody, but there is no ban on procreation. Should society intervene to sterilize such people for the protection of future unborn children? Some would regard this intervention as medieval and barbaric—but it has some bearing on the issue of criminalizing surrogacy.

The Government's Response

"Public policy" under the law in the United Kingdom, is based on the principle that no court will lend its aid to anyone who founds a course of action on an immoral or illegal act. However, the difficulty with invoking public policy is that it is not a dependable and unchanging set of moral values, but a shifting sand reflecting the changes in our society.

In the summer of 1983, before any commercial surrogacy agencies had been established in Britain, I wrote an article for *The Lancet*[5] in which I noted the almost universal disapproval of the practice of surrogacy, both commercial and voluntary, among Britain's medical, legal, scientific, and religious bodies. The article was a critique of the papers that were being reviewed by the Warnock Committee. In that article I made three recommendations with regard to surrogacy:

1. "The offer of reward of any kind to create a child by 'womb leasing' and/or surrogate motherhood should not be a criminal offence."

2. "Where the surrogate mother is not the biological mother of a child born as a result of embryo transfer with her informed consent, the donor of the ova should be the legal mother

of the child and the child the legitimate offspring of the biological mother. This situation is to be distinguished from that in which a surrogate of the prospective social mother receives a donated ova (as in AID) and the donor has relinquished all rights over the ova in favour of either the prospective social mother or surrogate."

3. "Contracts for surrogate motherhood or 'womb leasing' should remain unenforceable as a matter of public policy."

I stand by these recommendations.

Perhaps British society is not yet ready for total acceptance of surrogacy arrangements, but perhaps greater knowledge will bring increased public understanding and tolerance. Such arrangements could be legally conducted though a nonprofit-making agency with adequate safeguards for all concerned. In addition, profit-making agencies could be stringently licensed and controlled.

This kind of limited regulation would be more appropriate than the hastily passed legislation now in force. Even when the Warnock Committee's report was the subject of much public debate, the Government did not rush to introduce general legislation. Perhaps they thought (as I did in 1983), that the best way to discourage the large-scale practice of surrogate motherhood was to leave such contracts as legally unenforceable, since, regrettably, good faith is not the basis of much capitalist commercial enterprise! It was only the birth of Baby Cotton and the public outcry of dismay and disapproval that prompted Parliament to pass its hastily drafted Surrogacy Arrangements Act.

The grand plan was for comprehensive legislation taking into account most of the issues considered by Warnock. However, since commercial surrogacy appears to be halted in Britain and many other more urgent matters press for Parliamentary time, further legislation is unlikely for the moment. If and when it is introduced, there are likely to be some amendments to the 1985 Act. What direction they will take is anybody's guess!

References

[1] Report of the Committee of Inquiry in Human Fertilisation and Embryology. London: HM Stationery Office. Cmnd 9314. 1984.

[2] "Surrogacy Arrangements Act," *New Law Journal*, October 4, 1985.

[3] "Ethical Considerations of the New Reproductive Technologies," *Fertility and Sterility* 46(3), September 1986, Supplement 1.

[4] Opinion of the Judicial Council of the American Medical Association, in Proceedings of the House of Delegates, December 4-7, 1983.

[5] Diana Brahams, "In-vitro Fertilisation and Related Research," 1983 *Lancet*, September 24, 1983, p.726.

CASE STUDIES

When Baby's Mother is also Grandma— and Sister

Sally Morgan is forty-six years old and has been divorced for ten years. She has one child, a twenty-five-year-old daughter. Recently she married Frank Charlton, a forty-nine-year-old childless widower. They would like to start a family of their own, but she is now infertile.

Mrs. Charlton consults a university in vitro fertilization (IVF) program, where she is told that she is not a suitable candidate for the procedure. However, her husband's sperm could be used to fertilize an egg cell from an anonymous donor. The embryo could then be implanted in a surrogate mother and carried to term.

Since Mrs. Charlton would like her child to be genetically related, her daughter offers to donate the egg cell to be utilized in the in vitro fertilization process. Each of the daughter's cells contains 50 percent of her mother's genetic material; therefore the baby would have one-half of that amount, or 25 percent. In this manner, the child would be genetically related to Mrs. Charlton. Mrs. Charlton would be in the unusual position of being both mother and grandmother to the child; her daughter would be both its mother and sister.

Should the donation be approved?

—David Fassler, M.D.

COMMENTARY

by Lori B. Andrews

This case adds a twist to the debate raised by the involvement of third parties in procreation by asking whether a daughter may serve as a gamete donor. Although the advantages and disadvantages of such a situation will differ markedly depending on the particular individuals involved, such an arrangement should be allowed.

The donation would allow Mrs. Charlton and her husband to have a child genetically related to both of them. It may be the only realistic opportunity for her husband to have a child within the marriage since anonymously donated eggs may be scarce and costly (particularly in comparison to donor sperm).

The donation could give the daughter the chance to express her altruism. The prospective child might gain by experiencing greater love and support as well as a more definite identity than if produced by an anonymous donor. And permitting the donation would reinforce the strong moral and legal protection of autonomy regarding decisions about how to create and raise a family.

Some may object to the procedure because it seems unnatural, contrary to traditional notions of family, or may present risks to the parties. In attempting to assess the ethical merit of the donation, professional practices and the law should follow the model used for determining the scientific merit of a new therapy. Under the best of circumstances, a medical innovation is adopted when it is anticipated to be an improvement over the existing treatment modalities and is unlikely to cause risks that outweigh its potential benefits. In this ideal situation, as the procedure is done more frequently, its effects are closely monitored to determine whether it should continue to be used.

All forms of parenting, including traditional reproduction, present potential physical and psychological harm to the participants; yet society is reluctant to interfere with procreative decisions. This is the backdrop against which the donation of an egg from a daughter to a mother must be judged. I do not think that the risks presented by a

Hastings Center Report, October 1985

daughter's gamete donation are sufficiently different in type or greater in magnitude to warrant banning the procedure. Rather, such donations should be allowed and scrutinized for their actual, rather than possible effects.

The potential physical risks to the participants do not appear serious enough to preclude the procedure.

Since many women have undergone laparoscopies and pregnancies, the potential physical harm to the daughter and surrogate is readily quantifiable and can be explained during the informed consent process.When IVF first came into use, the potential physical risks to the child were unknown. Although there are still not enough births to assess whether IVF presents a slightly increased risk of anomalies in offspring (say, 5 percent), it is clear that IVF is generally safe and surely does not present the 25 percent risk of affected offspring that parents with a lethal recessive gene trait run when they choose to have children.

Although most of the human IVF births have involved pregnancies in which the embryo was implanted in the woman who provided the egg, the use of surrogate should not present additonal risks. Indeed, most of the animal IVF studies (showing no increase in anomalies) have involved transfers of the embryos to a surrogate.

Nor do the potential psychological ramifications for the participants seem a sufficient reason to ban the donation. Unlike the unknown risks presented by manipulations of embryos in the early attempts at IVF, the psychological harms can be predicted by analogy to existing situations, such as an adoption or a grandmother raising her daughter's child because of divorce or the daughter's young age.

In this case, three women and one man have an emotional investment in the creation of a child. The physician should discuss with the participants the ways in which the proposed donation arrangement might threaten their emotional well-being. This is in keeping with the approach taken by Great Britain's Warnock Committee and the Victoria,

Australia legislation, which require careful counseling when an identifiable egg donor is used.

The discussions should not be a form of licensing for parenting. Since we do not prohibit forty-six-year-old women from conceiving, bearing, and raising children naturally, Mrs. Charlton should not be discouraged because of her age from entering this arrangement. Rather, the interviews should focus on how the participants will handle the unique aspects of this case—the severing of the maternal genetic relationship and the maternal rearing relationship, with the former being provided by the daughter and the latter being provided by the mother.

One of the principal potential hazards lies in the possibility that the daughter could be coerced into donating her egg. In attempting to assure that the daughter has given her voluntary informed consent, the physician should make sure she has thought through the many possible future ramifications of the procedure. How would she feel if she lost her ability to conceive (perhaps as a result of the laparoscopic surgery itself) and her mother's child was her only link to motherhood?

How will the parties deal with the impression, though not the reality, of incest? Currently, stepfather-stepdaughter sexual relationships are considered incestuous and subject to civil penalties in eleven states and criminal penalties in five states. Although fertilizing the daughter's egg with her stepfather's sperm in a petri dish does not violate these laws, the unusual relationship may make the parties uneasy or cause them difficulties in dealing with outsiders who feel they have violated a basic taboo.

The physician should also discuss with the participants whether or not they will tell the child that its sister is the genetic mother. Because of the emotional harm unplanned disclosure can cause the child, the possibility of being candid with the child should at least be raised. It will clearly be stressful for the family unit if the parties do not agree on how to handle this point.

Yet the practitioner's ethical responsibilities do not end with the

application of appropriate policies and principles to this particular decision. Since the request for gamete donation between friends or relatives is likely to come up again, there is an ongoing responsibility to better inform the next decision. Just as a new medical procedure is monitored to collect information on the physical risks it presents, physicians and mental health professionals have a responsibility to research the psychological effects of the new reproductive technologies they introduce. The track record of the medical and psychiatric professions in conducting such studies is poor—witness the dearth of well-designed research about the psychological effects on the donor, recipient, recipient's spouse, and child of the century-old technique of artificial insemination by donor. But such studies are especially important where practitioners are helping to conceive a new individual in ways that give birth to new ethical dilemmas.

Lori B. Andrews, J.D., a project director at the American Bar Foundation, is the author of New Conceptions.

COMMENTARY

by Hans O. Tiefel

A forty-six-year-old mother of a twenty-five-year-old daughter who wants to start parenting all over again, who will not be denied by nature, who will be sixty-two with a husband of sixty-five when the hoped-for child will reach the mature age of fifteen—such a woman must be extraordinarily optimistic about what it means to raise a child. One cannot help but wonder whether a child out of season meant to enhance the marriage may prove extraordinarily taxing to a couple who normally would welcome the visits, and the departures, of grandchildren. Yet such doubts seem condescending since both Mr. and Mrs. Charlton are old enough to know what they are doing. Foolishness need not be immoral. Therefore one should assume that they are willing to pay the price for wanting to start "a family."

But not any child will do. A handicapped child, an abandoned child, a racially mixed child are not mentioned. The offspring must be their own genetically. This genetic connection necessitates the circuitous route of in vitro fertilization and surrogate motherhood. Yet the value of genetic linkage should be questioned when it is pursued in such a complex manner, when it draws other agents into this marriage as contributing agents, and when it raises the possibility of harm to the offspring since sperm deteriorate with aging. Moreover, since genetic percentages seem to matter in this case, 25 percent of the genetic inheritance will come from Mrs. Charlton's divorced husband. One expects that neither Mrs. Charlton nor her husband Frank care much for this genetic interloper. But this unhappy link does offer an opportunity to ascribe any undesirable characteristics of the child-to-be to that man who is well gone but not gone completely.

The role of Mrs. Charlton as both mother and grandmother does not seem troubling; both roles are nurturing and many grandmothers take over the functions of mothers by default. More questionable in this case is the exact meaning of "mother." There are three contenders for that title: the genetic mother (the daughter who contributes the egg), the surrogate, and the social mother (Mrs. Charlton). Whom shall the child call "Mom"?

And if that seems a trivial question, who will be responsible for the care and nurture of the child when it turns out differently than expected? Would Mrs. Charlton still acknowledge the child as hers if it were born with a genetic defect, since her genetic contribution is half that of her daughter? Would she claim to be the real mother if the child were born with a handicap that could be directly attributed to the carelessness of the surrogate mother during pregnancy? Normally mother and child are bound to each other by birth, for better or worse. When these natural ties disappear, bonds of loyalty and care for offspring may also weaken.

More interesting than the combined role of mother and grandmother is the dual status of the daughter and egg donor as both mother and sister. The arrangement assumes that the genetic relationship, which is decisive to the couple, should be disregarded by the daughter. The child-to-be will be half hers, genetically speaking, but this is considered irrelevant once the child is conceived. The parties seem to have contradictory value judgments about genetic derivation.

The surrogate's role is also problematic. Surrogates have been known to become unexpectedly attached to the children they have borne for profit or love. Assuming that the child is carried for love rather than money, would love require her to undergo amniocentesis and, if that showed the presence of defects, an abortion? If she refused abortion out of love for the child-to-be, would the child become hers in every sense, including responsibility for its medical care and upbringing?

And what of the child-to-be itself? It is still too early to tell if in vitro fertilization and embryo transfer pose long-term risks to the child. Even if aspiring parents take that risk (not for themselves but for their offspring), other problems remain. If our self-identity is shaped largely by lineage, if it is important to whom we belong and who belongs to us, then the child may want to relate to all three mothers. The couple cannot expect the child to be indifferent to "the woman who is my flesh and blood" or to "the woman who brought me into the world."

Even naturally born children complain of not being loved enough and of not belonging. Won't triple motherhood create additional tensions and resentment? Will the child not seek refuge from real or imagined grievances with the most sympathetic, and therefore the "real," mother? One might reply that the risks of dispersed kinship ties will not outweigh the good of this child's existence. But that begs the question, since such a value cannot be invoked before the child has come into being.

We live in relationships. But this case reads as if complex begetting were a private matter, as if the issues pertain only to this particular case and as if the wishes of the couple should be decisive. The case reads true enough in times in which morality is reduced to private choice, legality, and consumer satisfaction. But it is also misleading, especially in regard to medical matters. Medical professionals play an indispensable yet deplorably passive role here: Just tell us what you want and we will make it possible. Happily this is counterfactual; no institution is yet quite so accommodating.

Should physicians demur, the couple could claim that its rights have been violated. For rights remain the only powerful and public tool in otherwise privatized ethics. True, no one has a right to interfere with claims to beget children. But such rights remain negative. They establish no corresponding duty on the part of the physician to facilitate reproduction, any more than my right to marry obligates any woman to marry me. Moreover, relying on rights is rather self-centered. Rights cannot guide us in deciding who we should be as spouses or parents or what we owe one another in love.

The loving decision in this case is not what Mrs. Charlton and her husband "would like." It is one that seeks the good of all who are part of these relationships, especially the child-to-be. And the good of this envisioned offspring is obstructed by the risk of harm, by contradictory values about genetic ties, by confusion over who may claim the child and who is responsible for it (and whom the child may claim and be responsible to), and by a need for personal selflessness on the part of the genetic mother that exceeds realistic expectations. In this case moral judgment supports common sense: this foolishness is also immoral.

Hans O. Tiefel is professor of religion at the College of William and Mary.

What Price Parenthood?

by Paul Lauritzen

Current reproductive technology challenges us to think seriously about social values surrounding childbearing. Thoughtful discussion must combine careful attention to the experience of pursuing parenthood by technological means with principled reflection on the morality of this pursuit.

The ceremony goes as usual.

I lie on my back, fully clothed except for the healthy white cotton underdrawers. What I could see, if I were to open my eyes, would be the large white canopy of Serena Joy's outsized colonial-style four-poster bed, suspended like a sagging cloud above us…

Above me, towards the head of the bed, Serena Joy is arranged, outspread. Her legs are apart, I lie between them, my head on her stomach, her pubic bone on the base of my skull, her thighs on either side of me. She too is fully clothed.

My arms are raised; she holds my hands, each of mine in each of hers. This is supposed to signify that we are one flesh, one being. What it really means is that she is in control, of the process and thus of the product…

My red skirt is hitched up to my waist, though no higher. Below it the Commander is fucking. What he is fucking is the lower part of my body. I do not say making love, because this is not what he's doing. Copulating too would be inaccurate, because it would imply two people and only one is involved. (Margaret Atwood, *The Handmaid's Tale*).

Paul Lauritzen *is assistant professor of religious ethics in the Department of Religious Studies, John Carroll University, Cleveland, OH.*

This chilling depiction of the process of reproduction in the fictional Republic of Gilead provides a vision of what many feminists believe will soon be reality if the new reproductive technologies (NRTs) proceed unchecked. Children will be thought of exclusively as products. Women will be valuable merely as breeders. Reproductive prostitution will emerge as women are forced to sell wombs, ovaries, and eggs in reproductive brothels.[1] Men will be more fully in control than ever.

There was a time when I would have dismissed such claims as wildly alarmist. I still believe these worries to be overblown. Yet I have been haunted by this passage from *The Handmaid's Tale* as I have stood, month after month, holding my wife Lisa's hand as she, feet in stirrups, has received my sperm from the catheter that her doctor has maneuvered into her uterus. Indeed, once, when the nurse asked me to stand behind her to hold steady an uncooperative light, I wondered perversely whether I shouldn't, like Serena Joy, play my symbolic part by moving rhythmically as the nurse emptied the syringe.[2] Having experienced the world of reproductive medicine firsthand, I believe we need to take a closer look at feminist objections to NRTs.

Here, then, I will review objections that some feminists have raised to such technologies as *in vitro* fertilization (IVF), artificial insemination with donor sperm (AID), and surrogate motherhood, and relate these objections to my own experience. I take up feminist objections because, although there is no one "feminist" response to reproductive technology, some of the most forceful objections to this technology have come from writers who are self-consciously feminist and understand their opposition to the NRTs to be rooted in their feminism.[3] Moreover, the international feminist organization FINRRAGE (Feminist International Network of Resistance to Reproductive and Genetic Engineering) is committed to opposing the spread of reproductive technology, and it is from this group that we have the most sustained and systematic attack on NRTs in the literature.[4] I relate these objections to my own experience because, in my view, all serious moral reflection must attend to the concrete experience of particular individuals and thus inevitably involves a dialectical movement between general principles and our reactions to particular cases. The need to balance appeals to abstract rules and principles with attention to the affective responses of particular individuals has not always been sufficiently appreciated in moral theory or in medical ethics.[5] Yet such a balance is necessary if we are to understand both how moral decisions are actually made and how to act compassionately when faced with troubling moral situations.

Hastings Center Report, March/April 1990

My experience leads me to believe that there are some real dangers in pursuing these technologies, that individuals should resort to them only after much soul searching, and that society should resist efforts to expand their use in ways that would make them available as something other than a reproductive process of last resort. In the case of my wife and me, this soul searching is upon us. It now appears that artificial insemination with my sperm will not be successful. We are thus confronted with the decision of whether to pursue *in vitro* fertilization, artificial insemination with donor sperm, or adoption. This paper is one moment in that process of soul searching.

Like many couples of our generation and background, my wife and I delayed having children until we completed advanced degrees and began our jobs. With careful deliberation, we planned the best time to have children given our two careers, and were diligent in avoiding pregnancy until that time. What we had not planned on was the possibility that pregnancy would not follow quickly once we stopped using birth control. This had not been the experience of our friends whose equally carefully laid plans had all been realized. For them, birth control ended and pregnancy followed shortly thereafter. For us, a year of careful effort, including charting temperatures and cycles, yielded only frustration.

Because we had indeed been careful and deliberate in trying to conceive, we suspected early on that there might be a problem and we thus sought professional help. A post-coital examination by my wife's gynecologist revealed few, and rather immobile sperm. I was referred to a specialist for examination and diagnosed as having two unrelated problems: a varicocele and retrograde ejaculation. A varicocele is a varicose vein in the testicle that is sometimes associated with a reduction in both the numbers and quality of sperm. Retrograde ejaculation is a condition in which a muscle at the neck of the bladder does not contract sufficiently during ejaculation to prevent semen from entering the bladder. As a result, during intercourse semen is ejaculated into the bladder rather than into the vagina. Both conditions are treatable, in many cases. Indeed, the doctor's diagnosis was followed almost immediately by a presentation of possible "therapies," given roughly in the order of the doctor's preferences, all presented as points on the same therapeutic continuum. A varicocele can be repaired surgically. Retrograde ejaculation can sometimes be eliminated through the use of drugs and, failing that, can be circumvented by recovering sperm from urine and using it for artificial insemination. Should both these treatments fail, *in vitro* fertilization might

be successful. And, if all else fails, donor insemination is always a possibility.

Since surgery for a varicocele is not always successful and since surgery is more invasive than either of the treatments for retrograde ejaculation, I tried these latter treatments first. Unfortunately, neither drug therapy nor artificial insemination was of any avail. Possibly because of damage done to the sperm as the result of the varicocele, the numbers and quality of sperm recovered from urine for insemination were not such as to make conception likely. After trying artificial insemination (AIH) for six months, we decided to attempt to repair the varicocele. Following this surgery, there is generally a three to nine month period in which a patient can expect to see improvement in his sperm count. After nearly seven months, we have seen virtually no improvement. Although we have begun AIH once again, we do not have high hopes for success.

This is the bare chronicle of my infertility experience. A complete record would be too personal, too painful, and too long to present here. But something more should be said. For someone who loves children, who has always planned to have children, infertility is an agonizing experience. In a culture that defines virility so completely in phallocentric terms, infertility can also threaten male identity, for infertility is often confused with impotence. Infertility is damaging in other ways as well. The loss of intimacy as one's sex life is taken over by infertility specialists strains a relationship. More generally, the cycle of hope and then despair that repeats itself month after month in unsuccessful infertility treatment can become unbearable. Nor is the experience of infertility made easier by the unintended thoughtlessness or uncomfortable attempts at humor of others. It is hard to know which is worse: to endure a toast on Father's Day made with great fanfare by someone who knows full well your efforts to become a father or to suffer yet another comment about "shooting blanks."

With this as background, I would like to consider four interrelated, but distinct objections that have been raised to NRTs. According to feminist opponents, the new reproductive technologies are inescapably coercive; lead to the dismemberment of motherhood; treat women and children as products; and open the door to widespread genetic engineering.

The Tyranny of Technology

Although opponents of reproductive technology do not generally distinguish types of coercion, there are typically two sorts of claims made about NRTs. The first is that the very existence (and availability) of these technologies constitutes a sort of coercive *offer*; the second, that the future of these technologies is likely to include coercive *threats* to women's reproductive choices.[6] The first claim is often a response to the standard reasons given for developing these technologies. Advocates of NRTs typically argue that these techniques are developed exclusively to help infertile couples, expanding the range of choices open to them.[7] Moreover, the medical community is portrayed as responding to the needs and interest of infertile patients to find technological means to produce pregnancy if the natural ones fail. IVF programs, for example, are almost always defended on the grounds that however experimental, painful, or dangerous they may be to women, women choose to participate in them. Thus, it is said, IVF increases choice.

Feminists who believe NRTs to be coercive claim that such a choice is illusory, because in a culture that so thoroughly defines a woman's identity in terms of motherhood, the fact that women agree to participate in IVF programs does not mean they are truly free not to participate. According to this view, we must not focus too quickly on the private decisions of individuals.[8] Individual choices are almost always embedded in social contexts, and the context in our culture is such that a childless woman is an unenviable social anomaly. To choose to be childless is still socially disapproved and to be childless in fact is to be stigmatized as selfish and uncaring. In such a situation, to offer the hope of becoming a mother to a childless woman is a coercive offer. Such a woman may well not wish to undergo the trauma of an *in vitro* procedure, but unwillingly do so.

Robyn Rowland has appreciated the significance of this social context for infertile women. "In an ideological context where childbearing is claimed to be necessary for women to fulfill themselves," she writes, "whether this is reinforced by patriarchal structures or by feminist values, discovering that you are infertile is a devastating experience."[9] The response may be a desperate search to find any means of overcoming this infertility, a search that may render the idea of choice in this context largely meaningless.

Moreover, feminists insist, developing these technologies is not about increasing choice. They are not, by and large, available to single women— infertile or not—or to lesbian women. Further, if doctors were truly concerned for the suffering of infertile women, we would expect much greater effort to publicize and to prevent various causes of infertility, including physician-induced sterility, as well as to inform women more fully about the physical and emotional trauma that various types of fertility treatments involve.[10] This neglect became dramatically apparent to me when I discovered Lisa at home weeping quietly but uncontrollably after a "routine" salpingogram for which she was utterly unprepared by her doctor's description of the procedure.[11] I will return to this theme below but I hope the claim of feminist opponents of the NRTs is clear. If doctors were in fact concerned about the well-being of their infertile patients, they would treat them less as objects to be manipulated by technologies and more as persons. The fact that this is often not the case should reveal something about the underlying motivations.[12]

The second claim about the possibility of coercive threats is really a concern about the future. While we may debate whether a desperately infertile woman really is free to choose not to try *in vitro* fertilization, still, no one is forcing her to participate in an IVF program. But what about the future? This question is meant to point to how thoroughly medicine has encroached on the birth process. The use of ultrasound, amniocentesis, genetic testing and counseling, electronic fetal monitoring, and cesarean sections have all increased the medical community's control over the process of birth. Why should the process of conception be any different? If anything, a pattern suggests itself. What was originally introduced as a specialized treatment for a subclass of women quickly expanded to cover a far wider range of cases. What was originally an optional technology may quickly become the norm.[13]

Such interventions can be coercive not only in the sense that, once established as the norm they are difficult to avoid, but in the stricter sense that women may literally be forced to submit to them, as with court-ordered cesarean sections. Will compulsory treatment be true of the new technologies as well? Will the technology that allows for embryo flushing and transfer in surrogate cases be required in the future as part of a process of medical evaluation of the fetus? The concern that the answers to these questions is too likely to be "yes" stands behind some claims that the NRTs are dangerously coercive. The potential for a loss of control over one's reproductive destiny is increased with the development of these technologies. And the coercion that could follow such a loss of control is worrisome.

Have I experienced a loss of control or coercion? The answer is a qualified yes. I certainly have not felt coerced in the second sense. I have not been physically forced to undergo infertility treatment, nor has there been any threat, actual or implied, connected with the prospect of avoiding NRTs altogether. Still, I have experienced the existence of these technologies as coercive. And here the notion of a coercive offer is helpful. Although the inability to have children has not threatened my social identity in the same way it might were I a woman, nevertheless, the pressure is real. Having experienced this pressure, and having met others whose desperation to bear a child was almost palpable, I do not doubt that the offer of hope held out by available technologies, however slim and unrealistic in some cases, is indeed a form of coercion.

The problem here might reasonably be called the tyranny of available technologies. This "soft" form of coercion arises from the very existence of technologies of control. Increased control by the medical profession over the birth process, for example, has not resulted because of a conspiracy to gain control, but rather because, once the technology of control exists, it is nearly impossible not to make use of it. If, as I believe, this pressure to make use of existing technologies is a type of coercion, I have experienced this coercion powerfully during my infertility treatment. If surgery might repair the problem, even if the chances are not great, how can I not have surgery? If surgery and artificial insemination have not worked, but some new technique might, how can I not try the new technique?

The very existence of the technology inevitably changes the experience of infertility in ways that are not salutary. One of the peculiar aspects of infertility is that it is a condition that a couple suffers. Individuals can have retrograde ejaculation or blocked tubes, but only couples can be infertile. As Leon Kass has noted, infertility is as much a relationship as a condition.[14] Yet infertility treatment leads us to view infertility individually, with unfortunate consequences. The reason is that couples will often not be seen together in infertility treatment, and, even when they are, they will receive individual workups and be presented with individual treatment options. Now it might be said that providing individuals with options increases agency rather than diminishes it. Yet with this agency comes a responsibility that may not itself be chosen and that reduces the prospects for genuine choice. For once an individual is presented with a treatment option, *not* to pursue it is, in effect, to choose childlessness and to accept responsibility for it. From a situation in which infertility is a relational problem for which no one is to blame, it becomes an individual problem for which a woman or man who refuses treatment is to blame.[15] Reproductive technology structures the alternatives such that a patient is "free" to pursue every available form of assisted reproduction or to choose to be childless.

This problem is compounded by the fact that infertility specialists simply assume that patients will pursue all available treatments and typically present the variety of treatment options as just different points on the same therapeutic spectrum, distinguished primarily by degree of invasiveness. In our case, taking relatively mild drugs in an effort to make an incontinent muscle more efficient lies at one end of the continuum, at the other end of which lies IVF. Surgery, I suppose, falls somewhere in the middle. At no time in my experience, however, has anyone suggested that treatments differ qualitatively. (The only exception to this was my urologist's opposition to an experimental treatment for male-factor infertility.) It has generally been assumed that if one therapy fails, we will simply move on to the next. And that is the problem. If the technology exists, the expectation is that it will be used. Again, if IVF might work, how can we not try it? The force of these questions covers us like a weight as we consider what to do next.

The Dismemberment of Motherhood

A second objection raised against the NRTs is that they question the very meaning of motherhood. The reality of oocyte donation, embryo flushing, and embryo transfer produces another possible reality: the creation of a child for whom there are three mothers: the genetic mother, the gestational mother, and the social mother.[16] In such a situation, who is the *real* mother? In the absence of a compelling answer, the claim of each of these three women to the child will be tenuous. Maternity will be as much in dispute as paternity ever was. And whatever criteria are used to settle this issue, the result for women is that the reproductive experience may become discontinuous in much the way it has traditionally been for men. Just as paternity has been uncertain because the natural, biological relation between the father and child could always be questioned, so too might maternity become a sort of abstract idea rather than a concrete reality. Just as paternity has been a right rather than a natural relation, so too might maternity become.[17]

The significance of this can be seen if one takes seriously Mary O'Brien's claims that men's reproductive experience of discontinuity, that is, the inevitable uncertainty of genetic continuity, has contributed significantly to men's need to dominate. The problematic nature of paternity, O'Brien suggests, can account for the sense of isolation and separation so common in men, in part because for men the nature of paternity is such that the natural experiential relation of intimacy with another is missing.

Feminists' celebrations of motherhood have also

made much of the biological continuity women have traditionally experienced with their children. Caroline Whitbeck and Nancy Hartsock, for example, have both discussed how the biological differences between men and women, especially as they are manifested in reproduction, account for some of the differences in how men and women experience the world.[18] Many women do not experience the sharp separation between self and others so common to male experience, Hartsock and Whitbeck note, a fact both explain by appeal to the way in which female physiology mediates female experience. In the case of women who are mothers, the experience of pregnancy, labor, childbirth, and nursing shape a way of responding to the world and to others. For a mother whose milk lets down at the sound of her child's cry, a sense of deep connection and continuity is established.[19]

On this view, the danger of the new technologies of birth is precisely that they alienate women from procreation and thus rob them of one of the most significant sources of power and identity. It is precisely this realization that leads Connie Ramos, a character in Marge Piercy's *Woman on the Edge of Time*, to react with such horror at the division of motherhood envisioned by Piercy. In a world where gestation takes place in artificial wombs, where men as well as women nurse the young, women have lost something of tremendous value and men have gained something they always wanted: control of reproduction. Connie's response to seeing a breast feeding male poignantly expresses this point:

She felt angry. Yes, how dare any man share that pleasure. These women thought they had won, but they had abandoned to men the last refuge of women. What was special about being a woman here? They had given it all up, they had let men steal from them the last remnants of ancient power, those sealed in blood and in milk.[20]

One of the gravest concerns raised about the new technologies of birth, then, is that they represent the culmination of a patriarchal imperative: to gain for men what they have always lacked, namely, the power to reproduce. The fear is that this desire is close to realization. Gena Corea has put this point forcefully:

Now men are far beyond the stage at which they expressed their envy of woman's procreative power through couvade, transvestism, or subincision. They are beyond merely giving spiritual birth in their baptismal-font wombs, beyond giving physical birth with their electronic fetal monitors, their forceps, their knives. Now they have laboratories.[21]

Since this objection essentially focuses on the impact on women of the NRTs, my experience cannot speak directly to this issue. Nevertheless, because part of what is at stake is the importance of the unity of genetic and social parenthood, as well as the unity of genetic and gestational parenthood, this is not a concern exclusively of women; it is a concern I have confronted in reflecting about donor insemination and adoption. One of the most striking aspects of my experience is how powerfully I have felt the pull of biological connection. Does this mean that genetic and social parenthood should never be separated or that parenthood should be defined strictly as a biological relation? I believe the answer to both questions is "no," but my experience leads me to believe also that a unity of genetic, gestational, and social parenthood is an ideal that we ought to strive to maintain.

The Commodification of Reproduction

The third objection found in some of the feminist literature on NRTs is that they tend to treat human beings as products. Not only can these technologies divide up motherhood, they can divide up persons into parts. Even when they are used to treat infertility, it is often not men or women who are being treated, but testicles, sperm, ovaries, eggs, wombs, etc. While this is true to some extent of all treatment in the specialized world of modern medicine, it is acute in reproductive medicine. Robyn Rowland has described the situation as one in which women especially are treated as "living laboratories" in which body parts and systems are manipulated in dramatic fashion without knowledge about the consequences of such manipulation.[22] Clearly, this has been the case in the development of *in vitro* fertilization, where women have not been adequately informed about the experimental nature of the procedure, possible side effects, or poor success rates.

In addition, the language of reproductive medicine can also be dehumanizing. Eggs are "harvested" as one might bring in a crop. Body parts are personified and thus attributed a sort of individuality and intentionality; cervical mucus is said to be "hostile," the cervix itself is said to be "incompetent," and the list could go on.

Yet as troubling as the language and practice surrounding this technology may be in treating persons like products, it is the application of this technology that treats persons *as* products that is completely objectionable. This has clearly happened with the development of a commercial surrogate industry and donor sperm banks, and it is the danger that attends the establishment of oocyte donor programs. Indeed, Corea's idea of a reproductive brothel seems inescapable. If there are not yet houses of ill repute where one can go to purchase embryos and women to gestate them, there are brochures available containing pictures and biographical information of women willing to sell their services. Nor can the development of commercial surrogacy arrangements be dismissed as the misguided and unintended application of reproductive techniques, an application of NRTs mistakenly and uncharacteristically driven by the profit motive. Treatment of infertility is big business, and the drive to develop reproductive technology is clearly fueled by financial incentives.[23]

Nothing perhaps illustrates this more clearly than the development of an embryo flushing technique by a team of physicians at Harbor-UCLA Medical Center. In April 1983, this team successfully flushed an embryo from one woman and transferred it to a second woman who carried the fetus to term. The project was funded by Fertility and Genetics Research, a for-profit company begun by two physicians who envisioned the establishment of a chain of embryo transfer clinics where infertile women could purchase embryos to gestate themselves. Indeed, to insure maximum profits for themselves, the Harbor-UCLA team sought to patent the equipment and the technique they developed.[24]

Not only do men and women get treated as products, so do children. The logic here is clear enough. If women are paying for embryos or being paid for eggs, the embryos and the eggs cannot but be understood as products. Because they are products, buyers will place demands on them. We will expect our products to meet certain standards and, if they fail, we will want to be compensated or to return the damaged goods. In a society that sells embryos and eggs for profit, children will inevitably be treated as property to be bought and sold, and just as inevitably it follows that different children will carry different price tags. As Barbara Katz Rothman puts it, "some will be rejects, not salable at any price: too damaged, or the wrong colour, or too old, too long on the shelf."[25]

My own experience leads me to believe that this tendency toward the commodification of reproduction is one of the most worrisome aspects of the NRTs.[26] In part, this tendency is troubling because it manifests itself not simply in commercial surrogacy transactions—transactions that many if not most people find morally problematic—but in applications of these technologies that almost no one questions. For example, few, I believe, would have qualms about the sort of artificial insemination that Lisa and I have undertaken and yet perhaps the most difficult part of AIH for us has been the struggle to maintain a degree of intimacy in the process of reproduction in the midst of a clinical environment designed to achieve results. As Katz Rothman has pointed out, the ideology of technology that fuels this commodification is not reducible to particular technological tools or to particular commercial transactions. Rather it is a way of thinking of ourselves and our world in "mechanical, industrial terms," terms that are incompatible with intimacy.[27] Interestingly, the Roman Catholic Church has rejected AIH precisely because it separates procreation from sexual intercourse and the expression of love manifest in the conjugal act.[28] While I reject the act-oriented natural law reasoning that stands behind this position, there is an insight here that should not be overlooked. Once procreation is separated from sexual intercourse, it is difficult not to treat the process of procreation as the production of an object to which one has a right as the producer. It is also difficult under these circumstances not to place the end above the means; effectiveness in accomplishing one's goal can easily become the sole criterion by which decisions are made.

This anyway, has been my experience. Although Lisa and I tried for a time to maintain a degree of intimacy during the process of AIH by remaining together during all phases of the procedure as well as after the insemination, we quickly abandoned this as a charade. The system neither encourages nor facilitates intimacy. It is concerned, as it probably should be, with results. And so we have become pragmatists too. We do not much enjoy the process of AIH, to say the least, but we also do not try to make it something it is not. A conception, if it takes place, will not be the result of an act of bodily lovemaking, but a result of technology. We have come to accept this. Yet, such acceptance comes at a price, for our experience of reproduction is discontinuous. A child conceived by this method is lovingly willed into existence, but it is not conceived through a loving, bodily act.

Having accepted the separation of sexual intercourse and procreation, however, it is difficult to resist any sort of technological manipulation of gametes that might result in conception. We have, so to speak, relinquished our gametes to the doctors and once this has been done, how can various technological manipulations be judged other than by criteria of likelihood of success? This is precisely the problem: once one has begun a process that inevitably treats procreation as the production of a product, the methods of production can only be evaluated by the end result.

Reproductive Technologies and Genetic Engineering

The fourth objection to NRTs is that their general acceptance and use is an inevitable route to

80

widespread use of genetic engineering. It should be no mystery why this might be thought to be the case. Once the embryo, for example, is treated as a product to be bought and sold, there will be great pressure to produce the perfect product. The attraction of genetic engineering under such circumstances should be obvious. Genetic screening and therapy would be a sort of quality control mechanism by which to insure customer satisfaction.[29] Moreover, the greater access to embryos and to eggs provided by IVF and embryo flushing means that genetic manipulation of the eggs or the developing embryo is now more feasible than it once was. Even more importantly, however, this greater access to embryos and eggs, combined with the possibility of freezing and storing those not used to attempt a pregnancy, means that experimentation can go forward at a much faster rate. Scientists have experimented with the injection of genetic material into non-human eggs for some time, and a recent issue of *Cell* reported the introduction of foreign genetic material into mouse sperm.[30] It is not unreasonable to suppose that such manipulations will one day extend to human gametes. Indeed, one experimental technique being developed to treat forms of male infertility in which sperm is unable to penetrate the egg involves isolating a single sperm in order to introduce the sperm directly into the egg.[31] The obvious question is: How will this sperm be selected? The most likely answer will be: by a determination that it is not genetically abnormal.

Thus far, most genetic experimentation, manipulation, and screening has been defended by appeal to the goal of eliminating human suffering. If genetic abnormalities can be detected or even treated, much human suffering might either be avoided or alleviated. Yet, how does one distinguish between attempts to eliminate suffering and attempts at eugenics? The fact that it is so difficult to answer this question is one reason to be concerned about NRTs. Moreover, the equation of genetic abnormality or disability with suffering can be questioned. As Marsha Saxton has pointed out, we cannot simply assume that disabled people "suffer" from their physical conditions any more than any other group or category of individuals "suffer."[32] Indeed, decisions about bearing genetically damaged fetuses are generally made in relative ignorance of what sorts of lives potential offspring might actually have.[33] "Our exposure to disabled children," Saxton writes, "has been so limited by their isolation that most people have only stereotyped views which include telethons, [and] displays on drugstore counters depicting attractive 'crippled' youngsters soliciting our pity and loose change" (306).

If reproductive technology is developed because every person has a right to bear a child, does it not follow that every person has a right to bear a perfect child? Advocates of NRTs would not admit this, and yet it seems to be the logical conclusion of the commitment to produce a child, no matter the cost. To see the difficulties here, we need only ask how we are to define the perfect child, and whether a commitment to eliminate genetic abnormalities means that women will lose the freedom not to test for or to treat abnormalities.[34]

In my view, the concern here is a real one for, once one has begun to think in terms of producing a product, it becomes exceedingly difficult to distinguish between technological interventions except on the basis of the resulting product. And since the product one desires in this instance is a healthy baby, a technological intervention that helps to achieve this, even one that involves genetic manipulation, is likely to be both initially attractive and ultimately irresistible. My own reaction to the new technique of overcoming male infertility by isolating a single sperm and injecting it into an egg it would otherwise be unable to penetrate is instructive. My initial response was that of tremendous excitement. Here was a treatment that could clearly overcome our problem. The fact that I did not produce great numbers of sperm or that the ones I produced were not likely to be capable of penetrating an egg did not matter. In theory, very few sperm are required and the work of penetration is done for them. The fact that such a technique involves placing an extraordinary amount of control in the hands of the doctor who selects the single sperm from among the many millions that even a man with a low sperm count is likely to produce did not even occur to me. In fact, it was my doctor, who had moral reservations about this technique, who first pointed this out to me. What is perhaps more troubling, however, is that when the issue of control was pointed out to me, I found no immediately compelling reason to object. I had, after all, been routinely providing sperm for a lab to manipulate in an effort to produce a collection that was capable of penetrating my wife's egg. Was selecting a single sperm that could accomplish the goal really so different?

In light of these various objections and my own experience, then, my basic response is one of concern. I do not believe that the predominantly male medical profession is acting in bad faith in developing reproductive technologies, as some critics suggest. Much of the feminist literature on NRTs is cynical and deeply contemptuous of what is seen as a patriarchal and conspiratorial medical establishment. My own experience, however, does not bear this out. Although there is much about my treatment for infertility that I have found frustrating, anxiety-producing, and distasteful, and although I have felt at turns coerced by the existence of the technologies themselves; angry at the loss of intimacy in my relationship with Lisa; and worried by my own near obsession with the goal of achieving a pregnancy, I have never had reason to doubt the sincerity of my doctor's care and concern. That my experience has been so negative despite treating with a doctor who is very much aware of the potentially dehumanizing aspects of infertility treatment is further evidence of how serious the problems with these technologies may be.

This is not to deny that infertility specialists are too concerned with technological fixes; in my view, they are. While there is no conspiracy to gain control of the process of reproduction, there is increased control. And if one theme joins the various objections to the new reproductive technologies, it is that they increase the medical profession's control over the process of reproduction and that such control has deleterious consequences. We have not, by and large, thought through the consequences of this sort of intervention and control. Neither infertile couples nor those who try to alleviate their suffering, nor indeed the community that is generally supportive of the desire to have children has really asked whether that desire should be met at all costs. Is the desire to have children a desire for a basic human good? Can it be met through adoption or only through biological offspring? Are there other, competing social goods that set limits on how far we, as a community, should go to meet this need? These are certainly questions that I had not addressed before my experience of infertility. Even now I am not certain how to answer all of them. I am certain, however, that my desire to have children is strong. I am also equally certain that we need to attend to these questions as a society. For anyone not blinded by self deception will admit that wanting something does not always make it right.

Acknowledgments

A number of individuals both encouraged me to go forward with this essay, and provided me with very helpful suggestions for revisions. Thanks to Lisa Cahill, Lisa de Filippis, Howard Eilberg-Schwartz, Tom Kelly, Gilbert Meilaender, Louis Newman, John P. Reeder, Jr., David H. Smith, Claudia Spencer, John Spencer, and Brian Stiltner. I also received very helpful comments from the works-in-progress group at the Center for Bioethics at the Case Western Reserve University School of Medicine and the participants in a NEH sponsored Humanities and Medicine Institute at Hiram College held in collaboration with the Northeastern Ohio Universities College of Medicine.

References

1 See Gena Corea, "The Reproductive Brothel" in *Man-Made Woman*, Gena Corea *et al.*, eds. (Bloomington: Indiana University Press, 1987), 38-51.

2 The medical profession has gone to some lengths to insure that artificial insemination is defined as a medical procedure, and thus controlled by doctors. Most of my wife's inseminations have been administered by doctors, even when this has been inconvenient for us. The two exceptions have been when Lisa ovulated on the weekend and then, apparently, insemination did not need to be performed by a doctor.

3 Although for convenience I will refer in this paper to "feminist" objections, I cannot stress enough that there is not one feminist response to reproductive technology, but several. Indeed, feminist responses range from enthusiastic support to moderate and cautious support to radical opposition. See Anne Donchin, "The Future of Mothering: Reproductive Technology and Feminist Theory," *Hypatia* 1 (1986), 121-37.

4 Patricia Spallone and Deborah Lynn Steinberg, eds., *Made to Order* (Oxford: Pergamon Press, 1987).

5 But see Sidney Callahan, "The Role of Emotion in Ethical Decisionmaking," *Hastings Center Report* 18:3 (1988), 9-14.

6 On the difference between coercive offers and coercive threats, see Virginia Held, "Coercion and Coercive Offers," in *Coercion*, J. Roland Pennock and John Chapman, eds. (Chicago: Atherton, 1972), 49-62.

7 I use "couples" here intentionally. The justification for developing reproductive methods is almost always to help infertility within marriage. There is an irony in this: Although physicians tend to treat infertility as a problem for an individual, they insist that that individual be part of a heterosexual marriage. Thus it is not just infertility that is of concern, but infertility in certain types of situations.

8 For a discussion of the difficulty of providing an adequate account of free choice given the assumptions of modern liberalism, see Barbara Katz Rothman, *Recreating Motherhood* (New York: W.W. Norton, 1989), 62.

9 Robyn Rowland, "Of Woman Born, But for How Long?" in *Made to Order*, 70.

10 See Spallone and Steinberg, eds., *Made to Order*, 6-7.

11 The test involves injecting radiopaque dye into the uterine cavity after which x-rays are taken. The fallopian tubes are outlined wherever the dye has penetrated. Using this procedure, it is sometimes possible to determine whether a woman's tubes are blocked.

12 Here my experience and Lisa's differ dramatically. The infertility specialist I have seen could not be more sensitive or attentive to the human dimension of our difficulties. By contrast, Lisa's experience with the gynecologists involved with insemination has been almost entirely negative, in part because she has not been treated fully as a person by them.

13 Spallone and Steinberg, eds., *Made to Order*, 4-5.

14 Leon Kass, *Toward a More Natural Science* (New York: The Free Press, 1985), 45.

15 I am, in effect, suggesting that more choice is not always better. This is not a popular view in our culture, but it can be persuasively defended. For such a defense, see Gerald Dworkin, "Is More Choice Better than Less?," *Midwest Studies in Philosophy* 7, Peter A. French, Theodore E. Uehling, Jr., and Howard K. Wettstein, eds. (Minneapolis: University of Minnesota Press, 1982), 47-61.

16 Gena Corea, *The Mother Machine* (New York: Harper and Row, 1985), 290.

17 Mary O'Brien, *The Politics of Reproduction* (Boston: Routledge and Kegan Paul, 1981), 55.

18 See Nancy Hartsock, "The Feminist Standpoint: Developing

the Ground for a Specifically Feminist Historical Materialism," in *Discovering Reality*, Sandra Harding and Merrill B. Hintikka, eds. (Dordrecht: D. Reidel, 1983), 283-310; and Caroline Whitbeck, "A Different Reality: Feminist Ontology," in *Beyond Domination*, Carol C. Gould, ed. (Totowa, NJ: Rowman and Allanheld, 1983), 64-88.

[19] Emily Martin, *The Woman in the Body* (Boston: Beacon Press, 1987).

[20] Marge Piercy, *Woman on the Edge of Time* (New York: Ballantine Books, 1976), 134.

[21] Corea, *The Mother Machine*, 314.

[22] Robyn Rowland, "Women as Living Laboratories: The New Reproductive Technologies," in *The Trapped Woman*, Josefina Figueira-McDonough and Rosemary Sarri, eds. (Newbury Park, CA: Sage Publications, 1987), 81-112.

[23] According to the Office of Technology Assessment, $164 million is paid to close to 11,000 physicians every year for artificial inseminations alone. Add to this the variety of other infertility services provided every year to childless couples and the total cost is at least $1 billion (U.S. Congress, Office of Technology Assessment, *Artificial Insemination Practice in the U.S.: Summary of a 1987 Survey* [Washington: Government Printing Office, 1988]).

[24] Although there are currently no franchised clinics in the U.S., the ovum transfer procedure using uterine lavage is commonplace. See Leonard Formigli, Graziella Formigli, and Carlo Roccio, "Donation of Fertilized Uterine Ova to Infertile Women," *Fertility and Sterility* 47:1 (1987), 162-65.

[25] Barbara Katz Rothman, "The Products of Conception: The Social Context of Reproductive Choices," *Journal of Medical Ethics* 11 (1985), 191.

[26] The tendency to treat children as commodities is not solely the product of developing NRTs, of course, but the culmination of a process begun with the old reproductive technology of contraception. Once the inexorable connection between sexual intercourse and procreation was broken, it became possible to choose when to have children. From that point on, it made sense to treat children in some ways as products, the purchase of which, so to speak, could be planned as one planned the purchase of other expensive items.

[27] Katz Rothman, *Recreating Motherhood*, 49.

[28] Sacred Congregation for the Doctrine of the Faith, *Instruction on Respect for Human Life in Its Origin and on the Dignity of Procreation*, in *Origins* 16 (March 1987), 697-711.

[29] Katz Rothman, "The Products of Conception," 188.

[30] For a discussion of the transgenic animals that result from the genetic manipulation of eggs, see V.G. Pursel *et al.*, "Genetic Engineering of Livestock," *Science* 244 (1989), 1281-88. Also see M. Lavitrano *et al.*, "Sperm Cells as Vectors for Introducting Foreign DNA into Eggs: Genetic Transformation of Mice," *Cell* 57:5 (1989), 717-24.

[31] Actually, there are at least three different techniques being investigated. See Jon W. Gordon *et al.*, "Fertilization of Human Oocytes by Sperm from Infertile Males After Zona Pellucida Drilling," *Fertility and Sterility* 50:1 (1988), 68-73.

[32] Marsha Saxton, "Born and Unborn: The Implications of Reproductive Technologies for People with Disabilities," in *Test-Tube Women*, Rita Arditti, Renate Duelli Klein, and Shelley Minden, eds. (London: Pandora Press, 1984), 298-313.

[33] Anne Finger, "Claiming All of Our Bodies: Reproductive Rights and Disabilities," in *Test-Tube Women*, 281-97.

[34] See Ruth Hubbard, "'Fetal Rights' and the New Eugenics," *Science for the People* (March/April 1984), 7-9, 27-29.

The Argument for Unlimited Procreative Liberty: A Feminist Critique

by Maura A. Ryan

From a feminist perspective, unlimited procreative liberty risks treating children as property, distorts understanding of the family, and neglects moral concerns about how we reproduce.

As growing numbers of infertile heterosexual and gay and lesbian couples, along with single individuals, seek to parent through techniques that facilitate conception or permit the use of a genetic and/or gestational donor, and the boundaries of the "scientifically possible" enlarge, we are confronted with a host of increasingly urgent questions. Can the components of parenting—genetic, gestational, and social—be separated at will without harm to the participants? Do new forms of noncoital and donor-assisted reproduction threaten the foundations of the family, and hence, social existence as we know it? Are there "natural" limits to human intervention in the procreative process? Ought artificial reproduction be permitted to become a commercial venture? Does the right to engage in coital reproduction, protected for married couples under the U.S. Constitution, extend into a right to engage in noncoital reproduction; if so, for whom, and under

Maura A. Ryan is a graduate student in religious studies, Yale University. This manuscript won the first Jeanette Lappé Memorial Prize competition.

what circumstances?

Questions of liberty and individual rights are emotionally charged ones in American public discourse. Moreover, family autonomy has long been held as a value worthy of such firm protection in our courts and legislatures that policies of minimal interference by the state into domestic life have been maintained even where it has meant a certain institutional blindness to the reality of spousal and child abuse. This context explains why the question of procreative liberty is important in current public policy debates surrounding the "new reproduction." Decisions with respect to the limits that may be placed on efforts to procreate, on which parties may be permitted to seek technological assistance in procreation, on the amount of public protection or funding to be extended, and on the conditions under which funding or protection might be warranted turn, many legal scholars believe, on the question of whether we have a right to procreate. Some maintain that the Constitution provides for virtually unlimited right of access to reproductive means.

The freedom to decide whether one will bear and nurture children, and under what circumstances, has been a central issue in the won.en's liberation movement. As persons whose self-identity and social role have been defined historically in relation to their procreative capacities, women have a great deal at stake in questions of reproductive freedom. Early feminists expended significant energy to secure the right to use contraceptive measures and to seek legal abortion, as well as to gain recognition of their rights as consumers of gynecological and obstetrical care. To say that feminism has promoted procreative liberty for women is not, however, to say that contemporary feminists have welcomed recent developments in reproductive technology without reservation.[1] Nor is it to say, despite the central importance given to the protection of women's autonomy in reproductive decisions, that feminists in general would treat procreative liberty as an unrestricted value. Rather, a feminist perspective includes commitments to human relationality as well as autonomy, and attention to the social context of personal choices. Thus questions of individual freedom, even in matters of reproduction, must be raised in conjunction with other equally compelling considerations about what is needed for human flourishing and what is required for a just society.

I want to highlight these themes by attending to the arguments for an unlimited right to procreate raised most cogently by John Robertson.[2] This position, based primarily on the importance of procreation for individuals, contains several elements that are troubling from a feminist perspective. My concern will not be with matters of constitutional law, but instead with the underlying model of procreative liberty, and its consequences for our understanding of reproduction and our attitudes toward human persons in general and children in particular.

The Case for Full Procreative Liberty

Robertson's argument for the protection of a right to reproduce noncoitally or collaboratively (that is,

Hastings Center Report, July/August 1990

with the participation of a gamete donor or gestator who is not one's spouse) is based on a historical protection of intramarital reproductive rights and the societal interest in safeguarding family autonomy. Since courts have recognized persons' rights to reproduce coitally, and not to reproduce coitally, their right to pursue those ends by noncoital means, if necessary, must also be protected. As a consequence of the natural lottery, infertility ought not prevent some from pursuing what has been recognized as of value to all.

Because childbearing and rearing have been viewed as experiences of great significance to persons, constitutive of individual identity and notions of a meaningful life, the courts have tended to take a position of noninterference in procreative decisions, particularly where married couples were involved. However, while an individual's right *not* to conceive, gestate, and rear has been explicitly protected in cases like *Griswold v. Connecticut* and *Roe v. Wade*, as has the right of parents to rear according to their own beliefs in cases like *Wisconsin v. Yoder,* the right *to* procreate has been addressed only implicitly. Robertson argues that one could and should infer from the right of couples to avoid procreation a correlative right to procreate, and from the unregulated freedom of married couples to add to their families coitally a freedom to do so noncoitally. No clear distinction should be allowed to stand, when procreative means exist, between fertile and infertile couples:

The reason and values that support a right to reproduce coitally apply equally to noncoital activities involving external conception and collaborators. While the case is strongest for a couple's right to noncoital and external conception a strong argument for their right to enlist the aid of gamete and womb donors can also be made.[5]

Since reproductive rights are derived from the central importance of reproduction in an individual's life and are limited only by a capacity to participate meaningfully and an ability to accept or transfer rearing responsibilities, all those persons meeting this minimum criteria, whether married or not, ought to be free to pursue it.

Having argued that procreative autonomy is finally rooted in "the notion that individuals have a right to choose and live out the kind of life that they find meaningful and fulfilling," Robertson will allow for the use of technology for any reason that would realize the couple's "reproductive goals":

The right of married persons to use noncoital and collaborative means of conception to overcome infertility must extend to any purpose, including selecting the gender or genetic characteristics of the child or transferring the burden of gestation to another.[4]

Because procreative interests are for some persons dependent on the offspring's having certain gender or genetic characteristics, procreative liberty includes, according to Robertson, the freedom to manipulate egg, sperm, or embryo to achieve the desired offspring, and the freedom to stop implantation or abort a fetus with undesirable characteristics. A couple is not free to alter genetic material in a way that would cause serious harm to the offspring (that is, harm so great as to make life not worth living), but they may do whatever else will facilitate the development of an offspring possessing those characteristics and traits that make having a child meaningful for them.[5] Claims of harm made in the name of society (threats to the ideal of the family, etc.) are not compelling enough in his view to override individual rights.

Many people have taken issue with this position on the grounds that a right to assistance in reproduction simply does not follow from the right not to be compelled to bear a child.[6] It is one thing to say that no one ought to be made to reproduce, or no one ought to be prevented from reproducing by decree; it is quite another to say that society ought to provide whatever is necessary for reproduction to occur.[7]

While sharing these reservations, I wish to raise a different set of objections: The view of offspring presupposed in such a position is unacceptable from a feminist perspective; further, treating the act of reproducing in such a way has serious implications for efforts to bring about a society free of oppression. My

concerns lie chiefly in three areas: the tendency in this position to treat children as property; the use of "rights" language and a contract model to define the family; and an imbalance of concern for reproductive ends versus reproductive means.

Attitudes toward Children

The success of Robertson's argument depends upon accepting the view that persons can be the object of another's right. Since he is not arguing for the protection of the right to engage in procreative activities, but the freedom to "acquire that sort of child that would make one willing to bring a child into the world in the first place,"[8] he is asserting the right to acquire a human being (and one with particular characteristics). Nor is Robertson referring simply to the right of persons to share in the experience of child nurture (since ability to adopt would satisfy that), but to have a genetically related child. As a feminist, I would agree that persons ought to be protected in their right to determine when and in what manner they will reproduce, and that they should be free to shape familial life in a way meaningful for them. But such a right should not be understood as unlimited, as extending as far as the acquisition of a concrete human being. Every exercise of freedom has a history and a context; our liberty is thus conditioned both by our potential for causing harm to others and by our responsibility for the quality of our common lives. A view of unlimited procreative liberty does not give sufficient attention to the ways in which not only individual offspring could be harmed, but the human community. Nor does it take seriously enough the possibilities for conflicts between claims.

First, such a position fails to respect offspring as autonomous beings, as ends in themselves. While a child's special dependency requires a condition of compromised autonomy vis-à-vis his or her caretakers, still that child comes into this world as a human person with the potential for self-determination. Although we might grant that the experience of reproduction appropriately fulfills

85

needs and desires for the adults involved, advocating a model where children are brought into this world *chiefly* for that purpose gives too much weight to parental desires and too little to the protection of the offspring's essential autonomy. I am not saying that the desire to reproduce must be altruistic to be morally acceptable, nor that the experience of reproduction ought to be, or even could be, free of parental hopes and expectations for that offspring. My challenge is to a framework wherein the basis for unlimited procreative liberty is an individual desire for a particular type of child, a desire that is seldom weighed appropriately against the reality of the child-to-be as a potential autonomous human being. At what point does a being, who has been conceived, gestated, and born according to someone's specifications, become herself or himself? And if a child comes into the world primarily to fulfill parental need, are there limits to what a parent may do to ensure that the child will continue to meet the specified expectations?

With others, I share the fear that this understanding of procreative liberty incorporates a notion of children as products, on the assumption that individuals have a right to a particular kind of child and ought to be free, insofar as it is possible without causing grave physical harm, to manipulate the reproductive process so as to acquire the desired offspring. Currently, collaborative reproduction is a lengthy, arduous, and quite costly experience. How might parents look upon offspring when they enter the process with the belief that a certain kind of child is *owed* to them, and after they have paid a high price for that child? Certainly well-meaning people can bring children into the world through artificial reproduction and value them highly because of what they have gone through to have them. But this view of reproduction carries nonetheless the sense of "ordering" or "purchasing" children in accordance with specific parental desires, which in the end objectively devalues the child.

Not unlike, and just as dangerous as the thinking that makes women the property of their husbands, is the underlying view that children are not first and principally autonomous persons who also function as members of families and societies but rather the proper object of a parental right. We place our children at serious risk when we fail to see them first as existing for their own sakes and when we allow ourselves to think of them as malleable goods.

There are, in addition, serious problems in accepting as the standard for deciding how technology will be used to intervene in the reproductive process the adult initiator's definition of "procreative excellence." Since we are talking about a potentially autonomous human being, questions about the manipulation of genetic features, etc., ought to be asked first from the point of view of the offspring's best interests, not the prospective parent's desires. The decision then would be whether a certain genetic characteristic ought to be altered to facilitate that child's flourishing rather than whether a feature ought to be manipulated to make that offspring more acceptable to the parent.

A position of unlimited procreative liberty rooted in individual desire risks harming as well the quality of our lives together in community. Since reproduction in this view is tied so closely to one's private conception of a meaningful life, we are never talking about offspring per se, but a very specific type of offspring—a child with those genetic and gender characteristics that allow it to be incorporated into and contribute to the initiator's overall life project.

In a world where mixed-race and handicapped children are not now being adopted because they are "undesirable" we need to ask who determines, and should be permitted to so determine, what human characteristics are "desirable." My claim is not that parents are wrong to want a healthy, and genetically similar, child nor that persons may not have any good grounds for intervening in a pregnancy, for example one in which it is obvious that given certain characteristics the child will place great burdens on the parent or the family. My criticism is directed at an implied yardstick of acceptability, and the determination of reproductive standards based on personal whim.

Such a model stands at odds with a feminist vision of community where all are welcome and persons are challenged to deal creatively with differences.

In addition, we need to weigh the consequences of using a model of reproductive desirability which includes choices about the preferred sex of one's offspring, for efforts to promote equality between persons in society. This is not to suggest that such a practice, if widespread, would result in more boys being chosen than girls. We have no way to know that nor reason necessarily to assume it. What is dangerous, in light of the reality of sexism in our society, is the perpetuation of the belief that an offspring's gender should be a determinative factor in her or his value to parents, or to anyone else. The primary question is whether the project to provide the subjectively desirable child is where social energies and resources in reproductive medicine ought to be directed.

The underlying ideal of perfection shaping this perspective and the belief that all so-called imperfection, even in so complex a process as reproduction, can or should be eliminated, needs thus to be questioned seriously. Reproduction and nurture are processes that are never totally within our control, no matter how sophisticated our technology. The formation of a child's character and personality, the development of his or her talents, have to do with a great deal more (such as education, historical events, significant role models) than genetic blueprint. A genetically normal, or "genetically perfect" offspring in this model can for a variety of reasons turn out to be the sort of person his or her parents would not have objectively speaking "been willing to bring into the world." Thus the claim that a parental right to a satisfying reproductive experience justifies the manipulation of genetic material is flawed, for the sort of guarantee sought cannot be provided by control of conception.

The attempt to exert this level of control over the creation of offspring is not only an illusory project but a mistaken one. I do not want to advocate a total passivity toward nature or to suggest that the use of technology in altering the conditions of conception and gestation is always inappropriate. But the feminist value of cooperation with and humility toward nature suggests a middle road between technical domination of the natural reproductive process and passivity. This middle road entails, at least, some attention to the essential elements of particular personhood, and thus a weighing of which features of our offspring we ought to attempt to determine in advance and which we should accept as characteristics of that unique being.

It is not only the sense of "reproducing for excellence" that is troubling about the case for unlimited procreative liberty but the presupposition that since children are property, all relationships between offspring and interested adults can be wholly a matter of contract. This way of thinking about the family is in some ways reflective of an old and familiar pattern, one about which feminists ought to be very cautious.

The Contractual Model of Family

Robertson admits that when we begin to have multiple participants in reproduction "it becomes unclear which participants hold parental rights and duties and will function socially and psychologically as members of the child's family."[9] Such confusion can be alleviated, however, by a presumption that the contract between the parties will determine obligations and entitlements toward the child, rather than the commonly held definitions of paternity and maternity. Whether collaborative arrangements can or will result in family disruption and identity confusion for the offspring or in productive and satisfying "alternative" family experiences will depend in part on the clarity and quality of these contracts. Experience with donor sperm, Robertson argues, suggests that the contract between parties will play the decisive role in determining rearing rights and duties to the offspring. Generally speaking, the presumption of rightful parentage ought to go to the initiating couple according to the agreements made prior to conception.

If these practices become institutionalized, there is no doubt that well-constructed contracts will be enormously helpful for clarifying parental rights and duties and that all the parties, including potential offspring, would benefit from legal protection. There are serious problems, however, with accepting a simple contract solution to the confusion of collaborative reproduction; it is both inadequate and perpetuates an ideologically dangerous model of the family. For example, claiming that the preconception contract can be sufficiently clear as to determine parental relationships in advance denies the complexity of reproduction as an affective and social experience as well as a biological one. Accounts of surrogate mothering, for example, suggest it can be quite difficult to decide the shape of one's reproductive role beforehand when we are engaged in a project about which we can come to have very deep feelings. In addition, the nature of what reproductive initiators are contracting about is qualitatively different than the object of ordinary contracts. We do not have at this time, and may never have, a good way to determine the value of specific reproductive contributions or to weigh conflicts between contributors (for example, what is the market value of gestation versus gamete donation?) At the very least, to use sperm donation as a paradigm for workable contracts reflects inattention to the vast differences, emotional as well as physical, in the nature of various collaborative roles. Moreover, it masks inequalities between parties with respect to risk and benefit. A contract that may well be sufficient to determine rearing duties and rights with respect to a sperm donor may not address at all the complex physical and affective situation of the surrogate mother.

Our understanding of the experience can perhaps be reinterpreted as Robertson suggests, so that what comes to count as reproduction is the donation of genetic material for one person, or the experience of gestation for another. Yet while there are very good reasons for preserving the freedom of individuals to choose their level of participation in procreation, to say that the meaning of reproduction can be reduced to one of these partial roles is to perpetuate an impoverished notion of what it means to be a parent. Assigning various rights and obligations to abstract roles may facilitate the execution of collaborative contracts, but risks treating the various components of reproduction as though they fit into neat compartments, and as though the conception-gestation-rearing relationship is entirely negotiable. Feminists do not want to affirm a view of reproduction that makes the moral connections between conception, gestation, and rearing such that conception generates an absolute duty to rear; at the same time, however, concerns for embodiment and thus for reproduction as a whole process mitigate against treating parental obligations and entitlements in isolation from the experiences of conception, pregnancy, and birth.

There is, of course, a kind of tacit agreement, at least in our society, involved in every gestation and birth with respect to the resultant offspring's nurture (and in a sense, also with respect to parental entitlements). Whatever model has been used thus far to understand the relationship, however, has not taken the form of an entirely free contract. Prior to the development of technology, we identified the mother as the woman giving birth to the child and the father as the man whose sperm initially fertilized the egg—those persons with biological and experiential connection, rather than those who have contracted for parental rights and duties. Even when we describe situations where another individual has taken over rearing responsibilities for a child not his or her issue, we continue to refer to that person as an "adoptive" or "foster" parent. We do this not to say anything about the quality of rearing, but to preserve a truer sense of identity and biological continuity for the child, acknowledging that no matter what function the rearing adult serves, he or she cannot ever become the child's father or mother in the traditional sense. I do not want to hold that there could be no legitimate reasons for separating genetic, gestational, and rearing components of reproduction, or that persons who conceive a child will

87

always be the best rearers of that child and that they must therefore be the rearers in all cases. Experience shows that children can be raised well in situations other than the traditional biologically related family. However, the genetic-gestation-rearing connection in procreation ought not be disregarded a priori in the way suggested by the contract model, both for the sake of protecting the offspring's sense of identity as a value and for preserving an awareness of the importance of the task involved when human life is being created.

While "rights" and "entitlements" in childbearing do have much to do with an agreement to accept responsibility, the biological parent-child relationship is still deeply significant, particularly if we are speaking of the intimate mother-child bond in a normal gestation experience. It may be acceptable to say that a woman who has conceived, carried, and birthed a child may legitimately choose to transfer rearing obligations to another, but it does not seem correct to say then that this experience of procreation places *no* claim on her as a mother unless she chooses to assume one under the terms of a contract, or that her claim to this child is identical to the claims of all other contracting parties prior to the contract. Both the experience of having conceived and carried a child and the implicit agreement to nurture grounds parental entitlements; these two dimensions must be seen as elements of the same experience even where a decision is made to separate them. Given the significant burdens and challenges of childbearing and the length of time the commitment ordinarily encompasses, this interconnection is important to protect when possible. Implicit in my critique is the great irony of collaborative reproduction: it is precisely the value of this biological connection, which must be open for renunciation on the part of the donor or gestator, that drives the search for new methods and justifies the infertile party's right to assistance.

The Involuntary Nature of Kinship

The authority of the collaborative contract, coupled with a property view

of children, generates a troubling picture of the parent-child bond. One of the false notions perpetuated in such a model of parental entitlement is that we are free to choose all obligations, and able to formulate all the conditions of our lives to meet our expectations. While most contracts and commitments are based on things such as shared purpose, equal benefit, common attraction, etc., and are entered into and terminated voluntarily, until recently, the agreement to conceive, gestate, and rear a child has been of a different nature. While in the best of circumstances we make a choice to parent, and a series of choices about how children will be raised and the shape our family life will take, a great deal of the experience of reproduction is not in our control. The common expression "This child has a face only a mother could love" speaks, of course, to the fact that a parent's bond to her child transcends all cultural standards of beauty, etc., but also alludes to a deeply entrenched understanding of the "givenness" and duration of parental responsibilities. These have included acceptance of a relatively unknown outcome, of inequalities in benefits and burdens, and also of a certain irrevocability. "A face only a mother could love" says something as well about acceptance and fidelity to children, even to those whose looks or gender or genetic characteristics are not what the parent would have desired or what meets society's standards. We have accepted the fact that, unlike a product in the market, children cannot be returned or exchanged if found to be other than what was expected.

The commitment a parent undertakes is not dependent on that child's behavior or the return of like affection or the fulfillment of expectations in life, although those factors can certainly influence a parent's subjective experience and may at times modify obligations. A child does not enter into a committed relationship with his or her parents in the same way that a parent, by virtue of the decision to bear offspring, does with the child; still, there is some measure of givenness in the child-parent relationship as well. We are free

throughout life to choose friends, a mate, employers, etc. but not our family of origin. One of the things that family life can teach us is that we are born into some obligations, and some are born to us, and life includes the acceptance of those kinds of indissoluble and predefined obligations as well as the ones we freely incur. The involuntary quality of kinship can also teach us how to accept others as intimately connected to us, even when they fail to live up to our standards or when they do not possess the physical or personal qualities most attractive to us. To image reproduction as primarily a contractual process, where all the elements are open for negotiation, threatens to lose sight of this sense of transcendent commitment.

From the perspective of feminist ethics, the contractual view of procreative liberty assumes and perpetuates a traditional patriarchal model of the family (centered around rights and ownership), a model that has proven oppressive and sometimes dangerous for persons, especially women. A contract approach is initially attractive as it appears to bring about greater flexibility in the definition of family and the protection of procreative liberty (among the values feminists want to promote). But when persons are treated primarily as the object of another's right, and significant relationships are defined wholly according to legal arrangements rather than the experiences of nurture, the symbolic framework is that of the patriarchal family. Janet Farrell Smith has argued that this property model of parenting, having at its center a notion of rights, is inherently gender-biased and is protective of dangerous authority patterns. It is problematic in her view both because its structure of relationship is "male" in form and because males have traditionally been the exclusive holders of familial rights.[10]

What makes such a model destructively gender-biased, according to Smith, is its rootedness in an extractive view of power rather than a developmental one and its relation to the authority patterns of the traditional patriarchal family. The major elements of such a property model of human relations, namely ownership and proprietary control, have had more to do with fathering than with mothering. The realities of motherhood, on the other hand, have had more to do with care, nurturance and day-to-day responsibility. These represent a very different set of moral and political ideals.[11]

The concepts of right and entitlement used in the contractual model correspond to the values preserved in traditional notions of patriarchal fathering (control and ownership) rather than to those of care and responsibility associated with mothering. While many feminists would not want to posit "distinctively female" values or ideals, most would reject familiar structures that treat persons as property and would call instead for a style of parenting that is respectful of a child's autonomy and encourages individual flourishing. They would, as well, reject models of the family that attach authority to rigidly defined roles in favor of models based on equality between partners and cooperation in the performance of family tasks.

As Smith argues, promoting a property (or "rights-centered") model, whether through vigorous protection of familial autonomy or by the rhetoric of "right to procreate" can only reinforce an ideal of the family that not only does not encourage more respectful and cooperative parenting styles but may further facilitate the abuse of parental power. In the context of Robertson's argument, familial autonomy means a protection of parental control as rightful parent (owner) over minor children (a control that in the past has extended to wives). But this sort of familial autonomy underlying arguments for clarity of contract serves largely to protect proprietary interests rather than to facilitate intimacy or the development of creative, more humane forms of parenting for women and men.[12] Since the problem is not only that males have been the exclusive holders of rights to property (including their wives and children) but that this way of imaging the family denies the reality of women and children as fully human, it may not be enough simply for feminists to argue for equality between women and men in

the holding of these rights. Rather, the very language of rights, implying as it does some exclusive access to property, must be seen as inappropriate when describing the structure of the family.

Reproductive Ends and Means

One of the weaknesses of the argument for unlimited procreative liberty is a tendency to split ends from means, to overemphasize goals while giving little moral consideration to the methods employed to achieve them or to the price paid. Robertson's concern to promote the procreative initiator's interests is not adequately balanced, for example, by a concern for the persons who will participate as the means to the stated reproductive goals. Except where he discusses contract stipulations (requirements for informed consent, freedom from coercion, screening procedures, etc.) Robertson does not speak of donors and gestators as though they really have interests to be weighed; he argues, in fact, that unless grave harm is being done, their interests cannot override individual procreative liberty. As we saw earlier, the offspring as a particular child is treated not as an end in himself or herself, but as the means to a goal (a fulfilling parenting experience). The question of how such treatment may affect that child's quality of life, sense of identity, or development is hardly raised.

The problem is not that the holding of a reproductive end is wrong in itself, but that it may be mistaken to assume that an end-state can be clearly demarcated from the processes that lead up to it.[13] The primary assumption that reproduction is highly valued by individuals and therefore that freedom of access should be promoted treats reproductive freedom for the most part as a value that could be pursued in isolation of other claims (except the minimal obligation not to do grave harm to an offspring). Feminists reject such thinking as inadequately attentive to the reality of events as processes and to the fact that the means we use to bring about any end are part of the total reality of the event in question. Thus it is not enough to assert that providing genetically

related children to infertile individuals is a good to be promoted; questions must be raised about the nature of the arrangement by which that might occur, the impact of that project on the individuals involved and on the larger human community, and the claims other goods are simultaneously exerting.

It is wrong to suppose that an individual procreative right can be posited and its unlimited exercise upheld without careful consideration of the moral nature of the means necessary to attain its end. Interest in a genetically related child cannot be seen as an independent end, the value of which automatically discounts concerns for the present and future state of the offspring, for the physical and emotional safety of the collaborators, or for the place of the experience of reproduction in our collective value system. In addition, the particular techniques used in collaborative reproduction need separate evaluation. We might accept the use of artificial insemination by a donor, for example, on particular grounds (as that the risks to donor are small and the benefit great), but have serious reservations about the practice of surrogacy. An adequate argument for procreative liberty as a good would have to include a fair description of the necessary means since they cannot be separated from the end-state.

Because reproduction has a social dimension, and reproductive practices have profound real and symbolic impacts on the community, the promotion of individual procreative liberty can never be an abstract end. The value of collaborative reproduction for individuals needs to be weighed against the costs these practices may exact, not only in the lives of those individuals directly involved, but also with respect to the promotion of full human community. An assessment of procreative liberty that takes seriously the contextual nature of our choices asks, in addition to whether the "new reproduction" is good for individuals, how it relates to social concerns (to efforts to secure an adequate standard of living for all persons, to progress in the quality of class, gender, and race relations, etc.).

A commitment to the creation of a just society requires that an individual desire for a genetically related child cannot be held up as an end commanding significant public resources and energy if as a "good" it encourages the exploitation of vulnerable persons or fosters negative attitudes toward persons or groups of persons. At a minimum, questions need to be raised about the influence of institutionalizing these practices on our views toward women: will opportunities to serve as egg donors or gestators facilitate progress toward equality with men for women, or does this type of service further identify women in an oppressive way with their reproductive capabilities? If individuals have a right to a genetically related child, do others have an obligation to donate genetic material, and how will the extent of the obligation be determined? What are the potential consequences of medicalizing reproduction in terms of women's right to control over their own bodies? And who will the women be who serve as donors?— will the poor, who have always been exploited by the rich, be used to perform even this form of domestic service?

To take account of the context in which individual procreative liberty is pursued, we also need to weigh the expense and energy channelled in the direction of these reproductive services against the realities of poverty and overpopulation. We need to ask whether we should support the right of individuals to go to any length to acquire the type of child they want when there are so many children already living who are not being taken care of. And, recognizing that collaborative reproduction ordinarily has as its object a white child, we need as well to examine the kind of racial attitudes being perpetuated. We cannot treat the pursuit of a genetically related child, or the protection of individual procreative liberty, as though they are abstract goods that are never in conflict with other relevant goods, nor can we consider procreative liberty from the point of view of its end alone. Given the nature of the procreative task, *how* we reproduce is as significant as *whether* we do.

Promoting Full Humanity

The promotion of women's right to self-determination, especially in matters of reproduction, has indeed been a critical item on the feminist political agenda. But for most feminists, protection of individual autonomy is never treated as the single value to be considered in the analysis of a situation. A commitment to viewing persons as embodied and relational, as well as autonomous, mitigates against an abstract notion of freedom that does not take seriously enough the way in which personal choices alter the shape of the world in which they occur. Questions of personal liberty, including how far our right to procreate extends, can only properly be asked from the point of view of our reality as relational beings whose power for reproduction is a capacity with profound personal and social implications. It is never even theoretically unlimited.

The objectification of children, impoverishment of meaning in the experience of reproduction, damage to notions of kinship, the perpetuation of degrading views of women— all these concerns may be deemed "symbolic harms" that are not compelling enough to override personal liberty. But attention to women's experience has taught feminists that there are no "merely symbolic" harms; we interpret and shape experience through our symbols and therefore how we think about persons, events, and biological processes has a great deal to do with how we behave toward them. We need, then, to pay careful attention to what is being said of personhood, of parent-child relationships, of reproductive capacities, and so on in arguments for unlimited procreative liberty. If we hope to use reproductive technology in a way that promotes the full humanity of all persons, in a manner that is truly creative rather than destructive, then we must be attentive to the potential for harm on all levels. We have an ever-expanding power to reshape the experience of reproduction; whether we will prove in the future to have done so in the service of human life or not will have more than a little to do with how we came to think about it and what we allowed to be of value today.

Acknowledgments

The author would like to thank Professors Margaret Farley and Richard L. Fern for helpful comments on earlier drafts.

References

[1] While a few feminists have heralded developments in technology as the ground of possibility for women's true liberation, most have remained more cautious, foreseeing potential for further oppression as clearly as hope of equality. See Shulamith Firestone, *The Dialectic of Sex: The Case for Feminist Revolution* (New York: Bantam Books, 1971), 238; Christine Overall, *Ethics and Human Reproduction: A Feminist Analysis* (Boston: Allen and Unwin, 1987).

[2] John Robertson, "Procreative Liberty and the Control of Conception, Pregnancy and Childbirth," *Virginia Law Review* 69 (April 1983), 405-462; "Embryos, Families and Procreative Liberty: The Legal Structures of the New Reproduction," *Southern California Law Review* 59 (1986), 942-1041.

[3] Robertson, "Embryos, Families, and Procreative Liberty," 961.

[4] Robertson, "Procreative Liberty," 450.

[5] Robertson, "Procreative Liberty," 432.

[6] See Overall, *Ethics and Human Reproduction*, chapter 8; also Richard L. Fern, "The Fundamental Right to Marry and Raise a Family," unpublished manuscript (1987).

[7] The parallel would be marriage, that is, there is a recognized right to noninterference in the decision to marry but no obligation on society's part to provide a mate. See William J. Daniel, "Sexual Ethics in Relation to IVF and ET: The Fitting Use of Human Reproductive Power," in *Test-Tube Babies*, William Walters and Peter Singer, eds. (Melbourne: Oxford University Press, 1982), 73.

[8] Robertson, "Procreative Liberty," 430.

[9] Robertson, "Procreative Liberty," 424.

[10] Janet Farrell Smith, "Parenting and Property," in *Mothering: Essays in Feminist Theory*, Joyce Trebilcott, ed. (Totowa, NJ: Rowman and Allanheld, 1983), 199-210.

[11] Smith, "Parenting," 208.

[12] Smith, "Parenting," 206.

[13] For a discussion of a feminist critique of dualistic means-ends reasoning, see Jean Grimshaw, *Philosophy and Feminist Thinking* (Minneapolis: University of Minnesota Press, 1986), 187-226.

Reproductive Gifts and Gift Giving: The Altruistic Woman

by Janice G. Raymond

Reproductive gift relationships must be seen in their totality, not just as helping someone have a child. Noncommercial surrogacy cannot be treated as a mere act of altruism—any valorizing of altruistic surrogacy and reproductive gift-giving must be assessed within the wider context of women's political inequality.

I n the aftermath of the "Baby M" case, the surrogacy debate has mostly left the media forum and entered the state legislatures. Many of these legislatures are now debating the legal status of surrogate contracts. Where legislative committees have opposed commercial contracts, they have tended to view alternative non-commercial surrogate parenting arrangements as ethically and legally permissible. An underlying theme here is that noncommercial arrangements are seen as altruistic. This article examines the implications of an altruistic ethic, particularly in reference to surrogacy, and highlights its problems for women in the reproductive realm.

Janice G. Raymond is professor of women's studies and medical ethics, University of Massachusetts at Amherst, associate director of the Institute on Women and Technology at MIT, and author of the forthcoming Technological Justice: Women and the New Reproductive Medicine *(Beacon, 1991).*

Gifts and Gift Giving

In his well-known study, *The Gift Relationship: From Human Blood to Social Policy,* Richard Titmuss opposed commercial systems of blood supply to noncommercial and altruistic systems of blood giving. Titmuss's concern was to shore up the spirit of altruism and voluntarism which he saw declining in western societies. His analysis is, in the main, a positive assessment of the possibilities of altruistic blood donation. But Titmuss also understood that giving was influenced by "the relationships set up, social and economic, between the system and the donor," and that these relationships are "strongly determined by the values and cultural orientations permeating the donor system and the society in general."[1] The dialectic between values and structural factors emerges strongly in his work. We must ask, he wrote, if there is truly "no contract of custom, no legal bond, no functional determinism, no situations of discrimina-

tory power, domination, constraint or compulsion, no sense of shame or guilt, no gratitude imperative and no need for the penitence of a Chrysostom" (239). The role of cultural values and constraints in shaping gift-giving arrangements is vital.

In the case of many new reproductive practices, and surrogacy especially, "the donor system" mainly depends on women as the gift givers—women who donate the use of their bodies and the fruit of their wombs. Those who endorse altruistic surrogacy as an alternative to commercial surrogacy accept, without comment or criticism, that it is primarily women who constitute the altruistic population called upon to contribute gestating capacities.[2] The questions that Titmuss raised about "contract of custom," "functional determinism," "situations of discriminatory power," "domination, constraint or compulsion," as well as possible "shame or guilt" and a "gratitude imperative" form part of the unexamined hallowing of altruistic surrogacy.

This unexamined acceptance of women as reproductive gift givers is very much related to a longstanding patriarchal tradition of giving women away in other cultural contexts—for sex and in marriage, for example. Following Titmuss, we must continually in these discussions of altruism ask: who gives and why? But further, who has been given away historically and why? In this sense, women are not only the gift givers but the gift as well. The pervasiveness of women's personal and social obligation to give shapes the contexts of reproductive gifts and gift giving. We see this most clearly in the situation of so-called altruistic surrogacy.

Altruism versus Commercialism

Those critical of commercial surrogacy often contrast it to noncommercial or altruistic surrogacy. The New Jersey Supreme Court, in its appellate judgment, *In the Matter of Baby M,* found surrogate contracts contrary to the law and public policy of the state. Nonetheless, it concluded that there were no legal impediments to arrangements "when the surrogate mother volunteers, without any pay-

Hastings Center Report, November/December 1990

ment, to act as a surrogate."[3] Many state legislative committees are taking action to prohibit commercial surrogacy but are leaving untouched the whole area of noncommercial surrogate practices. Altruism and voluntarism emerge as moral virtues in opposition to commercialism. George Annas, who has opposed commercial surrogacy, is sympathetic to the view that "one can distinguish between doing something out of love and doing it for money. As long as existing adoption laws are followed voluntary relinquishment of a child to a close relative (such as an infertile sister) seems acceptable."[4] Such a scenario has in fact already been played out.

In this country, one publicized case of altruistic surrogacy occurred in 1985 when Sherry King offered to become pregnant for her sister, Carole, who had undergone a hysterectomy eighteen years before. Sherry King provided both egg and womb. "I know I couldn't be a surrogate mother for money....I'm doing this for love and for my sister."[5]

Such agreements have not been confined only to sisters. In 1987, a forty-eight-year-old woman, Pat Anthony, acted as a surrogate mother for her daughter and gave birth to triplets in South Africa. The attending obstetrician, Dr. Bernstein, commented: "We feel that what Pat Anthony has done for Karen is the acceptable face of surrogacy....There was no payment, no commercialism. It was an act of pure love."[6] Thus altruism becomes the ethical standard for an affirmative assessment of noncommercial surrogacy.

Altruism also is invoked to soften the pecuniary image of commercial surrogacy. Noel Keane, the well-known surrogate broker, has made an educational video called "A Special Lady," which is often shown to teenage girls in high schools and other contexts, encouraging them to consider "careers" as surrogates. The video promotes the idea that it takes a special kind of woman to bear babies for others, and that women who engage in surrogacy do so not mainly for the money but for the special joy it brings to the lives of those who can't have children themselves. A 1986 article in *The Australian* used exactly the same "special"

appeal to argue "Why rent-a-uterus is a noble calling." Sonia Humphrey, the author, stated:

It does take a special kind of woman to conceive, carry under her heart and bear a child which she knows she won't see grow and develop. It also takes a special kind of woman to take a baby which is not hers by blood and rear it with all the commitment of a biological mother without the hormonal hit which nature so kindly provides....But those special women do exist, both kinds. Why shouldn't both be honored?[7]

Altruism holds sway. Part of its dominance as an ethical norm derives from its accepted opposition to commercialism. Particularly in the current debate about legalizing surrogate contracts, opponents contend that these contracts make children into commodities to be bought and sold. They allege that this is tantamount to baby selling, and some have renamed the practice commercialized childbearing. Many have focused on the economic exploitation of the women who enter surrogate contracts, women who are in need of money or are financially dead-ended. In these perspectives, the ethical objection is restricted to the fact that a price tag is attached to that which should have no price. The corollary is often that surrogacy "for free" is morally and legally appropriate.

More significant for the dominance of altruism in the reproductive context, however, is the moral celebration of women's altruism. As Caroline Whitbeck has stated in a different context, "the moral expectation upon women is that they be nurturant, that is, that they ought to go beyond respecting rights and meet the needs of others."[8]

The Moral Celebration of Women's Altruism

The cultural norm of the altruistic woman who is infinitely giving and eternally accessible derives from a social context in which women give and are given away, and from a moral tradition that celebrates women's duty to meet and satisfy the needs of others. The cultural expectation of altruism has fallen most heavily on pregnant women, so that one could

say they are imaged as the archetypal altruists. As Beverly Harrison notes:

Many philosophers and theologians, although decrying gender inequality, still unconsciously assume that women's lives should express a different moral norm than men's, that women should exemplify moral purity and self-sacrifice, whereas men may live by the more minimal rational standards of moral obligation...perfection and self-sacrifice are never taken to be a day-to-day moral requirement for any moral agent except, it would seem, a pregnant woman.[9]

Harrison calls this a "supererogatory morality," acts that are expected to go beyond the accepted standards of obligation. Although traditionally women have been exhorted to be passive, simultaneously they are expected to be more responsible than men for meeting the needs of others. "We live in a world where many, perhaps most, of the voluntary sacrifices on behalf of human well-being are made by women, but the assumption of a special obligation to self-giving or sacrifice...is male-generated ideology" (62). The other side of this altruistic coin is male self-interest. A man is allowed to be more self-seeking, to go to great lengths to fulfill his self-interests, and this has been rationalized, in the case of surrogacy, as genetic continuity and "biological fulfillment."[10]

This is not merely an ideological pronouncement about female self-giving and male self-seeking. It raises complex questions about moral double standards in a cultural context where men as a class set the standards and women live them out, where inequality is systemic, and where women have an investment in their own subordination. This does not mean that every man is self-interested and every woman is altruistic. Were that the case, surely the biological determinists would be right!

There is, moreover, a distinct moral language that is part of this tradition that celebrates women's altruism. It is the language of selflessness and responsibility toward others in which women's very possibilities are framed. It is the discourse of maternalism, which traditionally has been the discourse of devotion and dedication in which women turn away from their own needs. It is also the discourse of maternal destiny in which a real woman is a mother, or one who acts like a mother, or more specifically, like the self-sacrificing, nurturant, and care-taking mothers women are supposed to be. If a woman chooses a different destiny and directs her self elsewhere, she risks placing herself outside female nature and culture. This language also encases women's activities in mothering metaphors, framing many of the creative endeavors that women undertake. Motherhood becomes an inspirational metaphor or symbol for the caring, the nurturing, and the sensitivity that women bring to a world ravaged by conflict.

A body of recent feminist literature, exemplified in the work of Carol Gilligan, has valorized women's altruistic development as the morality of responsibility, emphasizing that this is morality "in a different voice" from men. Formerly a mainstay of separate but equal ideology—as in "vive la différence"—this same discourse is now being transformed by some feminists into an endorsement of women's difference in human and moral development. Yet as Catharine MacKinnon notes,

For women to affirm difference, when difference means dominance, as it does with gender, means to affirm the qualities and characteristics of powerlessness…So I am critical of affirming what we have been, which necessarily is what we have been permitted….Women value care because men have valued us according to the care we give them.[11]

Altruism has been one of the most effective blocks to women's self-awareness and demand for self-determination. It has been an instrument structuring social organization and patterns of relationship in women's lives. The social relations set up by altruism and the giving of self have been among the most powerful forces that bind women to cultural roles and expectations.

The issue is not whether altruism can have any positive content in the lives of women, but rather that we cannot abstract this question from the gender-specific and gender-unequal situation of cultural values and structures in which new reproductive practices are arranged. This is not to claim that voluntary and genuine

magnanimity does not exist among women. It is to say that more is at stake than the womb, the egg, or the child as gift—and the woman as gift giver.

Creating Women in the Image of Victim

Altruism is not crudely obligatory. The more complex issue is what kind of choices women make within the context of a culture and tradition that orients them to give and give of themselves. To paraphrase Marx, women make their own choices, but they often do not make them just as they please. They often do not make them under conditions they create but under constraints they are powerless to change. The social construction of women's altruism should not reduce to creating women in the victim image.

Yet when feminists stress how women's choices are influenced by the social system and how women are channeled into giving, for example, they are reproached for portraying women as passive victims. Lori Andrews in her essay "Alternative Modes of Reproduction" for the Rutgers *Reproductive Laws for the 1990s* project faults feminist critics of the new reproductive technologies for embracing arguments based on "a presumed incapacity of women to make decisions."[12] For such detractors, pressure seems to exist only at the barrel of a gun.[13]

For women gifts play many roles. They generate identity, they protect status, and they often regulate guilt. Women who don't give—time, energy, care, sex—are often exposed to disapproval or penalty. But the more important element here is that on a cultural level women *are expected* to donate themselves in the form of time, energy, and body.

Emile Durkheim, in his classic work *Suicide,* maintained that suicide, seemingly the most individual of acts, must be viewed as the result of certain facts of the social milieu, what he called *courants suicidogènes.* One of these social currents was altruism. Durkheim discussed altruistic suicide as the manifestation of a *conscience collective*—the capacity of group values and forces to supersede the claims

of individuality and, in the case of soldiers and widows, for example, to influence a tendency to suicide. Durkheim observed that altruistic suicide involved a group attachment of great strength, such that individual assertion and fulfillment and even life itself became secondary. The ego was given over to and eventually absorbed in another, having been stripped of its individuality. Altruism resulted when social integration was strong, so binding that the individual became not only absorbed in the group but in the group's expectations.[14]

Durkheim's analysis of social integration is especially applicable to the social construction of women's altruism of which I speak. For women, family expectations often generate this kind of social integration, with family values and inducements overriding a woman's individuality. This is especially evident in the context of family surrogacy arrangements.

Family Ties, Gifts, and the Inducement of Altruism

The potential for women's exploitation is not necessarily less because no money is involved and reproductive arrangements may take place within a family setting. The family has not always been a safe place for women. And there are unique affective "inducements" in familial contexts that do not exist elsewhere. Although there is no "coercion of contract" or "inducement" of money, there could be the coercion of family ties in which having a baby for a sister or another family member may be rationalized as the "greatest gift" one woman can give to another.

Thus we must also examine the power and role of gifts in shaping social life. In *The Gift: Forms and Functions of Exchange in Archaic Society,* Marcel Mauss contends that gifts fulfill certain obligations. These obligations vary, but in all these instances—whether gifts are used to maintain social affection or to promote unity or loyalty within the group—they are experienced as prescriptive and exacting.[15] This is true on a cultural level, as Mauss has pointed out, but it is even more true on a family level, the context most often cited as the desirable site of altruistic reproductive exchanges.

Family opinion may not force a woman, in the sense of being outrightly coercive, to become pregnant for another family member. However, where family integration is strong, the nature of family opinion may be so engulfing that, for all practical purposes, it exacts a reproductive donation from a female source. And representing the surrogate arrangement as a gift holds the woman in tutelage to the norms of family duty, represented as giving to a family member in need.

Within family situations, it may also be considered selfish, uncaring, even dishonorable for a woman to deprive a relative of eggs or her gestating abilities. The category of altruism itself is *broadened* in family contexts to include all sorts of nontraditional reproductive "duties" that would be frowned on if women undertook them for money. Within families, it may be considered selfish for a woman to deprive her husband of children by not allowing the reproductive use of another female family member, especially *because* the arrangements will be kept within the family.

It is also highly likely that those with less power in the family will be expected to be more altruistic. Indeed they may be coerced to be so, as happened to Alejandra Muñoz. Muñoz, a poor, illiterate Mexican woman, was brought across the U.S. border illegally to bear a child for relatives at the urging of many family members. Muñoz was deceived about her role, having been told by family members that when she became pregnant, the embryo would be flushed out and transferred to the womb of her infertile cousin, Nattie. When this did not happen, she vowed to end the pregnancy but was beleaguered and thwarted by family members. Her relatives kept her under house confinement until the delivery. When she fought to keep her child, she was threatened with exposure as an illegal alien.[16]

In 1989, a New Jersey State Task Force on New Reproductive Practices recommended that unpaid surrogate arrangements between friends, relatives, or others be made legally unenforceable. One task force member specifically directed her criticism of noncommercial surrogacy to the family context. Arguing that surrogate arrangements between family members portend the same "disastrous implications" as the Baby M contract, Emily Arnow Alman said that she could foresee the "not-so-bright cousin" being exploited to bear a child for a relative.[17]

We might ask further what is suitable matter for exchange. When we speak of reproductive gifts and donations, but more especially in the case of surrogacy, where the gift and donation is the woman's body and ultimately the child who may be born of such a practice, we put the donation of persons side by side with the exchange of objects and things. The director of the New Jersey task force stated: "The task force feels that the state shouldn't confer any imprimatur of legitimacy on the practice of surrogacy in any form," and that "treating women and children and limiting their liberty by contracts enforceable by the state makes them less than human beings."[18]

Gender-Specific Ethics, Public Policy, and Legislation

While the altruistic woman may be at the center of noncommercial reproductive exchanges, so too is a portrait of science and technology as altruistic. A feature story on the mapping of the human genome in *The Economist* in May 1986 emphasized that "science's reputation—after *Challenger* and Chernobyl—could do with an altruistic megaplan."[19] The new reproductive technologies provide science with one part of this image: *in vitro* fertilization is represented as offering "new hope for the infertile"; surrogacy gives infertile couples the gift of a child; egg donation is helping others to have children. But it is not the technologies that are the sources of these reproductive gifts. It is women, and the historical medicalization of women's bodies in the reproductive context. Women are taken for granted in the name of reproductive research, the advancement of reproductive science, and, of course, the giving of life.

Altruism cannot be separated from the history, the values, and the political structures reinforcing women's reproductive inequality in our society. Questions such as, Who is my stranger? which Titmuss designates as the altruistic question with respect to blood donation, cannot be asked within the context of reproductive donations without asking the prior question of Who is my Samaritan?

Reproductive gift relationships must be seen in their totality, not just as helping someone to have a child. Noncommercial surrogacy cannot be treated as a mere act of altruism, for more is at issue than the ethics of altruism. Any valorizing of altruistic surrogacy and reproductive gift giving for women must be assessed within a context of political inequality, lest it help dignify inequality. Moral meaning and public policy should not be governed by the mere absence of market values. Moral meaning and public policy should be guided by the presence of gender specificity.

What does this mean? For one thing, it means that any assessment of reproductive exchanges, whether they involve commerce or not, takes as its ethical starting point the question of women's status and how the exchange enhances or diminishes gender inequality. Gender-specific ethics devotes primary attention to the consequences to women. It recognizes not only the harm but the devaluation that happens to all women when some are used for reproductive exchanges.

In *Feminism Unmodified: Discourses on Life and Law,* Catharine MacKinnon develops this notion of gender specificity as a foundation for legislation. Gender specificity recognizes "the most sex-differential abuses of women as a gender" and the reality that this is not a mere sex "difference" but "a socially situated subjection of women."[20] It also recognizes that treating women and men as the same in law, as if all things are equal at the starting point, is gender neutrality.

A gender-specific ethics and public policy confronts the degradation of women in the "private" sphere of reproduction and recognizes the gender inequality that exists as a result, for example, of women's expected altruism. Validating altruistic surrogacy on the level of public policy leaves intact the image and

94

reality of a woman as a *reproductive conduit*—someone through whom someone passes. The woman used as a conduit for someone else's procreative purposes, most evident in the case of surrogacy, becomes a mere instrument in reproductive exchanges, an incidental incubator detached from the total fabric of social, affective, and moral meanings associated with procreation. Thus the terminology of "donor" is inaccurate; women are more appropriately "sources" of eggs, wombs, and babies in the context of reproductive exchanges. Further, we are not really talking about "donations" here but about "procurement."

Surrogacy, situated within the larger context of gender inequality, is not simply the commercialization of women and children. On a political level, it reinforces the perception and use of women as a breeder class and reinforces the gender inequality of women as a group. This is not symbolic or intangible but strikes at the core of what a society allows women to be and become. Taking the commerce out of surrogacy but leaving the practice intact on a noncommercial and contractual basis glosses over that essential violation.

Proposals that the law keep clear of reproductive exchanges where no money changes hands are based on gender-neutral assumptions. If the harm of surrogacy, for example, is based only on the commercialization and commodification of reproduction, then the reality that *women* are always used in systems of surrogacy gets no fundamental legal notice. We must note that babies are not always born of surrogate contracts but women are always encumbered.

As a matter of public policy, the violation of a woman's person, dignity, and integrity have received no legal standing in most legislation opposed to surrogacy other than as mere allusion (the New Jersey Task Force recommendations are a notable exception). By not giving the violation of women primary standing in legislation opposing commercial surrogacy, women's systematic inequality is made invisible and kept in place. That inequality can then be romanticized as noble in so-called altruistic arrangements.

Gender-specific ethics and public policy raise serious doubt about the concept and reality of altruism and the ways it is used to dignify women's inequality. The focus on altruism sentimentalizes and thus obscures the ways women are medicalized and devalued by the new reproductive technologies and practices. An uncritical affirmation of reproductive gifts and gift givers—of egg donations, of "special ladies" who serve as so-called surrogate mothers for others who go to such lengths to have their own biological children, and of reproductive technology itself as a great gift to humanity—fails to examine the institutions of reproductive science, technology, and brokering that increasingly structure reproductive exchanges.

Women give their bodies over to painful and invasive IVF treatments when it is often their husbands who are infertile. Women are encouraged to offer their bodies in a myriad of ways so that others may have babies, health, and life. These noble-calling and gift-giving arguments reinforce women as self-sacrificing and ontological donors of wombs and what issues from them.

Altruistic reproductive exchanges leave intact the status of women as a breeder class. Women's bodies are still the raw material for other's needs, desires, and purposes. The normalization of altruistic exchanges may have, in fact, the effect of promoting the view that women *should* engage in reproductive exchanges free of charge. In the surrogate context, altruism reinforces the role of women as *mothers for others* and creates a new version of *relinquishing motherhood*.

The new reproductive altruism is very old in that it depends almost entirely upon women as the givers of these reproductive gifts. This is not to say that women cannot give freely. It is to say that things are not all that simple. It is also to say that this emphasis on giving has become an integral part of the technological propaganda performance. And finally, it is to say that the altruistic pedestal on which women are placed by these reproductive practices is one more way of glorifying women's inequality.

References

[1] Richard M. Titmuss, *The Gift Relationship: From Human Blood to Social Policy* (New York: Pantheon Books, 1971), 73.

[2] Men donate sperm, of course, but sperm donation is simple and short-lived. As one commentator put it, comparing the donation of eggs and wombs to the donation of sperm is like comparing the giving of an eye to the shedding of a tear.

[3] *Matter of Baby M*, 537 A2d 1265 (N.J. 1988).

[4] George J. Annas, "Death Without Dignity for Commercial Surrogacy: The Case of Baby M," *Hastings Center Report* 18:2 (1988), 21-24, at 23.

[5] "Florida Woman to Be Surrogate Mother for Sister," *Greenfield Recorder*, 12 November 1985.

[6] Eric Levin, "Motherly Love Works a Miracle," *People*, 19 October 1987, 43.

[7] Sonia Humphrey, "Why Rent-a-Uterus is a Noble Calling," *The Australian*, 19 December 1986.

[8] Caroline Whitbeck, "The Moral Implications of Regarding Women as People: New Perspectives on Pregnancy and Personhood," in *Abortion and the Status of the Fetus*, William Bondeson et al., eds. (Dordrecht: D. Reidel Publishing Co., 1983), 249.

[9] Beverly Wildung Harrison, *Our Right to Choose: Toward a New Ethic of Abortion* (Boston: Beacon Press, 1983), 39-40.

[10] *Matter of Baby M*, 217 N.J. Super, 313.

[11] Catharine A. MacKinnon, *Feminism Unmodified: Discourses on Life and Law* (Cambridge: Harvard University Press, 1987), 39.

[12] Lori B. Andrews, "Alternative Modes of Reproduction," in *Reproductive Laws for the 1990's: A Briefing Handbook*, Nadine Taub and Sherrill Cohen eds. (Newark, N.J.: The State University, Rutgers, 1989), 269.

[13] This reductionistic view has been challenged by many, including the New Jersey Supreme Court, which reversed the trial court's decision in the Whitehead-Stern surrogacy case. To its credit, the court recognized the complexity of consent in its assessment that for the so-called surrogate, money is an "inducement," as is the "coercion of contract."

[14] Emile Durkheim, *Suicide: A Study in Sociology*, trans. John A. Spaulding and George Simpson (New York: The Free Press, 1951), 217-40.

[15] Marcel Mauss, *The Gift: Forms and Functions of Exchange in Archaic Societies*, trans. Ian Cunnison (New York: W.W. Norton & Co., 1967), see especially ch. 1.

[16] Alejandra Muñoz, press conference on the founding of the National Coalition against Surrogacy, Washington, D.C., August 31, 1987.

[17] Robert Hanley, "Limits on Unpaid Surrogacy Backed," *New York Times*, 12 March 1989.

[18] Hanley, "Limits."

[19] "How to Build a Human Being," *The Economist*, 24 May 1986, 87.

[20] MacKinnon, *Feminism Unmodified*, 40-41.

CASE STUDIES

Selective Termination of Pregnancy

Ms. Q is a thirty-year-old woman who is pregnant for the first time, having spent several years in a local infertility program. She had been treated previously with clomiphene citrate, a fertility drug that increases the incidence of multiple births among those who subsequently become pregnant from 1 percent to 8 percent. Dr. G, the physician who prescribed the drug, had indicated to the patient that its use involved "some risk of multiple gestation."

At nine weeks gestation, ultrasound reveals the presence of triplets. After discussion with her husband, Ms. Q asks Dr. G to terminate two of the fetuses. She says she really wants to have a child and "be a good mother," but doesn't feel capable of caring for more than one child at a time. Even though all three fetuses appear healthy, her preference is to abort all rather than have triplets.

A technique similar to amniocentesis (in which the uterine cavity is entered) has been used to terminate selectively a defective fetus, when a serious fetal anomaly, such as Down syndrome, occurs in a multiple gestation. This technique could be used to terminate two of the triplets, but it entails an incremental risk of miscarriage. Legally, Dr. G could: (1) terminate the pregnancy through a standard method of abortion; (2) selectively terminate the gestation of two of the triplets; (3) refuse to terminate the pregnancy, with transfer of care to a physician who is willing to do so. Should Dr. G acquiesce in Ms. Q's request? Is this request morally valid?

COMMENTARY
by Angela R. Holder

The central question in this case is "What are the limits of a physician's duty to do what the patient wants?" No physician is legally obliged to provide treatment he or she deems unwise, dangerous, or not indicated simply because a patient wants it. Dr. G is no more required to abort one, some, or all of Ms. Q's fetuses than a physician is to give human growth hormone to a normal-sized child whose parents want a basketball star. The legal doctrine of informed consent means that a patient has the right to choose among reasonable medical alternatives; it does not mean that the physician must perform the chosen procedure if he or she thinks it is ill-advised. In case of necessary medical care, the physician may have a duty to refer the patient to someone who will comply with the patient's requests, but the condition of "necessary" would not apply to Ms. Q's situation.

Under normal circumstances, Ms. Q would have no trouble finding a physician who would perform a standard abortion, and, at this stage in the pregnancy, she has every legal right to decide to have one. (Since family finances have apparently presented no impediment to several years of infertility treatment, presumably she can afford this procedure.)

However, the procedure for selective abortion presents about a 45 percent risk of loss of all fetuses. There is also a risk that triplets will be sufficiently premature to have serious difficulties—many are born at 30 weeks' gestation. While some obstetricians might be willing to abort one fetus with a severe disorder, not many would agree to undertake a procedure still in its developmental stage only because a woman decided she was incapable of being a good mother to three children.

Ms. Q had been in the infertility program for several years. That experience surely should have presented opportunity for adequate counseling about the possibility of multiple births, since they cannot be predicted or prevented when fertility drugs are used, and what such a possibility would mean in terms of expenditure of energy and finances. In advance of her pregnancy, Ms. Q should have been able to think through for herself whether she could cope with this eventuality. Did she really want a baby, or was she in this program to satisfy the desires of other people—her husband, for example, or her parents who wanted a grandchild? Does she have any idea how much energy *one* baby requires? Several years of treatment should have provided Ms. Q with better counseling, rather than leaving her in this dilemma, since it was a reasonably foreseeable result of doing what she wanted to do.

Dr. G should attempt to mobilize family and child-care resources (including her husband, who presumably can learn to change diapers as well as she can) and facilitate contacts with mothers of triplets to find out how they cope with three children the same age. Perhaps Ms. Q will discover that the situation is not as difficult as she assumes and continue the pregnancy.

As Oscar Wilde wrote, "In this

Hastings Center Report, February/March 1988

world, there are only two tragedies. One is not getting what one wants, and the other is getting it."

Angela R. Holder *is counsel for medicolegal affairs at Yale University School of Medicine and Yale-New Haven Hospital, and clinical professor of pediatrics (law) at Yale University School of Medicine, New Haven, CT.*

This case study is one of a series demonstrating ethical dilemmas in medicine, science, the social sciences, and public policy. Although the case is based on fact, it has been edited to preserve confidentiality and to emphasize the ethical questions. Readers are invited to submit cases for consideration for this series. Case descriptions should be typed, double-spaced, and should not exceed 750 words.

COMMENTARY

by Mary Sue Henifin

Unlike the "old woman who lived in a shoe, she had so many children she didn't know what to do," Ms. Q has requested an available medical intervention as a solution. The question of whether Dr. G should acquiesce in her request for partial termination of her multiple pregnancy is one that tests the limits of a physician's obligation to respect patient autonomy.

Self-determination and autonomy apply to a patient's "negative" right to refuse as well as her "positive" right to choose among beneficial procedures, yet these principles do not guarantee the right to demand nonbeneficial or harmful treatment. Before providing a requested treatment, the physician should determine whether the patient can define a recognizable problem that medical treatment may benefit. If a requested treatment is beneficial, it should be among the options offered to the patient.

In this case, triplet pregnancy presents many recognizable problems to which partial termination is one solution. Once a benefit can be identified, the pregnant woman is in the best position to weigh the alternatives. Each woman brings her own ethical principles to decisions about her pregnancy based on her own life circumstances.

In an ideal relationship, physician and patient share their mutual knowledge and perspectives until they arrive at an agreed upon course of treatment *prior* to commencing therapy. In the case of inducing ovulation with clomaphene citrate, the discussion should include the eightfold increase in the risks of multiple gestation and accompanying maternal and fetal complications, not merely the vague warning provided by Dr. G that there is "some risk."

What information does Ms. Q need to make an autonomous decision? First, the physician must present those options that can provide benefit and discuss their risks. Three options could benefit Ms. Q: carrying the fetuses to term, complete abortion, or partial termination. A triplet pregnancy is by definition high risk, with stillbirth rates three times higher than for singleton pregnancy and perinatal mortality rates almost twenty times higher. Multiple gestation increases the strain on the pregnant woman's circulatory, renal, and endocrine systems, and she is more likely to suffer from hypertension, anemia, respiratory distress, preeclampsia, placenta previa, and placenta abrupta.

The fetuses are also at increased risk. The majority of multiple births are preterm; and intrauterine growth retardation is the rule, caused by placental insufficiency and crowding. Labor and delivery are particularly risky. Moreover, children born of multiple gestation have higher rates of congenital disabilities and developmental problems after birth.

Finally, multiple gestation severely disrupts the life of the pregnant woman and her family. Bedrest is usually prescribed beginning in the third trimester, and lengthy hospital stays may be required for both mother and newborns. Depression and, in rare cases, suicide have been reported to accompany multiple births as families try to cope with the caretaking, social, and economic pressures. Although support groups exist, such as The Triplet Connection in California and Central New Jersey Mothers of Multiples, reproductive choice may be circumscribed by inadequate access to medical coverage, housing, childcare, and other necessities.

Once risks have been identified, the physician should avoid paternalism and respect the patient's evaluation of her own unique circumstances. Just as it would be unethical for Dr. G to pressure Ms. Q to abort because of the *known* risks of multiple gestation, it would be wrong to try and pressure her to forgo partial termination because of alternative risks. Ms. Q's constitutionally protected right to privacy, including the right to make procreative decisions, supports her right to weigh the available options and their outcomes in selecting a course of treatment. Even when more accurate data are available on the relative risks of multiple gestation, abortion, and partial termination, privacy and procreative liberty must extend to protect the pregnant woman's choices. Dr. G should either respect Ms. Q's decision or transfer her care to a competent physician who is willing to do so.

Ms. Q's case illustrates how the development of new reproductive techniques leads to technological imperatives: If a technology exists it will be used. The critical focus is usually on the morality of "consumer demand." A more direct approach would examine the moral responsibility of researchers who develop and promote new reproductive technologies like selective termination.

Mary Sue Henifin *is a lawyer with the firm of Debevoise & Plimpton, New York, NY, editor of* Women & Health, *and a member of the Reproductive Rights Law and Policy Project at Rutgers University.*

Selective Termination of Pregnancy and Women's Reproductive Autonomy

by Christine Overall

The "demand" for selective termination of pregnancy is a socially constructed response to prior medical interventions in women's reproductive processes, themselves dependent on cultural views of infertility.

The development of techniques for selective termination of pregnancy has added further questions to debates about women's reproductive self-determination. The procedure is performed during the first or second trimester in some instances of multiple pregnancy, either to eliminate a fetus found through prenatal diagnosis to be handicapped or at risk of a disability, or simply to reduce the number of fetuses in the uterus. More than two hundred cases of selective termination are known to have been performed around the world.[1]

Physicians and ethicists have expressed reservations about selective termination, both with respect to its moral justification and to the formation of social policy governing access to and resource allocation for this

Christine Overall *is associate professor of philosophy at Queen's University, Kingston, Ontario, Canada.*

procedure. Selective termination has been viewed as invoking a right to kill a fetus rather than to control one's body, as with abortion,[2] and some commentators have recommended restricting the procedure to pregnancies of three or more[3] and even stipulated a need for national guidelines for the procedure.[4]

Many discussions appear to assume that selective termination is primarily a matter of acting against some fetus(es) on behalf of others. For example, Diana Brahams describes the issue as follows:

Is it ethical and legally appropriate to carry out a selective reduction of pregnancy—that is, to destroy one or more fetuses in order to give the remaining fetus or fetuses a better chance?[5]

However, this construction of the problem is radically incomplete, since it omits attention to the women—their bodies and their lives—who

should be at the center of any discussion of selective termination. When Margaret Somerville, for example, expresses concern about "the right to kill a fetus who is competing with another for space," she neglects to mention that the "space" in question is the pregnant woman's uterus. In fact, selective termination vividly instantiates many of the central ethical and policy concerns that must be raised about the technological manipulation of women's reproductive capacities.

Evans and colleagues state that "the ethical issues [of selective termination] are the same in multiple pregnancies whether the cause is spontaneous conception or infertility treatment" (293). Such a claim is typical of many discussions in contemporary bioethics, which abstract specific moral and social problems from the cultural context that produced them. But the issue of selective termination of pregnancy demonstrates the necessity of examining the social and political environment in which issues in biomedical ethics arise.

Selective termination itself must be understood and evaluated with reference to its own particular context. The apparent need or demand for selective termination in fact is created and elaborated in response to prior technological interventions in women's reproductive processes, themselves the result of prevailing cultural interpretations of infertility.

Hence, it is essential to explore the significance of selective termination for women's reproductive autonomy. The issue acquires added urgency at this point in both Canada and the United States when access to and allocation of funding for abortion are the focus of renewed controversy. Although not precisely the same as abortion, selective termination is similar insofar as in both cases one or more fetuses are destroyed. They differ in that in abortion the pregnancy ends whereas in selective termination, ideally, the pregnancy continues with one or more fetuses still present. I will argue that, provided a permissive abortion policy is justified (that is, a policy that allows abortion until the end of the second trimester), a concern for women's

Hastings Center Report, May/June 1990

reproductive autonomy precludes any general policy restricting access to selective termination of pregnancy, as well as clinical practices that discriminate on nonmedical grounds as to which women will be permitted to choose the procedure or how many fetuses they must retain.

A Technological Fix

In recent discussions of selective termination, women with multiple pregnancies are often represented as demanding the procedure—sometimes by threatening to abort the entire pregnancy if they are not allowed selective termination.[6]

The assumption that individual women "demand" selective termination of pregnancy places all moral responsibility for the procedure on the women themselves. However, neither the multiple pregnancies nor the "demands" for selective termination originated *ex nihilo*. An examination of their sources suggests both that moral responsibility for selective termination cannot rest solely on individual women and that the "demand" for selective termination is not just a straightforward exercise of reproductive freedom.

Deliberate societal and medical responses to the perceived problem of female infertility generate much of the demand for selective termination, which is but one result of a complex system of values and beliefs concerning fertility and infertility, maternity and children. Infertility is not merely a physical condition; it is both interpreted and evaluated within cultural contexts that help to specify the appropriate beliefs about and responses to the condition of being unable to reproduce. According to the prevailing ideology of pronatalism, women must reproduce, men must acquire offspring, and both parents should be biologically related to their offspring. A climate of acquisition and commodification encourages and reinforces the notion of child as possession. Infertility is seen as a problem for which the solution must be acquiring a child of one's own, biologically related to oneself, at almost any emotional, physical, or economic costs.[7]

The recent increase in numbers of multiple pregnancies comes largely from two steps taken in the treatment of infertility. The use of fertility drugs to prod women's bodies into ovulating and producing more than one ovum at a time results in an incidence of multiple gestation ranging from 16 to 39 percent.[8] Gamete intrafallopian transfer (GIFT) using several eggs, and in vitro fertilization (IVF) with subsequent implantation of several embryos in the woman's uterus to increase the likelihood that she will become pregnant may also result in multiple gestation. As Brahams notes, "Pregnancy rate increments are about 8 percent for each pre-embryo replaced in IVF, giving expected pregnancy rates of 8, 16, 24, and 32 percent for 1, 2, 3, and 4 pre-embryos, respectively" (1409). A "try anything" mentality is fostered by the fact that prospective IVF patients are often not adequately informed about the very low clinical success rates ("failure rates" would be a more appropriate term) of the procedure.[9] A case reported by Evans and colleagues dramatically illustrates the potential effects of these treatments: One woman's reproductive history included three cesarean sections, a tubal ligation, a tuboplasty (after which she remained infertile), in vitro fertilization with subsequent implantation of four embryos, selective termination of two of the fetuses, revelation via ultrasound that one of the remaining twins had "severe oligohydramnios and no evidence of a bladder or kidneys," spontaneous miscarriage of the abnormal twin, and intrauterine death of the remaining fetus (291).

In a commentary critical of selective termination, Angela Holder quotes Oscar Wilde's dictum: "In this world, there are only two tragedies. One is not getting what one wants, and the other is getting it" (22). But this begs the question of what is meant by saying that women "want" multiple pregnancy, or "want" selective termination of pregnancy.[10] What factors led these women to take infertility drugs and/or participate in an IVF program? How do they evaluate fertility, pregnancy, motherhood, children? How do they perceive themselves as women, as potential mothers, as infertile, and where do children fit into these visions? To what degree were they adequately informed of the likelihood that they would gestate more than one fetus? Were they provided with adequate support to enable them to clarify their own reasons and goals for seeking reproductive interventions, and to provide assistance throughout the emotionally and physically demanding aspects of the treatment? Barbara Katz Rothman's appraisal of women who abort fetuses with genetic defects has more general applicability:

They are the victims of a social system that fails to take collective responsibility for the needs of its members, and leaves individual women to make impossible choices. We are spared collective responsibility, because we individualize the problem. We make it the woman's own. She "chooses," and so we owe her nothing.[11]

Uncritical use of the claim that certain women "demand" selective termination implies that they are just selfish, unable to extend their caring to more than one or two infants, particularly if one has a disability. But this interpretation appears unjustified. In general, participants in IVF programs are extremely eager for a child. They are encouraged to be self-sacrificing, to be acquiescent in the manipulations the medical system requires their bodies to undergo. As John C. Hobbins notes, these women "have often already volunteered for innovative treatments and may be desperate to try another." The little evidence so far available suggests that if anything these women are, by comparison to their male partners, somewhat passive in regard to the making of reproductive decisions.[12] There is no evidence to suggest that most are not willing to assume the challenges of multiple pregnancy.

An additional cause of multiple pregnancy is the conflicting attitudes toward the embryo and fetus manifested in infertility research and clinical practice. One report suggests that multiple pregnancies resulting from IVF are generated not only because clinicians are driven by the motive to succeed—and implantation of large numbers of embryos appears to offer that prospect—but also because of "intimidation of medical

99

practitioners by critics and authorities who insist that all fertilized eggs or pre-embryos be immediately returned to the patient."[13] Such "intimidation" does not, of course, excuse clinicians who may sacrifice their patients' well-being. Nevertheless, conservative beliefs in the necessity and inevitability of procreation and the sacredness and "personhood" of the embryo may contribute to the production of multiple pregnancies.

Thus, the technological "solutions" to some forms of female infertility create an additional problem of female hyperfertility—to which a further technological "solution" of selective termination is then offered. Women's so-called "demand" for selective termination of pregnancy is not a primordial expression of individual need, but a socially constructed response to prior medical interventions.

The debate over access to selective pregnancy termination exemplifies a classic no-win situation for women, in which medical technology generates a solution to a problem itself generated by medical technology—yet women are regarded as immoral for seeking that solution. While women have been, in part, victimized through the use of reproductive interventions that fail to respect and facilitate their reproductive autonomy, they are nevertheless unjustifiably held responsible for their attempts to cope with the outcomes of these interventions in the forms made available to them. From this perspective, selective termination is not so much an extension of women's reproductive choice as it is the extension of control over women's reproductive capacity—through the use of fertility drugs, GIFT, and IVF as "solutions" to infertility that often result, when successful, in multiple gestations; through the provision of a technology, selective termination, to respond to multiple gestation that may create much of the same ambivalence for women as is generated by abortion; and finally through the imposition of limitations on women's access to the procedure.

In decisions about selective termination, women are not simply feckless, selfish, and irresponsible. Nor are they mere victims of their social conditioning and the machinations of the medical and scientific establishments. But they must make their choices in the face of extensive socialization for maternity, a limited range of options, and sometimes inadequate information about outcomes. When women "demand" selective termination of pregnancy they are attempting to take action in response to a situation not of their own making, in the only way that seems available to them. Hence my argument is not that women are merely helpless victims and therefore must be permitted access to selective termination, but rather that it would be both socially irresponsible and unjust for a health care system that contributes to the generation of problematic multiple pregnancies to withhold access to a potential, if flawed, response to the situation.

Selective Termination and Abortion

There is reason to believe that women's attitudes toward selective termination may be similar to their attitudes toward abortion. Although abortion is a solution to the problem of unwanted pregnancy, and the general availability of abortion accords women significant and essential reproductive freedom, it is often an occasion for ambivalence, and remains, as Caroline Whitbeck has pointed out, a "grim option" for most women.[14] Women who abort are, after all, undergoing a surgical invasion of their bodies, and some may also experience emotional distress. Moreover, for some women the death of the fetus is a source of grief, particularly when the pregnancy is wanted and the abortion is sought because of severe fetal disabilities.[15]

Comparable factors may contribute to women's reservations about selective termination of pregnancy. Those who resort to this procedure surely do not desire the invasion of their uterus, nor do they make it their aim to kill fetuses. In fact, unlike women who request abortions because their pregnancy is unwanted, most of those who seek selective termination are originally pregnant by choice. And as Evans and colleagues note, such pregnancies are "not only wanted but achieved at great psychological and economic cost after a lengthy struggle with infertility" (292).

For such women a procedure that risks the loss of all fetuses as selective termination does, may be especially troubling. The procedure is still experimental, and its short- and long-term outcomes are largely unknown. Richard C. Berkowitz and colleagues suggest that "[a]lthough the risks associated with selective reduction are known, the dearth of experience with the procedure to date makes it impossible to assess their likelihood" (1046). Further, in their report on four cases of selective termination, Evans and coworkers state that:

[A]ny attempt to reduce the number of fetuses [is] experimental and [can] result in miscarriage, and…infection, bleeding, and other unknown risks [are] possible. If successful, the attempt could theoretically damage the remaining fetuses (290).

Note that "success" in the latter case would be seriously limited, assuming that the pregnant woman's goal is to gestate and subsequently deliver one or more healthy infants. In fact, success in this more plausible sense is fairly low.[16] As a consequence, in their study of first trimester selective termination, Berkowitz *et al.* mention the "psychological difficulty of making the decision [to undergo selective termination]," a difficulty partly resulting from "emotional bonding" with the fetuses after repeated ultrasound examinations (1046).

Thus, women undergoing selective termination, like those undergoing abortion, are choosing a grim option; they are ending the existence of one or more fetuses because the alternatives—aborting all the fetuses (and taking the risk that they will never again succeed in becoming pregnant), or attempting to maintain all the fetuses through pregnancy, delivery, and childrearing—are unacceptable, morally, medically, or practically.

The Challenges of Multiple Gestation

Why don't women who seek selective termination simply continue their pregnancies? No matter how much it is taken for granted, the accomplishment of gestating and birthing even

> **Thus, the technological "solutions" to some forms of female infertility create an additional problem of female hyperfertility—to which a further technological "solution" of selective termination is then offered. Women's so-called "demand" for selective termination of pregnancy is not a primordial expression of individual need, but a socially constructed response to prior medical interventions.**

one child is an extraordinary event; perhaps even more praise should be given to the woman who births twins or triplets or quadruplets. Rather than setting policy limits on women who are not able or willing to gestate more than one or two fetuses, we should recognize and understand the extraordinary challenges posed by multiple pregnancies.

There are good consequentialist reasons why a woman might choose to reduce the number of fetuses she carries. For the pregnant woman, continuation of a multiple pregnancy means, Evans notes, "almost certain preterm delivery, prefaced by early and lengthy hospitalization, higher risks of pregnancy-induced hypertension, polyhydramnios, severe anemia, preeclampsia, and postpartum blood transfusions" (292).[17]

The so-called "minor discomforts" of pregnancy are increased in a multiple pregnancy, and women may suffer severe nausea and vomiting or become depressed or anxious. There is also an increased likelihood of cesarean delivery, entailing more pain and a longer recovery time after the birth.[18]

Infants born of multiple pregnancy risk "premature delivery, low infant birthweight, birth defects, and problems of infant immaturity, including physical and mental retardation."[19] Moreover, as Evans and colleagues note, there is a high likelihood that these infants "may...suffer a lengthy, costly process of dying in neonatal intensive care" (295). Thus a woman carrying more than one fetus also faces the possibility of becoming a mother to infants who will be seriously physically impaired or will die.

It is also important to count the social costs of bearing several children simultaneously, where the responsibilities, burdens, and lost opportunities occasioned by child-rearing fall primarily if not exclusively upon the woman rather than upon her male partner (if any) or more equitably upon the society as a whole—particularly when the infants are disabled. A recent article on Canada's first set of "test-tube quintuplets" reported that the babies' mother, Mae Collier, changes diapers fifty times a day, and goes through twelve litres of milk a day and 150 jars of baby food a week. Her husband works full time outside of the home and "spends much of his spare time building the family's new house."[20]

Moreover, while North American culture is strongly pronatalist, it is simultaneously anti-child. One of the most prevalent myths of the West is that North Americans love and spoil their children. A sensitive examination—perhaps from the perspective of a child or a loving parent—of the conditions in which many children grow up puts the lie to this myth.[21] Children are among the most vulnerable victims of poverty and malnutrition. Subjected to physical and sexual abuse, educated in schools that more often aim for custody and confinement than growth and learning, exploited as opportunities for the mass marketing of useless and sometimes dangerous foods and toys, children, the weakest members of our society, are often the least protected. Children are virtually the last social group in North America for whom discrimination and segregation are routinely countenanced. In many residential areas, businesses, restaurants, hotels, and other "public" places, children are not welcome, and except in preschools and nurseries, there is usually little or no accommodation to their physical needs and capacities.

A society that is simultaneously pronatalist but anti-child and only minimally supportive of mothering is unlikely to welcome quintuplets and other multiples—except for their novelty—any more than it welcomes single children. The issue, then, is not just how many fetuses a woman can be required to gestate, but also how many children she can be required to raise, and under what sort of societal conditions.

To this argument it is no adequate rejoinder to say that such women should continue their pregnancies and then surrender some but not all of the infants for adoption by eager childless and infertile couples. It is one thing for a woman to have the choice of making this decision after careful thought and with full support throughout the pregnancy and afterward when the infants have been given up. Such a choice may be hard enough. It would be another matter, however, to advocate a policy that would restrict selective termination in such a way that gestating all the fetuses and surrendering some becomes a woman's only option.

First, the presence of each additional fetus places further demands on the woman's physical and emotional resources; gestating triplets or quadruplets is not just the same as gestating twins. Second, to compel a woman to continue to gestate fetuses she does not want for the sake of others who do is to treat the woman as a mere breeder, a biological machine for the production of new human beings. Finally, it would be callous indeed to ignore the emotional turmoil and pain of the woman who must gestate and deliver a baby only to surrender it to others. In the case of a multiple gestation an added distress would arise because of the necessity of somehow choosing which infant(s) to keep and which to give up.

Within the existing social context, therefore, access to selective termination must be understood as an essential component of women's reproductive rights. But it is important to distinguish between the right to reproduce and the right not to reproduce. Entitlement to access to selective termination, like entitlement to access to abortion, falls within the right not to reproduce.[22]

Entitlement to choose how many fetuses to gestate, and of what sort, is in this context a limited and negative one. If women are entitled to choose to end their pregnancies altogether, then they are also entitled to choose how many fetuses and of what sort they will carry. If it is unjustified to deny a woman access to an abortion of all fetuses in her uterus, then it is also unjustified to deny her access to the termination of some of those fetuses. Furthermore, if abortion is legally permitted in cases where the fetus is seriously handicapped, it is inconsistent to refuse to permit the termination of one handicapped fetus in a multiple pregnancy.

One way of understanding abortion as an exercise of the right not to reproduce is to see it as the premature emptying of the uterus, or the deliberate termination of the fetus's occupancy of the womb. If a woman has an entitlement to an abortion, that is to the emptying of her uterus of all of its occupants, then there is no ground to compel her to maintain all the occupants of her uterus if she chooses to retain only some of them. While the risks of multiple pregnancy for both the fetuses and the pregnant woman increase with the number of fetuses involved, it does not follow that restrictions on selective termination for pregnancies with smaller numbers of fetuses would be justified. Legal or medical policy cannot consistently say, "you may choose whether to be pregnant, that is, whether your uterus shall be occupied, but you may not choose how many shall occupy your uterus."

More generally, if abortion of a healthy singleton pregnancy is permitted for any reason, as a matter of the woman's choice, within the first five months or so of pregnancy, it is inconsistent to refuse to permit the termination of one or more healthy fetuses in a multiple pregnancy. To say otherwise is unjustifiably to accord the fetuses a right to occupancy of the woman's uterus. It is to say that two or more human entities, at an extremely immature stage in their development, have the right to use a human person's body. But no embryo or fetus has a right to the use of a pregnant woman's body—any more than any other human being, at whatever stage of development, has a right to use another's body.[23] The absence of that right is recognized through state-sanctioned access to abortion. Fetuses do not acquire a right, either collectively or individually, to use a woman's uterus simply because there are several of them present simultaneously. Even if a woman is willingly and happily pregnant she does not surrender her entitlement to bodily self-determination, and she does not, specifically, surrender her entitlement to determine how many human entities may occupy her uterus.

Although I defend a social policy that does not set limits on access to selective termination of pregnancy, there can be no denying that the procedure may raise serious moral problems. As some persons with disabilities have pointed out, there is a special moral significance to the termination of a fetus with a disability such as Down syndrome.[24] The use of prenatal diagnosis followed by abortion or selective termination may have eugenic overtones, when the presupposition is that we can ensure only high quality babies will be born, and that "defective" fetuses can be eliminated before birth.[25] The fetus is treated as a product for which "quality control" measures are appropriate. Moreover, as amniocentesis and chorionic villus sampling reveal the sex of offspring, there is also a possibility that selective termination of pregnancy could be used, as abortion already is, to eliminate fetuses of the "wrong" sex—in most cases, that is, those that are female.[26]

These possibilities are distressing and potentially dangerous to disabled persons and to women generally. The way to deal with these and other moral reservations about selective termination is not to prohibit the procedure or to limit access to it on such grounds as fetal disability or fetal sex choice. Instead, part of the answer is to change the conditions that promote large numbers of embryos and fetuses. For example, since as Evans and colleagues astutely note, "[m]any of the currently known instances of grand multiple pregnancies should have never happened" (296), the administration of fertility drugs to induce ovulation can be carefully monitored, and for IVF and GIFT procedures, more use can be made of the natural ovulatory cycle and of cryopreservation of embryos.[27] The number of eggs implanted through GIFT and the number of embryos implanted after IVF can be limited—not by unilateral decision of the physician, but after careful consultation with the woman about the chances of multiple pregnancy and her attitudes toward it.[28] To that end, there is a need for further research on predicting the likelihood

> Fetuses do not acquire a right, either collectively or individually, to use a woman's uterus simply because there are several of them present simultaneously. Even if a woman is willingly and happily pregnant she does not surrender her entitlement to bodily self-determination, and she does not, specifically, surrender her entitlement to determine how many human entities may occupy her uterus.

of multiple pregnancy.[29] And, given the experimental nature of selective termination, genuinely informed choice should be mandatory for prospective patients, who need to know both the short- and long-term risks and outcomes of the procedure. Acquiring this information will necessitate the "long-term follow-up of parents and children...to assess the psychological and physical effects of fetal reduction."[30] By these means the numbers of selective terminations can be reduced, and the women who seek selective termination can be both protected and empowered.

More generally, however, we should carefully reevaluate both the pronatalist ideology and the system of treatments of infertility that constitute the context in which selective termination of pregnancy comes to seem essential. There is also a need to improve social support for parenting, and to transform the conditions that make it difficult or impossible to be the mother of triplets, quadruplets, etc. or of a baby with a severe disability. Only through the provision of committed care for children and support for women's self-determination will genuine reproductive freedom and responsibility be attained.

Acknowledgment

I would like to acknowledge the assistance of Monica Webster, Queen's University Health Sciences Library, in locating resource material for this paper.

References

1. Marie T. Mulcahy, Brian Roberman, and S.E. Reid, "Chorion Biopsy, Cytogenetic Diagnosis, and Selective Termination in a Twin Pregnancy at Risk of Haemophilia" (letter), *The Lancet*, 13 October 1984, 866; "Selective Fetal Reduction" (review article), *The Lancet*, 1 October 1988, 773; Dorothy Lipovenko, "Infertility Technology Forces People to Make Life and Death Choices," *The Globe and Mail*, 21 January 1989, A4.

2. "Multiple Pregnancies Create Moral Dilemma," *Kingston Whig Standard*, 21 January 1989, 3.

3. Mark I. Evans *et al.*, "Selective First-Trimester Termination in Octuplet and Quadruplet Pregnancies: Clinical and Ethical Issues," *Obstetrics and Gynecology* 71:3, pt. 1 (1988), 289-296, at 293; Richard L. Berkowitz *et al.*, "Selective Reduction of Multifetal Pregnancies in the First Trimester," *New England Journal of Medicine* 118:16 (1988), 1043.

4. Lipovenko, "Infertility Technology."

5. Diana Brahams, "Assisted Reproduction and Selective Reduction of Pregnancy," *The Lancet*, 12 December 1987, 1409; cf. John C. Hobbins, "Selective Reduction—A Perinatal Necessity?," *New England Journal of Medicine* 318:16 (1988), 1063; Evans *et al.*, "Selective First-Trimester Termination," 295.

6. One television interviewer who talked to me about this issue described women as "forcing" doctors to provide the procedure! See also "Multiple Pregnancies Create Moral Dilemma"; Angela R. Holder and Mary Sue Henifin, "Selective Termination of Pregnancy," *Hastings Center Report* 18:1 (1988), 21-22.

7. Christine Overall, *Ethics and Human Reproduction: A Feminist Analysis* (Boston: Allen & Unwin, 1987), 139-56.

8. Hobbins, "Selective Reduction," 1062.

9. Gena Corea and Susan Ince, "Report of a Survey of IVF Clinics in the U.S.," in *Made to Order: The Myth of Reproductive and Genetic Progress*, Patricia Spallone and Deborah Lynn Steinberg, eds. (Oxford: Pergamon Press, 1987), 133-45.

10. Compare the ambiguity of the claim "women want it" in connection with in vitro fertilization. See Christine Crowe, "Women Want It: In Vitro Fertilization and Women's Motivations for Participation" in Spallone and Steinberg, *Made to Order*, 84-93.

11. Barbara Katz Rothman, *The Tentative Pregnancy: Prenatal Diagnosis and the Future of Motherhood* (New York: Viking, 1986), 189.

12. Judith Lorber, "In Vitro Fertilization and Gender Politics," in *Embryos, Ethics, and Women's Rights*, Elaine Hoffman Baruch, Amadeo F. D'Adamo, Jr., and Joni Seager, eds. (New York: Haworth Press, 1988), 123-26.

13. "Selective Fetal Reduction," 774

14. Caroline Whitbeck, "The Moral Implications of Regarding Women as People: New Perspectives on Pregnancy and Personhood," in *Abortion and the Status of the Fetus*, William B. Bondeson *et al.*, eds. (Boston: Reidel, 1984), 251-52.

15. Rothman, *The Tentative Pregnancy*, 177-216. She describes abortion in the case of fetal defect as "the chosen tragedy" (180).

16. Evans *et al.* give a success rate of 50% (p. 289), while Berkowitz *et al.* give 66-2/3% (1043). Angela Holder quotes a success rate of 55% (21).

17. Cf. Berkowitz *et al.*, "Selective Reduction," 1045; and Alastair H. MacLennan, "Multiple Gestation: Clinical Characteristics and Management," in *Maternal-Fetal Medicine: Principles and Practice*, Robert K. Creasy and Robert Resnick, eds. (Philadelphia: W.B. Saunders, 2nd ed., 1989), 581-84.

18. Jose C. Scerbo, Powan Rattan, and Joan E. Drukker, "Twins and Other Multiple Gestations," in *High-Risk Pregnancy: A Team Approach*, Robert A. Knuppel and Joan E. Drukker, eds. (Philadelphia: W.B. Saunders, 1986) 347-48, 358; Martin L. Pernoll, Gerda I. Benda, and S. Gorham Babson, *Diagnosis and Management of the Fetus and Neonate at Risk: A Guide for Team Care* (St. Louis: C.V. Mosby, 5th ed., 1986), 192-93.

19. "Selective Fetal Reduction," 773.

20. Victoria Stevens, "Test-Tube Quints Celebrate First Birthday," *The Toronto Star*, 6 February 1989, A7.

21. See Letty Cottin Pogrebin, *Family Politics: Love and Power on an Intimate Frontier* (New York: McGraw-Hill, 1983), 42.

22. Overall, *Ethics and Human Reproduction*, 166-68.

23. Overall, *Ethics and Human Reproduction*, 76-79.

24. Adrienne Asch, "Reproductive Technology and Disability," in *Reproductive Laws for the 1990s*, Sherrill Cohen and Nadine Taub, eds. (Clifton, NJ: Humana Press, 1989), 69-117; Marsha Saxton, "Prenatal Screening and Discriminatory Attitudes About Disability," in *Embryos, Ethics, and Women's Rights*, 217-24.

25. Ruth Hubbard, "Eugenics: New Tools, Old Ideas," in *Embryos, Ethics, and Women's Rights*, 225-35.

26. Cf. Robyn Rowland, "Motherhood, Patriarchal Power, Alienation and the Issue of 'Choice' in Sex Preselection," in *Man-Made Women*, 74-87.

27. Hobbins, "Selective Reduction," 1063; "Selective Fetal Reduction," 773, 774.

28. Brahams, "Assisted Reproduction," 1409.

29. Ian Craft *et al.*, "Multiple Pregnancy, Selective Reduction, and Flexible Treatment" (letter), *The Lancet*, 5 November 1988, 1087.

30. "Selective Fetal Reduction," 775.

Ethics and New Reproductive Technologies: An International Review of Committee Statements

by LeRoy Walters

LeRoy Walters is director of the Center for Bioethics at the Kennedy Institute of Ethics, Georgetown University, Washington, D.C. He is coeditor of the annual *Bibliography of Bioethics* and of an anthology entitled *Contemporary Issues in Bioethics.* He was a consultant to the HEW Ethics Advisory Board (1979) and a member of the American Fertility Society's Ethics Committee (1986).

What factors might account for the extraordinary worldwide interest in the new reproductive technologies during the past decade? The answer must of necessity be impressionistic. First, the reproductive technologies associated with clinical in vitro fertilization (IVF) and the reproductive arrangements that involve a paid surrogate mother are relatively new phenomena. Before 1978 it was unclear whether clinical IVF would be technically feasible. Less than ten years later there are already approximately 4,600 children in the world whose conception was achieved with its aid. Similarly, fee-for-service surrogacy has become a public issue only in the 1980s, especially in the United States, where the Baby M case has galvanized public opinion.

Second, because clinical IVF and surrogate motherhood are predominantly means for overcoming involuntary infertility, they are topics of great interest to the large numbers (perhaps 10 percent) of infertile couples in the world, as well as to anyone considering what he or she *would* do if faced with an infertility problem. Decisions about whether and how to start a family are important elements in the life-plans of many people. The new possibilities for donation of eggs or embryos or for temporary engagement of a gestational mother may also require a rethinking of conventional notions of "family."

A third factor is public concern about future directions in biomedical research. Human embryo research provides, in the eyes of some commentators, an example of a right-to-life issue that involves no conflicts with the rights of pregnant women. The capacity of researchers to culture unattached human embryos in vitro for seven to ten days raises in a new form the question: "What moral obligations, if any, do we have to early human embryos, and why?" In the future, the issue of human embryo research may be increasingly linked with the issues of genetic diagnosis and germ-line approaches to genetic intervention. The 1985 Benda Commission report from the Federal Republic of Germany took precisely this tack, reviewing in vitro fertilization, genetic diagnosis, and gene therapy as, in some sense, parallel phenomena. If a single term were used to characterize the often unarticulated public concern about these potential developments, the word would be "manipulation." Behind this word lie the questions, "Under what circumstances, if any, should scientists create human embryos solely for research purposes?" and "Under what circumstances, if any, should scientists modify human embryos genetically in the effort to convey benefits to embryos and their potential offspring?"

The Practices and the Statements

This essay will focus on three relatively new practices associated with the fertilization of human eggs and/or human procreation: (1) clinical in vitro fertilization; (2) surrogate motherhood; and (3) human embryo research. The first of these practices is a "new reproductive technology" in the strict sense. The second practice, at least in its fee-for-service mode, involves a relatively new reproductive arrangement; the technology usually employed, artificial insemination, is relatively old. The third practice, human embryo research, need not be connected with human reproduction at all; however, it necessarily involves the use of human reproductive cells. A fourth related technology, artificial insemination, is omitted here in the interest of brevity. This exclusion should not cause us to overlook important issues, given the close parallels between artificial insemination and clinical in vitro fertilization.

My approach to discussing the ethics of these three new practices will be to analyze the issues raised and the positions adopted in committee statements on the new reproductive technologies. Since 1979 at least eighty-five committee statements on the new reproductive technologies have been prepared by committees representing at least twenty-five countries. Nineteen statements are from Australia; sixteen from the U.K., and thirteen from the U.S. Eight are from Western Europe, five from the Federal Republic of Germany, and New Zealand produced three. Japan has produced two statements and the German Democratic Republic one; theirs are the only statements from Asia and Eastern Europe that I was able to discover. The Middle East and the continents of Africa and Latin America are not represented.[1]

It would obviously be difficult to analyze all eighty-five statements within the scope of a single essay. I have therefore adopted the simplifying strategy of focusing the analysis only on statements that cover multiple topics in greater depth.[2] For this purpose I have combined series of statements from the same committee into a single composite statement, then set a minimum-length cutoff of fifty text pages for each simple or composite statement.[3] The fifteen statements that fulfill the inclusion criteria for length and coverage of multiple topics are listed in Table 1. These fifteen extended statements represent eight nations: Australia, U.K., U.S., Canada, Federal Republic of Germany, France, The Netherlands, and Spain.

Since the mid-1970s the committee (or commission) mode has emerged as an extremely important method for both ethical analysis and public policy making in the bioethics field. In many cases the committees are officially appointed by governments to help resolve controversial or technically complex issues in a more academic

TABLE 1

THE FIFTEEN EXTENDED COMMITTEE STATEMENTS ON THE NEW REPRODUCTIVE TECHNOLOGIES: 1979-1987

A. U.S., Department of Health, Education and Welfare (HEW), Ethics Advisory Board, *HEW Support of Research Involving Human In Vitro Fertilization and Embryo Transfer* (May 4, 1979)[4]

B. Victoria, Australia, Committee to Consider the Social, Ethical and Legal Issues Arising from In Vitro Fertilization
  1. *Interim Report* (= Waller I) (September 1982)[5]
  2. *Issues Paper on Donor Gametes* (= Waller II) (April 1983)[6]
  3. *Report on Donor Gametes and In Vitro Fertilization* (= Waller III) (April 1983)[7]
  4. *Report on the Disposition of Embryos Produced by In Vitro Fertilization* (= Waller IV) (April 1984)[8]

C. South Australia, *Report of the Working Party on In Vitro Fertilization and Artificial Insemination by Donor* (January 1984)[9]

D. Queensland, Australia, *Report of the Special Committee Appointed by the Queensland Government to Enquire into the Laws Relating to Artificial Insemination, In Vitro Fertilization and Other Related Matters* (= Demack, Queensland) (March 1, 1984)[10]

E. Council for Science and Society (United Kingdom), Working Party, *Human Procreation: Ethical Aspects of the New Techniques* (May 1984)[11]

F. United Kingdom, Department of Health and Social Security, *Report of the Committee of Inquiry into Human Fertilisation and Embryology* (=Warnock, United Kingdom) (July 1984)[12]

G. Tasmania, Australia, Committee to Investigate Artificial Conception and Related Matters
  1. *Interim Report* (= Tasmania I) (December 1984)[13]
  2. *Final Report* (= Tasmania II) (June 1985)[14]

H. Ontario, Law Reform Commission, *Report on Human Artificial Reproduction and Related Matters* (tabled June 13, 1985)[15]

I. Australia, Family Law Council
  1. *Interim Report* (= Family Law Council I) (July 1984)[16]
  2. *Creating Children: A Uniform Approach to the Law and Practice of Reproductive Technology in Australia* (= Family Law Council II) (July 1985)[17]

J. Federal Republic of Germany, Minister for Research and Technology and Justice Minister, Working Group, *In Vitro Fertilization, Genome Analysis, and Gene Therapy* (= Benda, German Federal Republic) (November 1985)[18]

K. Spain, Congress of Deputies, General Secretariat, Special Commission for the Study of Human In Vitro Fertilization and Artificial Insemination, *Report* (April 10, 1986)[19]

L. American Fertility Society, Ethics Committee, *Ethical Considerations of the New Reproductive Technologies* (September 1986)[20]

M. Western Australia, Committee to Enquire into the Social, Legal and Ethical Issues Relating to In Vitro Fertilization and Its Supervision
  1. *Interim Report* (= Western Australia I) (August 1984)[21]
  2. *Report* (= Western Australia II) (October 1986)[22]

N. Netherlands, Health Council, Committee on In Vitro Fertilization and Artificial Insemination by Donor
  1. *Interim Report on In Vitro Fertilization* (= Dutch Health Council I) (October 10, 1984)[23]
  2. *Report on Artificial Reproduction, with Special Reference to In Vitro Fertilization, Artificial Insemination with Donor Sperm, and Surrogate Motherhood* (= Dutch Health Council II) (October 16, 1986)[24]

O. France, National Consultative Committee on Ethics
  1. *Report on Ethical Problems Related to Techniques of Artificial Reproduction* (= National Ethics Committee I) (October 23, 1984)[25]
  2. *Report on Research Involving Human Embryos In Vitro and Their Use for Medical and Scientific Purposes* (= National Ethics Committee II) (December 15, 1986)[26]

mode than the rough-and-tumble of day-to-day politics allows.

Officially appointed committees, in turn, often receive testimony from *other* committees representing various interest groups, as well as from technical experts and laypeople. The committees then typically seek to reach ethical judgments that are both rationally defensible and politically acceptable to large segments of a given society. In other words, publicly appointed committees frequently seek the middle ground on an issue. The committees may or may not recommend formal legislation or regulation as part of the resolution of an issue.

An alternative mode of committee activity is also evident in the discussion of the new reproductive technologies. Professional societies sometimes appoint committees to develop ethical or other standards for the profession. One goal of such private bodies may be to forestall legislation or government regulation by asserting, in effect, that the profession is capable of regulating itself. In other cases, however, professional bodies recommend specific content for legislation or regulation.

As examples of bioethical discussion, committee statements possess certain advantages. In contrast to bills and laws on the new reproductive technologies, these statements have the virtue of allowing scope for the presentation of reasons and arguments. As contrasted with court decisions in this sphere, of which there are few, committee statements can take a general approach to new practices rather than reacting to particular—often tragic—circumstances. In contrast to scholarly or popular articles written by individuals or groups, committee statements build on a process—sometimes a public process—of give-and-take directed toward achieving a consensus document. Disagreements on the issues are often reflected in written dissenting opinions.

Issues in Clinical In Vitro Fertilization

The judgments reached by fifteen committees on several pivotal issues in clinical IVF are summarized in Table 2. Row 1 indicates that an important conclusion has been unanimously reached

in the fifteen extended statements—namely, that a new reproductive technique that has been with us for less than ten years is, in principle, ethically acceptable. Several of the committees received submissions from groups that argued the natural-reproduction-only position. None of the committees finally accepted this anti-IVF view.

Rows 2a and 2b reflect both agreement and disagreement on eligibility for clinical IVF. All fifteen extended committee statements accept the use of this technique for heterosexual couples who have completed the prescribed procedures for matrimony that are required by statute or regulation. In addition, eleven of the fifteen committees expressly include heterosexual couples living together in de facto stable relationships as appropriate candidates for IVF. A minority of committees, five of the fifteen, also regard either single women or members of homosexual couples or both as appropriate candidates for clinical IVF in some circumstances (see the five negative answers in Row 2a).

As Row 2c indicates, all fifteen committee statements restrict clinical IVF to situations where there are "medical" indications for the procedure—usually an infertility problem, but sometimes a concern to avoid transmitting a genetic disease or trait to one's offspring. What the committees are at pains to discourage is the use of clinical IVF for social or eugenic reasons, such as the desire to produce superior babies.

Emerging cryopreservation techniques raise almost unprecedented ethical and public-policy questions. These issues are covered in Row 3. The fifteen extended statements accept the potential clinical usefulness of embryo freezing but clearly regard the technique as experimental. Eleven of the statements approved embryo freezing, one could not achieve resolution on the issue, and one disapproved the practice for the time being (see Row 3a). Two contrasting public policy approaches can be distinguished. The Ethics Committee of the American Fertility Society urged that embryo freezing be performed as a clinical experiment, subject to prior review and approval by

a local institutional review board. In contrast, the French National Ethics Committee stipulated that clinicians should await the results of further laboratory studies, to be concluded in the next two to three years, before employing embryo freezing with patients.

The committees were sure that a time limit should be set for the cryopreservation of frozen embryos but disagreed on the appropriate length of time (see Rows 3c and 3d). All of the groups commenting on the issue agreed that the couple providing the gametes used in IVF have the authority to decide about the disposal of the embryos, but several of the committees argued that the frozen embryos should not be regarded as their *property*, in the strict sense of the word (see Row 3e). An alternative to embryo freezing, namely, egg freezing, was discussed by nine committees (see Row 3b). If this new technique is demonstrated to be safe and effective, it may in the future be regarded as the preferred cryopreservation approach because it involves gametes rather than embryos.

Rows 4a to 4h summarize a series of questions surrounding the donation or sale of human eggs or embryos. The number of rows in this section alone attests to the possible complications of third-party involvement. Egg donation in conjunction with clinical IVF seems closely analogous to semen donation in connection with artificial insemination by donor (AID). Perhaps in part for this reason, twelve of the fifteen extended committee statements found egg donation to be ethically acceptable without qualification. A thirteenth approved egg donation in rare circumstances. Only the 1979 HEW Ethics Advisory Board Report flatly opposed donation of any kind (see Row 4d).

Embryo donation is somewhat more complicated than egg donation because there is no direct genetic link between the embryo and the future rearing parents—although there will be a gestational link. Several of the fifteen extended committee statements reflect a more cautious approach to embryo donation than to egg donation, as Row 4e indicates. Nine of the fifteen statements explicitly approved embryo donation without qualification, two approved the practice in rare cases, two opposed the practice in principle, and one opposed the practice until juridical rules can be drawn up to regulate it.

Generally, the committees agreed that donation should be genuine donation rather than sale, but some drew fine distinctions between reimbursement of donor expenses, payment for "time and inconvenience," and reimbursement for "discomfort." On the question of donor anonymity, the committees disagreed. Some committees wanted to allow patients to choose their own donors, such as siblings or close friends, where anonymity would obviously be impossible. The Benda Commission adopted a unique position on this question, arguing that the offspring of IVF must be permitted access to the name and address of the donor when they attain the age of seventeen (see Rows 4a and 4g in Column J). This policy parallels the general West German policy of allowing adopted children to learn the identities of their genetic parents when the children become adults. The Tasmanian committee recommended a similar policy for clinical IVF but would require the consent of the donor(s) before identifying information could be released.

Issues in Surrogate Motherhood

In contrast to the strong support for clinical IVF and its variations, there is strong opposition to surrogate motherhood in the fifteen extended committee statements. As Table 3 indicates, eleven of the fifteen statements found surrogate motherhood arrangements with payment of a fee to the surrogate to be ethically unacceptable.

Only the Ontario Law Reform Commission statement, the Report of the American Fertility Society Ethics Committee, and the Dutch Health Council committee found fee-based surrogacy to be ethically acceptable (see the first row of Table 3). All three committees that adopted the minority position required medical reasons for surrogate motherhood arrangements and specifically rejected surrogacy for reasons of convenience. The three committees also advocated stricter oversight measures than currently exist in the United States. The Ethics Committee of the American Fertility Society argued that not enough reliable data about surrogate motherhood arrangements exist and that, therefore, if surrogate motherhood is practiced, it should be practiced only as a clinical experiment. This stipulation means that surrogate motherhood should be offered only according to a research protocol that has had prior approval by a local IRB or ethics committee. The American Fertility Society committee also urged surrogate motherhood clinics to publish data about the process and the outcome of surrogate motherhood arrangements, so that the professions and the public will have a firmer basis for evaluating the practice.

The Ontario Law Reform Commission took a rather different tack. It advocated the practice of surrogate motherhood only with the prior and continuing involvement of a family law court. In its view, the court should supervise the screening and counseling of both the surrogate and the commissioning parents. It should also assist in drawing up the contract and supervise the setting of a fee for the surrogate. Finally, the court would ensure that the contract would be enforced. The Canadian effort clearly means to take the practice of surrogate motherhood out of the commercial sphere and to have the courts involved in a prior and ongoing way. Whether the court system would be equipped to handle a heavy surrogate motherhood caseload, the commission does not say.

The Dutch Health Council proposed a third oversight mechanism, the appointment of a special noncommercial government-supervised body. The role of this body would resemble that of a traditional adoption agency: it would help to find suitable surrogate mothers and would then oversee all arrangements, including the payment of appropriate fees. A unique feature of this proposed system is that it provides each surrogate mother a three-month grace period after the birth of the infant in which she can decide to keep the infant as her own.

The opposition to surrogate motherhood in the fifteen extended committee statements is reduced only slightly when the payment of a fee is removed from the arrangement. The working party of the British Council for Science and Society approved nonfee-based surrogacy but disapproved fee-based surrogacy. Thus, a minority of four committees approved the noncommercial form of surrogacy while ten remained opposed. Six of the ten statements opposing both forms of surrogacy originated in Australia.

Issues in Human Embryo Research

The first major decision to be made about research on early human embryos, or preimplantation embryos, is whether such research is ethically acceptable under any circumstances. Four extended committee statements answered this question in the negative, as Row 1 in Table 4 indicates. The four committees that said a categorical no to human embryo research were all Australian. The remaining eleven committee statements approved at least some kinds of research with early embryos.

The proponents of human embryo research fall into two groups. The first and larger group allows for research only on embryos that are left over from the clinical context. Six committee statements adopted this position—those from Victoria, Australia, West Germany, Spain, Western Australia, The Netherlands, and France. (See the yes/no pattern in Rows 2a and 2b of Table 4.) The five remaining committee statements from Great Britain, Canada, and the United States would permit the deliberate creation of embryos through IVF for research purposes. On this issue one can, I think, distinguish between a Western European and liberal Australian viewpoint, on the one hand, and an Anglo-American viewpoint on the other.

There are major differences in the committees' views on the appropriate duration of embryo culture for research purposes (see rows 3a and 3b in Table 4). The majority view clearly favors fourteen days, but the French committee adopted a seven-day limit, while the West German commission would permit research only through the first cleavages. When specific research procedures were discussed, special concern was expressed about several procedures: interspecies fertilization or fusion, genetic alteration of

TABLE 2 ISSUES IN CLINICAL IN VITRO FERTILIZATION

	A HEW Ethics Advisory Board 1979	B Waller I-IV Victoria 1982-84	C South Australia 1984	D Demack, Queensland 1984	E Council for Science and Society U.K. 1984	F Warnock, United Kingdom 1984	G Tasmania I-II 1984-85	H Ontario Law Reform Commission 1985	I Australia, Family Law Council I-II 1984-85
1. Acceptability in principle	yes	yes	yes	yes	yes	yes	yes	yes	yes
2. Eligibility and counseling requirements (recipients)									
a. Couples only	yes	yes	yes	yes	no	yes	yes	no	yes
b. Marriage required	yes	(yes)	(no)	no[3]	no	no	no	no	NR
c. "Medical" grounds only	(yes)	yes	yes	yes	(yes)	(yes)	(yes)	(yes)	(yes)
d. Counseling required	—	yes	yes	yes	yes	yes	yes	—	yes
3. Freezing or disposal									
a. Freezing of embryos permissible	—	yes	yes	yes	yes	yes[4]	yes	yes	—
b. Freezing of eggs permissible	—	yes[1]	yes[1]	—	yes[1]	yes[1]	yes[1]	(yes)	—
c. Time limit on storage of embryos	—	yes	yes	yes	—	yes	yes[6]	yes	—
d. Duration of storage time permitted	—	5 yrs.	10 yrs.	2 yrs.	—	10 yrs.	—[6]	10 yrs	—
e. Disposal of embryos permitted	—	yes	yes	yes	(yes)	yes	yes	yes	—
4. Third-party involvement (donation)									
a. Acceptability in principle	no	yes	yes	yes	yes	yes	yes	yes	yes
b. Donor screening required	—	yes	yes	yes	yes	yes	yes	(yes)[9]	yes
c. Counseling of donors required	—	yes	yes	yes	—	yes	yes	—	yes
d. Donation of eggs permissible	no	yes	yes	yes	yes	yes	yes[7]	yes	yes
e. Donation of embryos permissible	no	yes	no	yes	yes	yes	yes[7]	yes	(yes)
f. Limit on number of donations	—	—	yes	—	—	yes	yes	(yes)[9]	—
g. Anonymity required	—	no	yes	no	yes	yes[5]	no	(yes)	no[11]
h. Payment permissible	—	no[2]	(no)	no	no	no[2]	no[8]	no[10]	—

TABLE 3 ISSUES IN SURROGATE MOTHERHOOD

	A HEW Ethics Advisory Board 1979	B Waller I-IV Victoria 1982-84	C South Australia 1984	D Demack, Queensland 1984	E Council for Science and Society U.K. 1984	F Warnock, United Kingdom 1984	G Tasmania I-II 1984-85	H Ontario Law Reform Commission 1985	I Australia, Family Law Council I-II 1984-85
With Payment of a Fee Acceptability in principle	(no)	no	no	no	no[2]	no	no[4]	yes[5]	no
Without Payment of a Fee Acceptability in principle	(no)	no[1]	no	no	yes[5]	no	no[4]	yes[5]	no

TABLE 4 ISSUES IN HUMAN EMBRYO RESEARCH

1. Acceptability in principle	yes	yes	no	no	yes	yes	no[1]	yes	no
2. Source of embryos									
a. Unneeded embryos from the clinic	—	yes	—	—	yes	yes	—	yes	no[5]
b. Embryos created for research purposes	—	no	—	—	(yes)	yes	—	yes	no
3. Time limit on duration of embryo culture									
a. Time limit set	yes	yes	—	—	yes	yes	—	yes	—
b. Duration, in days	14 days	14 days	—	—	2 weeks	14 days	—	14 days[2]	—

( ) = implicitly   NR = not resolved   — = not discussed

J Benda, German Federal Republic 1985	K Spain, Special Commission 1986	L American Fertility Society 1986	M Western Australia I-II 1984-86	N Dutch Health Council I-II 1984-86	O National Ethics Committee I-II, France 1984-86
yes	yes	yes	yes	yes	yes
yes	no	no	yes	no[23]	yes
no	no	no	no	no	no
yes	yes	(yes)	yes	yes	yes
yes	yes	—	yes	yes	yes
yes	yes	yes[17]	NR[21]	yes[24]	no[26]
—	no[15]	yes[1]	no[15]	—	—
yes	yes	yes	—	yes	yes
2 yrs	5 yrs.	variable[18]	—	1 yr.[25]	1 yr.[27]
yes[12]	—	yes	yes	yes	yes[28]
yes[13]	yes	yes	yes	yes	no[29]
yes	yes	yes	yes	yes	—
—	(yes)	—	yes	—	—
yes[13]	yes	yes	yes	yes	—
yes[14]	yes	yes	yes[22]	yes	no[29]
yes	yes	no[19]	—	yes	—
no	yes	no	yes	yes	—
(no)	no[16]	no[20]	—	no	no

[1] If the technology improves.
[2] Reimbursement of expenses only.
[3] Preference may be given to legally married couples.
[4] As an experimental technique.
[5] As a general rule.
[6] All frozen embryos to be thawed and transferred before another laparoscopic procedure is performed.
[7] Child born after donation to have access to identifying information about donor(s), upon child's turning 18, if donor or donors consent.
[8] Only for "bona fide medical expenses."
[9] Matter to be regulated by professional standards.
[10] For "reasonable expenses," based on "time and inconvenience," but not on "discomfort."
[11] But gamete donors should not be related to recipient couples.
[12] If pregnancy becomes infeasible for the couple that provided the gametes.
[13] In rare circumstances, and only with the possibility of the child's learning the identity of the donor when the child turns 17.
[14] Only if necessary to preserve the lives of "surplus" embryos.
[15] Not until the technique is demonstrated to be feasible.
[16] But payment for loss of income and for transportation expenses is permitted.
[17] As a clinical experiment.
[18] As long as the normal reproductive capability of the egg provider continues.
[19] Because donation of eggs is a self-limiting procedure.
[20] Only "reimbursement for expenses and inconvenience associated with the donation."
[21] Insufficient data exist to substantiate a definitive recommendation.
[22] But only in rare cases; practice "should not normally be permitted."
[23] IVF for an infertile woman without a male partner is "acceptable in certain circumstances."
[24] Provided that the practice is properly regulated.
[25] Unless the couple requests an extension.
[26] Not until an assessment of research work on the freezing of embryos can be carried out, within 2-3 years.
[27] Except for medical reasons, and with the approval of an ethics committee.
[28] As the lesser evil.
[29] Not until juridical rules have been drawn up to regulate the practice.

J Benda, German Federal Republic 1985	K Spain, Special Commission 1986	L American Fertility Society 1986	M Western Australia I-II 1984-86	N Dutch Health Council I-II 1984-86	O National Ethics Committee I-II, France 1984-86
no	no	yes[6]	no[7]	yes[8]	no
no	no	yes[6]	no[7]	yes[8]	no
yes	yes[5]	yes[6]	yes	yes[6,7]	yes[8]
yes	yes[5]	yes	yes	yes[7]	yes[8]
no	no	yes	no	no	no
yes[4]	yes	yes	yes	yes	yes
—[4]	14 days	14 days	14 days	14 days	7 days

[1] Not "at present."
[2] However, the practice should not be outlawed.
[3] "In very exceptional circumstances," with the assistance of non-profit adoption agencies; not "for purposes of convenience."
[4] But this prohibition should be reviewed in 5 years.
[5] Provided that a court gives prior approval for all payments, as well as for all other terms of the agreement.
[6] As a clinical experiment.
[7] Not at this time.
[8] A non-commercial government-supervised body would help find the suitable surrogate mothers and supervise all arrangements.

[1] But a National Bio-Technology Committee should periodically review current community attitudes on the subject.
[2] Subject to alteration if circumstances warrant.
[3] Majority opinion.
[4] Through the first cleavages.
[5] But only with embryos that are nonviable and are not implantable, i.e., that are anomalous or biologically disturbed
[6] This report employs the term "pre-embryo" for the conceptus during the first 14 days after fertilization.
[7] "By way of exception."
[8] But only after approval of the research project by the National Ethics Committee and only under its supervision.

embryos, cloning, and gestation in a nonhuman environment.

The Contribution of Committees

As a former consultant and committee member, I am perhaps unduly impressed with the value of committee statements. However, the foregoing analysis has made clear that, quantitatively at least, committee statements represent a substantial contribution to the bioethics literature on the new reproductive technologies. One can, in fact, trace a kind of evolution in international ethical reflection on these technologies.

Periodic committee statements and reports may emerge as the preferred mode of public oversight and social control in at least selected areas of biology and medicine. Because biomedical technology is so dynamic, specific statutes and regulations run the risk of instant obsolescence. Litigation is likely to lag behind technological innovation by at least several years. In contrast, properly structured committees can undertake necessary research, receive public input, perform in-depth analyses, and indicate to policy makers and the public areas requiring special attention. Committees, commissions, and boards will surely not replace the essential functions played by legislatures, executive agencies, and the courts. At their best, however, committees can provide the factual and analytical basis for enlightened public policy making. ■

Acknowledgments

I acknowledge with gratitude the assistance of the following persons in the acquisition of committee statements: in Australia, Jacqueline Anstead, J.F. Corrie, Helga Kuhse, Helen L'Orange, Russell Scott, and Louis Waller; in New Zealand, Graham Duncan and Margaret Nixon; in The Netherlands, Henk Rigter and J.F. Beernink; in Spain, Francisco Abel; in Norway, Rune Dyve; in Scotland, Deborah Adams; in Ireland, Robert Harrison; at the Council of Europe in Strasbourg, Elisabeth Rohmer; at the British Embassy in Washington, D.C., Margot Bellman; at the Dutch Embassy in Washington, D.C., Theo Evers; at the Office of Technology Assessment, Timothy Condon; at the Library of Congress, Irene Smith-Coleman; at the National Institutes of Health, John Fletcher; in New York State, Tracy Miller; and at the Kennedy Institute of Ethics, Mary Coutts,

Rihito Kimura, Patricia McCarrick, Sue Meinke, Hans-Martin Sass, and Warren Reich. I also thank Lori Andrews, Robert Cook-Deegan, Bernard Dickens, John Fletcher, Howard Jones, John Robertson, Russell Scott, and Gladys White for their helpful comments on earlier drafts. Finally, I thank Michael Stanley for his excellent assistance in the manuscript preparation. This work was supported in part by a grant from the Joseph P. Kennedy, Jr. Foundation.

References

[1] The remaining countries or organizations are: Canada, France, The Netherlands, Sweden, Switzerland, and the World Medical Association, which produced 2 statements each; the Catholic Church, Denmark, Ireland, Norway, Spain, and the Third World Congress on IVF and ET, each produced 1 statement. This total of eighty-five does not include many of the unpublished committee statements submitted as testimony or evidence to such government-appointed bodies as the HEW Ethics Advisory Board in the United States, the Warnock committee in the United Kingdom, and the Waller committee in Victoria, Australia. If these statements were added to the eighty-five, the total number of committee statements worldwide from 1979 through 1987 would probably increase to at least 200.

[2] At least two of the three topics discussed in this essay must be covered in the statement.

[3] The fifty-page minimum was chosen before the publication of the *Vatican Instruction* of March 1987 and was not selected to exclude this statement.

[4] 2 vols. Washington, D.C.: U.S. Department of Health, Education, and Welfare, May 4, 1979. Chairman: James C. Gaither.

[5] Victoria, Australia: Unpublished document, September, 1982. Chairman: Louis Waller.

[6] *Issues Paper on Donor Gametes in IVF.* Victoria: Unpublished document, April 1983. Chairman: Louis Waller.

[7] Victoria, Australia: Unpublished document, August 1983. Chairman: Louis Waller.

[8] Melbourne: F.D. Atkinson Government Printer, August 1984. Chairman: Louis Waller.

[9] Adelaide: South Australian Health Commission, January 1984. Chairpersons: Aileen F. Connon and Philippa Kelly.

[10] 2 vols. Queensland: Unpublished document presented to the Minister for Justice and Attorney-General, March 1, 1984. Chairman: Mr. Justice Demack.

[11] New York: Oxford University Press, 1984. Chairman: G.R. Dunstan.

[12] London: Her Majesty's Stationery Office, July 1984. Cmnd. 9314. Chairman: Dame Mary Warnock.

[13] Hobart, Tasmania, Australia: Director-General of Health Services, December 1984. Chairman: Don Chalmers.

[14] Hobart, Tasmania, Australia: Director-General of Health Services, June 1985. Chairman: Don Chalmers.

[15] 2 vols. Toronto, Ontario: Ministry of the Attorney General, 1985. Chairman: James R. Breithaupt.

[16] Melbourne: Family Law Council, July 1984. Chairman: Mr. Justice Asche.

[17] Canberra: Attorney General's Department, Australian Government Publishing Service, July 1985. Chairman: Mr. Justice Asche.

[18] *Bericht der Arbeitsgruppe: In-vitro-Fertilisation, Genomanalyse und Gentherapie.* Bonn: Bundesminister der Justiz und Bundesminister fur Forschung und Technologie, 1985. Chairman, Mr. Justice Ernst Benda.

[19] Congress de los Diputados, Secretaría General, Comisión Especial de Estudio de la Fecundació "In Vitro" y la Inseminación Artificial Humanas. *Informe.* Madrid: Congreso de los Diputados, Secretari General, approved April 10, 1986. Chairman: Marcelo Palacios.

[20] *Fertility and Sterility* 46(3, Supplement 1): i-94S, September 1986.

[21] Perth, Western Australia: Minister for Health, August 16, 1984. Chairman: Robert Meadows.

[22] Perth, Western Australia: Minister for Health, October 1986. Chairman: C.A. Michael.

[23] Gezondheidsraad, de Commissie IVF/KID. *Interimadvies inzake In Vitro Fertilisatie.* 's-Gravenhage: Gezondheidsraad, October 10, 1984. Chairman: S.A. de Lange.

[24] Gezondheidsraad, de Commisie IVF/KID. *Advies inzake Kunstmatige Voortplanting, in het bijzonder In Vitro Fertilisatie, Kunstmatige Inseminatie met Donorzaad en Draagmoederschap.* 's-Gravenhage: Gezondheidsraad, October 16, 1986. Chairman: S.A. de Lange.

[25] Comité Consultatif National d'Ethique pour les Sciences de la Vie et de la Santé. *Avis sur les Problemes Ethiques Nes des Techniques de Reproduction Artificielle.* Paris: Le Comité October 23, 1984. Chairman: Jean Bernard.

[26] Comité Consultatif National d'Ethique pour les Sciences de la Vie et de la Santé. *Avis relatif aux Recherches sur les Embryons Humains In Vitro et a Leur Utilisation a des Fins Medicales et Scientifiques.* Paris: Le Comité, December 15, 1986. Chairman: Jean Bernard.

Reproductive Technology

In France,
Debate and Indecision

by Anne Fagot-Largeault

Anne Fagot-Largeault is professor of philosophy and consultant in psychiatry at the University of Paris XII.

An estimated 16,000 French people owe their existence to artificial insemination by donor, although most of them don't know this. In recent years the rate of AID births has remained at about 1,700 children per year or one out of 450 births. Over 300 IVF children were born from 1982 to 1985, and their number is increasing steadily; most will presumably be told something about their test-tube origin because of the glory currently attached to being an IVF baby. Ninety percent of AID customers order their sperm from one of France's twenty CECOS or sperm banks such as Bicêtre, which was the first, created in 1973. These are semi-public institutions, which deal only with stable heterosexual couples where the male is infertile or is at risk of transmitting a hereditary disease. Other, less influential institutions, some of them private, and some private practitioners have more flexible rules and less open policies of insemination.

IVF was first promoted by a few teaching hospitals, such as Beclère, Sèvres-Necker, with research teams backed by the National Institute of Health and Medical Research (INSERM). Recently, however, IVF centers have mushroomed in public and private settings. There were over a hundred in 1986, though the Ministry of Health reckoned that the maximum needed were forty. Only the large and experienced centers have an acceptable success rate and substantial waiting lists (up to four years), as well as programs of embryo or egg donation. IVF is theoretically accessible to couples facing a problem of female (fallopian tube) infertility, but the tendency is to extend availability to couples with low sperm count or infertility from unknown causes.

One peculiarity of the French situation concerns financing. Due to a law passed in 1978 which had among its objectives encouraging people to have children, the cost of infertility diagnosis and treatment is entirely covered by the medicare system (*sécurité sociale*). This is a glaring exception to the overall principle of 80 percent coverage for health expenses under the national health insurance plan, with the beneficiary's share of 20 percent often, but optionally, covered by personal health insurance. This total coverage, together with the decriminalization of abortion (1975), which is partially paid for by the medicare system, tends to make procreative autonomy a basic right presumably implied by the constitutional right to health.

This development does not please everyone. Some people object on religious grounds, others for ecological reasons (because artificial procreation is not natural), and a few economists and public health specialists recently pointed out that for society the financial burden of new procreation techniques outweighs their feeble beneficial impact on the birth rate. (In 1986 the average cost of "manufacturing" an IVF child was estimated to be $50,000; an AID child costs about $5,000.) These critics find it paradoxical to support the "artificial" child more than the natural or the adopted one, and absurd to give preference to treating infertility, rather than investigating and preventing sexually transmitted diseases, which are the main causes of infertility. Thus, quite apart from moral reservations, there appears to be an inclination to curb procreative demands by bringing artificial technologies back within the common law, and/or limiting the number of free attempted inseminations or embryo implants.

A second feature of the French landscape concerns public attitudes. Artificial reproduction techniques have been, and still are, under the control of a medical profession endowed with a strong tradition of secrecy and moral autonomy, in a society extremely tolerant of the individual's right to procreate. The recourse to marginal means of procreation is deemed a matter of privacy and personal choice. A 1985 opinion poll showed that most people were far more willing to let others use AID or the new artificial reproduction techniques than to use them themselves, and that they widely preferred regulation by physicians (or medical ethics committees) than by law.

The ethics of AID is essentially defined by the physicians running the CECOS. A large majority of the public approves of their restrictive rules but does not object to other physicians following more relaxed ethical criteria (such as using paid donors, or inseminating unmarried people, or advocating surrogate motherhood, as in one Marseille center). The French Medical Association (*Ordre des Médecins*) has issued recommendations, and reminded practitioners that they are responsible for their choices and should act according to their conscience. This is compatible with the fact that various IVF centers have different ethical codes and may or may not choose to consult with a local IRB where there is one. (For example, in 1985 the IRB in Bicêtre issued recommendations on the use of frozen embryos and on egg donation at the request of the Beclère IVF center.)

Public and Professional Debates

Only in the early eighties did it become clear that important social values were at stake, and that doctors alone could no longer define what should or should not be done. Family associations started discussing the changes that had occurred in the structure of the family. Some within the medical and scientific community asked for systematic ethical review and legislative action concerning the new reproductive technologies. A large public became aware of situations hitherto overlooked because they were kept confidential.

In February 1982, Amandine, the first French test-tube baby, was born. The little girl appeared nightly on the television news. From 1983 to 1985 the media reported other striking events: a woman in Nîmes bore a child for her twin sister; a widow sued the CECOS to recover her dead husband's frozen sperm with a view to *postmortem* insemination, and won; an association recruiting surrogate mothers was barred in Strasbourg, etc. Patricia, the first paid surrogate mother in France, became a star and declared how happy she was to have discovered her own generosity. In the spring of 1986 the first two test-tube babies created from *frozen* embryos were born in France, and exhibited on TV. Also in 1986 one of Amandine's two "scientific fathers" spoke out forcefully against selectively implanting embryos on the basis of their gender. The procreation show culminated in 1986 with an informative series of four broadcasts entitled "the wizards of life" (*les sorciers de la vie*).

During the same years a variety of professionals from the biological and social sciences, law, philosophy, and religion engaged in transdisciplinary discussions and reflection, encouraged by the government. In January 1985, a major symposium in Paris on "Genetics, Procreation and Law," initiated by the ministers of Justice, Health, and Research, publicly debated whether legislators should intervene, for example, to prohibit surrogacy arrangements, or to make the presumption of paternity irrebuttable for the social fathers of children conceived from donated sperm. Later the same year, an international conference in Paris compared the legislation relating to human artificial procreation in various countries.

Despite a wide diversity of opinions, French legal specialists have tended to counsel against a rush to alter the parentage law. They have argued that a certain amount of legal insecurity for the parents of "artificial" children is not necessarily a bad thing; and that the current law, although ignoring artificial reproduction altogether, can accommodate some of the problematic cases. In particular, the Kantian doctrine that the human person has dignity, and does not have a price, and that no part of a person can be sold, bought, or traded, is a fundamental principle in the French judicial tradition. This makes surrogacy arrangements void, which discourages many lawyers from defending them. The legal status of human embryos is not clear, however, and this, together with the complexity of parental links implied by the use of donated gametes, embryos, or hired wombs, confuses the legal criteria now in effect.

The National Committee

The National Consultative Ethics Committee (CCNE) was created in 1983. It established several working groups, which have issued Reports and Recommendations (*Avis*) on problems related to IVF and human reproduction. The 1984 *Avis* on the use of fetal tissue for therapeutic, diagnostic, or research purposes, expressly stated that the human embryo or fetus, as a "potential human person" from the time of conception, should be treated with respect, and never as merely material for the laboratory or trade. Another 1984 *Avis* on the ethical problems arising from artificial reproduction techniques acknowledged that infertile couples had "a right to be treated," and noted that the French tradition had been to interfere as little as possible with the freedom to procreate. However, due to passionate opposition between those who wanted to stop all treatment and those who would be satisfied with minimal controls, the report recommended that a large national consultation should be organized, to educate the people and discover how the French community at large wanted to proceed.

In response to this suggestion, in 1985 Prime Minister Laurent Fabius entrusted a group of five with the task of gathering information about the feelings and opinions of experts and the general public on artificial procreation and the status of embryos. After a huge amount of work, the group issued a preliminary report in 1986, which examined the state of the new techniques within the country, and the ways they are perceived by various scientific, religious, and cultural groups, by the press, by professional associations, and by the public. The report called for a more systematic consultation, to be conducted by sociologists using a comprehensive questionnaire, but this was not pursued, apparently for financial reasons.

At the end of 1986, the CCNE published a long Report and Recommendations on the ethical acceptability of research on IVF and human embryos. This states (1) that the creation of embryos is legitimate only in the context of a "parental project"; (2) that in vitro fertilization should not take place for the specific purpose of research even with the consent of both gamete producers; and (3) that IVF should be carried out only in centers approved by public authorities. However the practice of fertilizing more eggs than the number of embryos strictly intended for transfer, and freezing the surplus embryos, is accepted as a "least evil," and the problem of how surplus embryos may be used is faced openly, although the members of the CCNE did not reach consensus on the issue. Donating embryos for the purpose of research is deemed tolerable to the extent that the research is strictly regulated.

The main feature of the report that the press seized on calls for a three-year moratorium on any research aimed at making a genetic diagnosis prior to implantation. The CCNE's rationale is that the moral cost of getting a standard prenatal diagnosis and eventually deciding to have an abortion is more acceptable than the risk of eugenic practices, should a genetic sorting of embryos become routinely available. An "ethical report," which accompanies the main document, explains that it is important for our culture to maintain that a person is not an object that can be programmed, and that the element of chance in the "genetic lottery" should be respected as constituting the biological basis of individuality and liberty.

Thus at this point there are con-

trasting attitudes in France. On the one hand there is a growing concern within the community as reflected in a fair amount of psychological, sociological, and legal research, and a set of ethical recommendations from the National Ethics Committee. On the other hand, neither the Government nor Parliament has called for a systematic ethical

review of research protocols, or attempted to reform the law. The delay is partly attributable to the political changes that occurred in 1986. Some members of the CCNE along with others fear that, as researchers run ahead and politicians procrastinate, we will confront irreversible facts, *le fait accompli*.■

In Israel, Law, Religious Orthodoxy, and Reproductive Technologies

by Amos Shapira

Amos Shapira holds the Kalman Lubowski Chair in Law and Biomedical Ethics, Faculty of Law, Tel Aviv University, Israel.

Israel is a community fraught with contradictions: a Jewish national home with a sizable non-Jewish ethnic minority; an immigrant society bent on nation building while still beset by lingering tensions generated in the process of absorbing Jews from all over the world; a liberal democracy that has not determined the appropriate role of religious values, practices, and institutions.

The continuing debate over religion and state involves sharply contending values. Tensions between Orthodox Jews and secularists have occasionally thrown the entire political system into turmoil and have made the specter of a *Kulturkampf* (cultural war) a constant threat to communal life.

Against this background of diversity, normative arrangements, often based on compromise and expediency, have had to be forged. Israel does not

subscribe to the American model of the separation of religion and state (a model that is quite extraordinary from a global perspective). Religious institutions, including judicial tribunals and political parties, are formally recognized. Religious social services, such as parochial education, are state-supported. Religious injunctions concerning, for example, the observance of Sabbath and Kashruth (dietary rules) and marriage and divorce, are enshrined in state legislation. Yet in their daily affairs most Israelis lead an essentially secular life.

Thus the Israeli experience displays a unique mix of religious orthodoxy and secularist lifestyle, of fundamentalist paternalism and permissive individualism, of traditional proscriptive tenets and liberal precepts of privacy, autonomy, and self-determination. This is the frequently inconsistent cultural context in which ethical themes surrounding the development and use of artificial means of reproduction are raised, argued, and shaped.

Demographic considerations, contrary to expectations, have not played a role in support of technologies to facilitate fertility and increase the birth rate. The current Jewish majority in the Jewish state seems to many rather precarious and even dubious for the distant future unless there is a further increase

in the Jewish population birth rate and in Jewish immigration to Israel. But there has been no explicit public and political impetus to promote infertility treatment framed in demographic terms. The most significant force behind the new technologies has been the medical profession, first and foremost the senior physicians and their support staff involved in this endeavor. Somber recollection of the atrocities committed by Nazi doctors and medical staff under the pretext of scientific experimentation certainly forms an integral part of the Israeli psyche. Yet, whatever words of caution or reservation are voiced in the debate surrounding reproductive technologies, they do not refer to the gruesome Nazi experience. Concerns have centered mainly on such issues as risk-benefit calculus, informed consent, and religious and legal considerations.

Artificial Insemination: The Law of Bastardy

Artificial insemination by donor (AID) was the first reproductive technology to be partially regulated in Israel. For many years AID had been practiced in hospitals and clinics without any formal and explicit legislative, administrative, or judicial direction. In June 1979, the Minister of Health decreed that the operation of a sperm bank and the artificial insemination of a woman may be conducted only under the Health Ministry's control. Shortly thereafter, the director general of the ministry issued a circular to all hospitals in Israel, setting out rules concerning sperm banks and AID. This document stipulates, among other things, that multiple donations of sperm are not to be accepted from the same donor, that access to records and documents in a sperm bank is strictly limited, that AID may be performed only after it is determined that the woman cannot become pregnant from the sperm of her husband, that the sperm to be used for AID will be chosen by the physician alone, and that the identity of the donor and that of the husband and wife may be revealed to no one, including either party.

Both the woman and her husband must give written consent, and the husband must declare that the child that is born will be considered as his own for all purposes, including support and inheritance. The donor, too, is required to give his written consent to the use of his sperm for AID, and to abide scrupulously by the principle of anonymity. Several stipulations are of special cultural and religious significance: The sperm of a particular donor must not be used if sexual relations between the woman and that donor (were they to exist) would be incestuous. The sperm of the husband combined with that of the donor ought to be used insofar as possible. And AID may not be performed if the donor is married.

The legal foundation of these rules and directives is rather shaky for several juridical reasons. In particular, it is inconceivable that matters of personal status, such as the determination of paternity of a child born of artificial insemination, can be decreed normatively except by primary legislation, that is, a statute enacted by the Knesset (Israeli Parliament). Yet the Knesset is unlikely to embark upon such a legislative program in the foreseeable future, in view of the generally negative attitude to AID displayed by the politically influential religious establishment. This attitude stems mainly from an age-old Jewish religious law, which attaches the stigma of bastardy to a child born to a married woman and not fathered by her Jewish husband. Any premature legislative initiative may indeed threaten the widespread practice of AID in Israel; it is likely to provoke dormant religious objections into public opposition.

In Vitro Fertilization and Research Regulation

In December 1980, the director general of the Ministry of Health promulgated the Public Health Regulations (Human Experimentation), the first attempt to devise a regulatory framework for biomedical research involving human subjects. These regulations provide for a Supreme Helsinki Committee for Medical Experiments on Humans (the name refers to the Helsinki Declaration of 1964, revised in 1975, an international statement of research ethics). The committee's opinion must be sought, among other things, prior to conducting "an experiment concerning the artificial fertilization of a woman." The committee's ten-member panel includes a jurist, a clergyman, six university professors (of whom at least three are physicians), the director general of the Ministry of Health or his representative (provided that they are licensed physicians), and the head of the Medical Association of Israel.

Given the relative scarcity of preformulated standards, the Supreme Helsinki Committee has had to break new paths. It functions as a semilegislator, fashioning general directives in the course of scrutinizing specific research proposals. The principal field assigned to the committee to date has been in vitro fertilization (IVF) and embryo replacement. The committee's piecemeal but consistent, cautious yet steadfast handling of its assignment reveals the diverse and occasionally conflicting legal, religious, and sociopolitical factors that shape the ethical debate on new reproductive technologies.

In mid-1981 the director general, upon the advice of the Supreme Helsinki Committee, granted two leading medical centers qualified authorization to perform IVF. Later, a few other major hospitals were accorded similar permits. Ova could be removed from a woman solely for subsequent fertilization and replacement. Consequently, women who were not candidates for ovum replacement (for reasons of, for example, age or physical condition) were ineligible. Also, considering the risks inherent in laparoscopy (which was then the prevalent procedure for

harvesting eggs), participation was restricted to women for whom laparoscopy was indicated, irrespective of the proposed IVF treatment.

The committee carefully outlined an informed consent process, including the provision of written explanatory material, counseling, and ultimately the signing of a detailed consent document. A system of monitoring and reporting was established. Mindful of public sensitivities (primarily religious sentiments) and possible political repercussions, the committee at first limited participation in the IVF and embryo replacement program to married couples. Subsequently, it extended eligibility to single women, as a rule those with a stable family environment, that is, those who have an ongoing relationship with a man.

The issue of ovum donation was considered next. The Supreme Helsinki Committee's handling of this question has been clouded with some ambiguity. Initially, the committee advised permitting human egg donation from unmarried women only, because of the Jewish religious law of bastardy. According to some religious law authorities, the injunction making the child of a married Jewish woman not fathered by her husband a bastard could be interpreted as extending to the situation of an egg donated by a married Jewish woman to be fertilized by the sperm of the recipient woman's husband. Inevitably, the exclusion of ovum donation by married women has severely limited the natural reservoir for such donations, namely, surplus eggs retrieved from married women themselves undergoing IVF treatment. In addition, singling out unmarried women as the only eligible egg donors might expose young donors (not themselves undergoing IVF treatment) to unnecessary risks. It could also encourage the practice of offering payment for such donations.

The situation was mitigated when single women also became eligible for IVF treatment. Also, some medical centers have voluntarily adopted a policy of rejecting offers of egg donation (with or without pecuniary reward) made by young unmarried volunteers not themselves receiving IVF treatment. Furthermore, the director general of the Ministry of Health and the committee have expressly indicated a preference for accepting egg donations from single women who have already borne children of their own. Finally, at a later stage, the Supreme Helsinki Committee authorized the acceptance of an ovum donation from a married woman in exceptional instances of identified, within-the-family egg donations.

After the practice of IVF and embryo replacement had become established and egg donation had received a qualified endorsement, the Supreme Helsinki Committee was asked to approve the performance of IVF and embryo transfer to a "host" or "carrier," that is, gestational mother. The committee summarily dismissed such applications without thoroughly considering the ethical and other problems entailed in the different variations of the so-called "surrogacy" situation.

In 1984, the Supreme Helsinki Committee considered the freezing and storage of pre-implantation embryos. The committee resolved to authorize, during a trial period of two years, the freezing of fertilized ova for up to six months but only for the use of the couple involved. A subcommittee was appointed to explore in detail the scientific, ethical, and legal implications of frozen embryo storage, implantation, donation, and thawing. The subcommittee's report was discussed but not fully endorsed by the full committee.

In May 1986 the Ministry of Health published draft regulations dealing with various aspects of extracorporeal fertilization. Ova may be recovered for purposes of replacement, donation, freezing, and implantation only from women themselves undergoing infertility treatment and in the course of such treatment. Freezing of fertilized eggs is usually limited to a period not exceeding five years. Single women are explicitly recognized in the proposed regulations as eligible for fertilized egg implantation, provided that a hospital's social worker certifies in writing that the woman is psychologically and economically capable of raising the child. But implantation of a fertilized ovum may be performed in a woman only if the ovum is her own or if it was retrieved from a "woman of the same People [i.e. ethnic-national

origin]….on grounds of the welfare [i.e. best interests] of the child." It is also proposed that an egg donor be limited in her donation or donations to only one woman recipient, in order to preclude the possibility of numerous half-siblings being born into different families, and to minimize the risk of future incestuous marriages.

The draft regulations stipulate that no extracorporeal fertilization may be performed unless both spouses have received an explanation from the physician in charge and have signed a written consent form. Research and experiments on a fertilized egg are totally banned. Implantation of a fertilized egg in a woman "not designed to be the child's mother" is forbidden. Violation of the proposed regulations' injunctions is punishable by imprisonment and/or fine.

The Need for Legislation

The Ministry of Health's attempt to subject new reproductive technologies to systematic normative regulation is definitely welcome. However, the specific standards proposed are not impeccable. Thus, for instance, the directive that a fertilized ovum may be implanted in a woman only if the ovum was retrieved from "a woman of the same People [i.e. ethnic-national origin]" is patently problematic and disturbing. In addition to raising intriguing questions of interpretation (what is the precise meaning of "people" or "ethnic-national origin" in this context?), such a proscription could provoke accusations, whether justified or not, of segregationist or even racist attitudes. The stated rationale for this directive, formulated in terms of "the welfare [i.e. best interests] of the child" to be born is not likely to ameliorate this negative response. To be sure, the parties involved in an egg donation arrangement may voluntarily wish to stipulate terms and conditions, including the ethnic origin or religious affiliation of the egg donor. But formally enshrining such a restriction in a legislative measure is another matter.

The real reason for the restriction lies in the traditional principle of Jewish religious law that a Jew is only one who is born to a Jewish mother (or one duly converted to Judaism). The fear is

that a child born as a result of the implantation of a fertilized ovum recovered from a non-Jewish woman donor would not be considered Jewish, a serious disadvantage given Israeli realities (concerning, for instance, matters of marriage and divorce). This is a real problem. Yet the solution offered by the draft regulations is like an overdose of a strong medicine, which cures the disease while killing the patient.

A solution should and can be found elsewhere. The religious law decrees that only the offspring of a Jewish mother is regarded as a Jew. But who is the mother in a situation where woman A is implanted with an ovum retrieved from woman B and then carries the pregnancy to term and gives birth to a child? If one adopts the position that, for purposes of lineage, the gestational-carrier woman rather than the ovum donor is the mother (although the latter is certainly the genetic parent), a position not without religious foundation, then the solution becomes obvious. The child of the (Jewish) gestational mother would be Jewish.

Finally, when the process of procreation is no longer limited to one man and one woman, baffling legal questions as to the juridical identities, rights, and obligations of parents and children are bound to arise. What relative weight ought to be accorded to genetic, gestational, contractual, and social factors in establishing personal status relationships of parents and children?

Many of these questions cannot be answered except by primary legislation. Yet conceiving and delivering legislative measures on such issues is no small feat in a heterogeneous society like Israel. The Knesset is unlikely to act in the foreseeable future. ■

In The Netherlands, Tolerance and Debate

by Maurice A.M. de Wachter and Guido M.W.R. de Wert

Maurice A.M. de Wachter is director of the Institute for Bioethics, Maastricht, The Netherlands; Guido M.W.R. de Wert is a research associate at the same Institute.

Dutch society has a tradition of tolerance. In the nineteenth century The Netherlands was among the few nations in Europe that decriminalized suicide and suicide attempts. In this century religious factions have (for the most part) abandoned their public antagonism in matters of sexuality as well as abortion and euthanasia to become tolerant of divergent opinions, ways of life, and practices. Recently, the Dutch people seem to have found ways of dealing tolerantly with the dilemmas of AIDS by creating a climate of openness and compassion, by obtaining the effective cooperation of the major risk-groups, and primarily by refusing to turn a policy of health prevention into a moralistic campaign.

Dutch citizens not only profit from this climate of tolerance; they also contribute to it. After the Second World War, especially during the late 50s and 60s, the Dutch people turned extremely critical of authority and authoritarian morality. Among the various religious groups, the Roman Catholic Church bore the brunt of the attack. The emancipation of citizen and believer seems

to have firmly established a tradition of autonomy of conscience and respect for anyone's definition of what "the good life" means. In The Netherlands everything seems possible. At the least, everything can be said if not done.

In this climate, it is not surprising that most modern means of artificial reproduction, such as AID, IVF, and surrogate motherhood, are available; and that research on the embryo and genetic diagnosis in vitro are being planned. But all of these techniques have attracted public attention, both as topics for ethical debate and as subjects of public policy.

The public policy interest in these issues is reflected in an October 1986 advisory report from the independent Netherlands' Health Council on Artificial Reproduction to the Minister of Health. (An executive summary of the Health Council's report on "artificial reproduction" is available from the Health Council, P.O. Box 90517, The Hague.) Under Dutch law the Minister of Health has in principle (though exceptions have occurred) the power to control the functions of hospitals—particularly the specialists' facilities and equipment, and to "stipulate the procedure for determining need and for granting licenses."

The Minister also receives advice from the National Council for Public Health, as well as from various health insurance companies and professional medical organizations. Most of these groups have taken the opportunity of offering advice to the government in matters of artificial reproduction.

Underlying the public policy

reports is an ongoing debate on the ethical issues surrounding the development, introduction, and use of artificial means of reproduction. This debate has two major components. First, there are themes and issues common to AID, IVF, and surrogacy such as the value of parenthood, the involvement of third parties, and the question of who should have access. Second, there are ethical issues that are specific to IVF only, in particular, embryo research.

AID, IVF, and Surrogacy

Ethical arguments about AID and IVF are to some extent shaped by attitudes toward infertility. Some people attach extremely high importance to biological parenthood. For them, to beget your "own" child is more important than to beget a child. Others radically disagree. They state that infertility is not a medical problem and suggest that infertile couples should seek nonmedical solutions, such as accepting their childlessness or adopting a baby, although adoption is for a number of reasons difficult to accomplish in this country.

The Health Council is convinced that medical solutions to infertility are ethically right and recommends an extension of medical indications for IVF. The use of a third party is still controversial. Some call it a violation of the child's right to be born as the true offspring of the parents who will be responsible for his or her upbringing. In The Netherlands the practice of donating sperm for AID is nevertheless widespread, leading to the birth of about 1,000 children yearly. The ethical discussion focuses on secrecy, anonymity, and selection of donors. Recently a working group of the Association of Family and Youth Law recommended that the law state unequivocally that the sperm donor has no responsibility for the child.

More and more people oppose the traditional practice of not telling the child about his or her AID origins. Secrecy is seen as possibly harmful to the child. It certainly goes against the right to know one's genetic identity, a position which is gaining support in The Netherlands. The Health Council, accordingly, pleads for informing the child, but is cautious that information regarding the child's genetic identity must not lead to the identification of the donor. This position was primarily taken to protect the donor's privacy. The Health Council also rejects the use of AID for positive eugenic purposes. Thus donors may be rejected only in a few specific cases, for example, when they pose an increased genetic risk. For the same reason registering specific endowments of the donor (such as intelligence) is not permitted. Similar recommendations exist about egg donation and embryo donation.

Although surrogate motherhood remains quite rare in The Netherlands (probably fewer than ten cases annually) the public debate is violent. The possible harms to mother, child, and social parents cause many people to have serious reservations. However, an absolute prohibition is regarded by many as impractical. The Council's report on artificial reproduction recommends counseling for both parents-to-be and surrogate mothers in order to reduce possible conflicts. Furthermore, when things run according to plan, it recommends expediting the procedure for adoption.

In general, recourse to surrogate motherhood for nonmedical reasons is considered ethically unacceptable. The Health Council recommends intensifying professional interventions in order to treat infertility and suggests that commercial arrangements through agencies be forbidden by law. The same report prefers anonymous surrogacy to the current Dutch practice of seeking surrogates among relatives or friends. The latter is seen as detrimental to the child who will be living with two mothers and will very likely develop identity problems.

Basic to the use of artificial reproduction is the question of people's right to have access to services that will help them in realizing their desire to procreate. Over and above the general acknowledgment that married or stable couples are entitled to such help, there is a trend to include celibate women and lesbian couples.

Embryo research has become in The Netherlands, as in many other countries, a hotly debated issue. The national Health Council considers

embryo research justifiable in principle provided only leftover embryos (which were developed for therapy, yet have not been transplanted) are used and provided the research period does not exceed fourteen days. Moreover, the Council recommends that no local committee alone should decide on the matter, but that a national committee be established to review all such research protocols. The report says nothing about either the future technical feasibility or the ethical implications of genetic diagnosis in vitro. (The Council holds very negative views about sex preselection in embryos.)

Reimbursement for IVF is also controversial. All Dutch citizens have health insurance coverage. Depending on their income, they are insured either by a company associated with the Union of Dutch Health Insurers (if their yearly income is below fl. 50,000) or by one of the ten so-called private insurers. While most of the private insurance companies cover IVF, the Minister of Health, on advice of the Council of the Union of Dutch Health

Insurers, decided during 1985 that for the time being IVF would not be covered by the companies associated with the Union. This decision created an exception to the usual policy that common medical practices are automatically covered.

Meanwhile the Council of the Union is subsidizing a three-year research program in a few clinics and for a limited number of patients covered by the Union. The goal is to study cost-effectiveness of IVF in a context of limits to health care. It is expected that this type of technology assessment will help to decide whether or not IVF will be covered for members of the Union. On this issue the Health Council found IVF to be at least as cost-effective as microsurgical tubal repair; and soon possibly more cost-effective.

Critics find the Government's policy too restrictive. They point to long waiting lists, and injustice for those who cannot travel abroad for IVF. Their position illustrates that the issue of allocation and priorities in health care resources remains unsolved.■

In Britain, the Debate after the Warnock Report

by Raanan Gillon

Raanan Gillon, a physician who is also trained in philosophy, is director of the Imperial College Health Service, London University, and editor of the *Journal of Medical Ethics*. He is a senior fellow at the Center for Medical Law and Ethics, King's College, University of London, and a deputy director of the Institute for Medical Ethics, London.

The pioneering of in vitro fertilization by the British scientists Patrick Steptoe and Robert G. Edwards in 1978

can be seen as the start of a new era—a paradigm shift in human ability to intervene in human reproduction. The power for bad as well as the potential for good of IVF and its associated technologies was rapidly recognized in Britain, and in 1982 the Thatcher Government appointed a multidisciplinary Inquiry chaired by Lady Warnock, an Oxford philosopher, to consider medical and scientific developments "related to human fertilization and embryology." Two years and reams of evidence later the Committee made some sixty-three, mostly unanimous, recommendations, including a variety of proposed legislative reforms.

The most controversial recommendation would have permitted

117

research (followed by destruction) on human embryos up to fourteen days after fertilization. Three bills to ban such research, subsequently introduced by members of Parliament independently of the government, were ultimately defeated. The other controversial recommendation—to ban all commercial surrogacy arrangements (and to ban participation by health workers in *any* surrogacy arrangements)—hit the headlines and the television screens when an American commercial surrogacy arrangement found its way to Britain. Very rapidly the government brought in the Surrogacy Arrangements Act 1985 banning commercial surrogacy and advertising of and for surrogacy services (see Diana Brahams, "The Hasty British Ban on Commercial Surrogacy," *Hastings Center Report*, February 1987, pp. 16-18).

Interestingly, while the Act defines "commercial surrogacy" in part on the basis of the receipt of any payment in connection with the surrogacy arrangements, it specifically excludes payment to or for the benefit of the surrogate mother as affording evidence of commercial surrogacy. Nor does the Act go so far as the majority of the Warnock committee recommended, for it does *not* make "criminally liable the actions of professionals and others who knowingly assist in the establishment of a surrogate pregnancy," assuming of course that they are not participating in a commercial surrogacy arrangement.

The government did nothing further at that time to implement the Warnock recommendations. In 1985, however, the Committee's recommendation for a statutory licensing authority to control artificial reproduction and associated techniques was given the shadow of a response when the Medical Research Council (MRC) and the Royal College of Obstetricians and Gynecologists (RCOG), independently of legislation, set up a *voluntary* licensing authority (VLA). This authority offered guidelines partly based on the Warnock Report's recommendations and partly on recommendations in reports of the two sponsoring organizations. The guidelines included redesignating the preimplantation embryo of up to fourteen days development as a "pre-embryo" rather than an embryo. Four

of the twelve members of the VLA, including its chairwoman, are nondoctors, and include the eminent Church of England theologian Professor Gordon Dunstan.

In late 1986, the government, apparently eager to postpone further parliamentary controversy until after the election anticipated in 1987, issued a "consultation paper" outlining the Warnock Report's proposals for legislation and urging more public discussion. As the consultation paper points out, public discussion, though vigorous, had been largely restricted to the two most controversial proposals made by the Warnock Report, those to permit embryo research and to ban surrogacy.

The Unborn Children Protection Bill

It was Enoch Powell, a previous Conservative Minister of Health, who first set the legislative cat among the pigeons to respond to Warnock. He expressed a sense of revulsion and repugnance that any human embryo should be experimented on and destroyed merely for the acquisition of knowledge. Despite the government's request for a period of wide public discussion about all the Warnock proposals, Mr. Powell's Unborn Children Protection Bill sought to preempt this and to prohibit all nontherapeutic experimentation on human embryos. In February 1986 his bill, on a free vote (according to conscience rather than party lines), obtained a second reading majority of 172 (236 to 66) and seemed, as senior politicians reportedly claimed, "unstoppable." However, as a result of the parliamentary tactics of opponents (and lack of support from the Government), the bill did not get through its committee stages. Similar fates befell the two subsequent similar bills introduced by MP Ken Hargreaves.

The main arguments of Mr. Powell and his supporters were pro-life: the embryo was a human being; doctors should not play God (or "usurp the authority of God," as the Northern Irish Protestant fundamentalist, the Rev. Ian Paisley put it); helpless unborn children should be protected against experimentation, which offended the dignity of man. In addition, they said, there were risks of dreadful consequences if genetic engi-

neering were applied to human beings; and the ends did not justify the means.

Arguments in favor of research on human embryos rested on the benefits that could be anticipated from such research, especially in alleviating infertility and handicap. Some MPs, including the then Minister of Health, argued that Mr. Powell's bill was premature, preempting wide public debate and focusing too narrowly on only one aspect of the Warnock Report.

Lady Warnock's Warning

In the *London Times* a furious debate raged over embryo experimentation, with Paul Johnson, a past editor of the *New Statesman*, linking the Holocaust, abortion, and "embryocide," and suggesting that Lady Warnock's reasoning would vindicate Dr. Joseph Mengele. Lady Warnock herself wrote to oppose the Powell Bill, under the title "Absolutely Wrong," and warned: "The great tide of moral fundamentalism sweeping across from America is in my view a genuine threat. It cannot be wholly distinguished from dogmatism, intolerance, and fanaticism; forces not just theoretically objectionable, but as we all know, in practice terrifying."

With the exception of the Royal College of General Practitioners, which had flatly rejected Warnock's recommendation to allow nontherapeutic experimentation on human embryos, the medical professional organizations almost unanimously opposed banning carefully controlled research on early embryos. Thus the BMA, the RCOG, and the MRC all favored carefully regulated research on early embryos, as did editorials in the *British Medical Journal* and *The Lancet*. And a multidisciplinary working party convened by the CIBA Foundation, an independent and respected academic organization supported by the CIBA-GEIGY Corporation, argued forcefully for the benefits and justifiability of such research.

Other Recommendations

As the government says in its consultation paper, there have been relatively few public responses to the other recommendations for legislation in the Warnock Report. Among these were the central recommendation to establish a statutory licensing body to control most services connected with artificial reproduction; a statutory obligation to provide counseling for prospective artificial insemination and in vitro fertilization parents; legal acceptance of AID and IVF children as children of the women giving birth and legitimate children of their marriages when the husbands have also consented to the treatment, with the husband's consent presumed unless proved otherwise; provision of "basic information about the donor's ethnic origin and genetic health" to children of AID and egg or embryo donation procedures; limitation on storage of embryos to no longer than ten years with no legal right of ownership in the human embryos; various provisions about the use, disposal, and rights of succession (none) of stored embryos when the father dies before transfer to the mother; and the outlawing of transfer of a human embryo into the uterus of another species for gestation. The government's consultation paper invites comment on all these proposals as well as further comments on the more controversial Warnock proposals concerning embryo research and surrogacy.

Future Directions

On the issue of embryo research, Britain's existing liberal abortion law would seem to point against a total ban. For Britain already permits in its abortion law the destruction of fetuses in the interests of others, even (exceptionally) as late as twenty-eight weeks into pregnancy; and given the philosophical presuppositions about the moral status of the embryo and fetus that such a law implies, it would seem quixotic indeed to criminalize potentially beneficial nontherapeutic medical research on one- or two-week embryos, *provided* that they are not allowed to develop. But a sincere and often very vocal minority of the population totally rejects the premises.

The establishment of a statutory licensing authority to control the application and development of artificial means of reproduction seems likely to be generally acceptable and a sensible and reasonably flexible way for society and the medical and scientific communities to cooperate in controlling the use of human gametes and embryos.

Its functioning would depend crucially on its composition and the readiness of its members to compromise between opposing views.

However, it would be foolish to predict which path legislation, when and if it is enacted, will finally take. A safer prophecy is that an election will be called before the current consultation process is completed and a new government will have to pick up the Warnock hot potato. ■

In Japan, Consensus Has Limits

by Koichi Bai, Yasuko Shirai, and Michiko Ishii

Koichi Bai is professor of law and director of the Institute of Medical Humanitics at Kitasato University, Sagamihara, Kanagawa. *Yasuko Shirai* is senior researcher, Department of Social Welfare, Institute for Developmental Research, Aichi Prefectural Colony, Aichi. *Michiko Ishii* is a lecturer in the Faculty of Law at Teikyo University, Tokyo.

Japan is sometimes called a country of consensus and harmony.[1] This properly describes one feature, but should not be overemphasized, especially at present when we face some critical issues raised by the new reproductive technologies. Not only are Japanese attitudes divided pro and con over the use of these technologies; we also find,

surprisingly, that the new technology is occasionally accepted by traditional minds and rejected by progressive spirits.

We must beware of drawing general conclusions as to "Japanese" characteristics on these issues. We ought not to assume too readily a uniformity in Japanese culture; nor, needless to say, can we ignore Japanese peculiarity. The key is to observe the situation as it exists.

Artificial Insemination by Donor

In 1949 the first AID child was reportedly born in Japan. At that time, several institutions were performing AID. Keio University Hospital was the first to do this procedure, and is the only hospital that continues to do so, and then only when a married woman has obtained her husband's consent. Japan has no sperm bank facilities. Sperm donors are medical students and other people with some connection to the hospital who receive money for their donation. Estimates are that nearly 10,000 AID children have now been born in Japan.

Until now, there has been little serious opposition to AID. No one is

119

advocating legal prohibitions. Even though no law *clearly* establishes the child's legal status, there have been no lawsuits regarding AID children.

Ever since the legal problems relating to AID were discussed at a symposium of the Japanese Association of Civil Law in 1953, many legal scholars have construed the law in such a way that the AID baby of a married woman is presumed to be a legitimate child of her husband, so long as the procedure is carried out according to current practice (Japanese Civil Act Article 772). A minority, myself included, feel that the AID child should not be presumed to be the legitimate child of the husband. Thus, in the minority view, anybody can challenge the paternity at any time.

Both opinions take as their starting point the medical practice of preserving sperm donors' anonymity. Hospitals keep records but no information is made available. Very few people have argued that the AID child has a right to identify his or her biological father. Indeed, in most cases no one tells the AID child any facts about his or her birth.

In Vitro Fertilization

Unlike AID, which had its origins in the late 1940s, in vitro fertilization (IVF) is rather controversial. Since the news about England's first "test-tube baby" reached Japan, interest in the procedure has increased. The first test-tube baby in Japan was born on March 14, 1983, at Tohoku national university hospital. Currently, about thirty institutions perform in vitro fertilization. It is difficult to say how many IVF babies have been born because there has been no official count, but according to a recent study,[2] forty-seven babies have now been born, and increasing numbers of people are attempting the procedure.

According to the guidelines of the Japanese Obstetrics and Gynecological Society, in vitro fertilization is limited to married couples. Eggs are not donated for in vitro fertilization in Japan, nor does any "lending" or "leasing" of wombs take place. Moreover, the fact that an ethics committee at a university hospital other than Tohoku deliberated on the propriety of IVF before the

procedure was done for the first time reflects a different social consciousness from the climate at the start of AID. The following are some distinctive points at issue:

The definition of IVF. The Japanese Obstetrics and Gynecological Society defines IVF as a medical practice for treating infertility. But others view IVF as a distinctly nonmedical technology. Some want to put IVF in the legal category of a nonmedical service performed exclusively by a physician. In addition, there is concern about the possibility of IVF children being born handicapped, or developing psychological problems, though no research has yet been done on this question. They say that IVF is still a changing technology. The element of experimentation in the procedure should be uncovered and clarified in each case.

Limitations on the procedure. As has been said, IVF is performed only on married couples. This debatable limitation is based on an interest in the child's well-being. Some people, however, insist that such a limitation is inappropriate. Others claim that even if such a limitation could be accepted, it has nothing to do with medical considerations; therefore physicians alone should not decide whether to introduce it into the criteria; the agreement of the general public is required as well.

Impact on individuals and society. Doctors who support IVF maintain that they have a responsibility to respond to the patient's needs. But others argue that how a new technology is used affects not only the patient, but also the entire society. On these grounds, some people oppose the introduction of new technology, particularly if the doctor is thinking only about the patient; they argue that this approach diminishes the social responsibility of the medical profession.

When life begins. Another criticism of IVF focuses on the loss of many fertilized eggs in the process of creating one IVF child. This relates to the question of when human life begins. According to the Japanese Civil Act, Article 1.3, the capacity to enjoy rights as a person commences at the time of birth. However, according to the same Act, (Arts. 886 and 721,) a fetus is regarded as a born child for purposes

of inheritance and claiming compensation for damage, provided that it is born alive. The view of one person in the Ministry of Justice, which the Diet referred to in passing, is that the fertilized egg also has the status of a fetus. This does not mean that the Ministry has concluded that a frozen fertilized egg can inherit even many years after the death of its parents.

Possibility of abortion. In August 1986, it was reported that the use of fertility drugs resulted in the conception of four children, two of which were selectively aborted. Arguments for and against such selective abortions filled the newspaper columns. While the case had nothing to do with IVF, this procedure can raise similar questions regarding future IVF.

Gene manipulation and embryo research. Should fertilized eggs not destined for implantation be used for experimentation? The Japanese Obstetrics and Gynecological Society has recommended that a fertilized egg can be used for experimentation during the first two weeks after fertilization, with the consent of the donors. It also stated that gene manipulation should not be performed on these eggs. Members of the society must report their experimental work. Nevertheless, no sanctions are in place for those who violate these prohibitions. Some question whether these rules are adequate.

Privacy issues. When the first IVF child was born, the name of the family was reported in one newspaper, although those doctors directly involved in the case intended to maintain the privacy of the couple and child. Because of the publicity, the family had to move out of their home and the doctors did not disclose anything further about the case. Critics of such practices believe that while on the one hand the hospitals should openly publicize such procedures, on the other hand society should guard the privacy of the families involved. In this case, neither of these conditions was fulfilled.

In Japan, a ready acceptance of IVF stands side by side with a bias against the parties involved. We need to make a sincere effort to resolve this issue.

Gender Selection

In 1984, for the first time in Japan, a girl was born through a process of gender selection, which separates X and Y sperm. Before this, there were few ethical debates over gender selection in Japan; but since then ethics committees have begun to examine the questions surrounding this technology. As a result, the hospital and the medical association have decided that gender selection should be performed only in order to prevent gender-linked diseases. At present, gender selection is still controversial and not yet socially acceptable. We need to establish a clear process by which such reproductive technologies become socially accepted, to provide guidance for each future situation.

Social Attitudes

In light of the various arguments mentioned above, it is difficult to generalize about the attitude of the Japanese people. Taken collectively, the numerous opinions do not suggest any uniform perspective. Japanese attitudes have not been examined closely because of misinformation and lack of research. However, the following four opinion surveys have been done:

- Before the first successful IVF birth, Keio University law students examined the attitudes of health care personnel toward IVF by surveying gynecologists, nurses, and midwives between July and October 1982. Seventy-five percent of 271 gynecologists agreed with the idea that IVF falls within the realm of traditional infertility treatment, while 43.6 percent of nurses (out of 218 questioned) and 37.1 percent of midwives (out of 259) agreed. Sixty-eight percent of doctors approved of the clinical use of IVF in general, while only 20 percent of nurses and midwives approved.
- In May 1983, after the first IVF birth, Shirai and Shirai questioned all the members of the Japanese Society of Social Psychology. Of the 186 respondents (161 male and 25 female) were involved and 57 percent agreed on using the husband's sperm and the wife's egg in IVF. Fifteen percent were opposed and 28 percent abstained.
- In May 1984, the Mainichi news organization questioned 2,759 married women under age fifty across the nation. The women were asked if a husband and wife unable to have their own child except by external fertilization should be allowed to proceed; 62.2 percent responded in the affirmative, while 32.7 percent disagreed. The younger women responded more positively than the older (76.3 percent of 351 women in their late twenties approved, for example, in contrast to 52.3 percent of 515 women in their late forties).
- In December 1985, the Prime Minister's office conducted a national survey of 3,307 men and 4,134 women age twenty and older. The question was whether or not IVF should be performed on humans; 28.5 percent answered yes, while 54.8 percent answered no; 16.7 percent did not respond. This survey detected no attitudinal differences between the sexes. As in the Mainichi news survey, the younger respondents were more receptive to IVF, with 46.8 percent of the sample in their twenties (944) favoring the clinical use of IVF. Of those over sixty, only 17.2 percent of the 1,408 questioned favored IVF. In light of this study, it also appears that highly educated Japanese have a more positive attitude toward IVF.

Based on the results of these few studies, it is difficult to designate clearly the Japanese attitude toward IVF and we prefer to withhold any judgment. At this point, we would like to introduce two interesting provisional arguments.

First, in the research by Shirai and Shirai, the respondents provided supporting reasons for their positions. Those who support IVF said that (1) the right to privacy includes the reproductive process, (2) IVF is a treatment for infertility, and (3) it is acceptable to separate sex and reproduction. Those who do not support IVF argued that (1) it fails to respect human dignity, (2) it conflicts with the ways of nature. Those who withheld a response mentioned that they are unable to resolve the tension between privacy rights in the reproductive sphere and "nature's providence." All the respondents pointed out that the establishment of community values and comprehensive guidelines are indispensable for the practice of IVF. Their statements reflect serious concerns that the new reproductive technology will spread without thought and appropriate guidelines or regulation.

The second point is suggested by Dr. K. Nakamura.[3] Paradoxically, modern reproductive technologies can become the instruments to preserve traditional family structure and values. Even in contemporary Japan, traditional values such as the desire for a male heir still persist to some extent. And technologies that at one level threaten traditional values and practices, at another allow the traditional belief in the woman's responsibility for infertility to go unchallenged. That is what has happened in Japan, where the new reproductive technologies create a tension and a link between traditional belief and contemporary practice. We must not lose sight of such delicate bearings in accepting the new technology. ∎

References

[1] Eric Feldman, "Medical Ethics the Japanese Way," *Hastings Center Report* 15:5 (October 1985), 21-24.

[2] Personal communication with Professor T. Mori, Kyoto University.

[3] Keiko Nakamura, "Medical Ethics and Bioethics from the Viewpoint of Life Science," in *Medicine and Ethics* edited by Koichi Bai (Tokyo: Nihonhyoronsha, 1987).

In Australia, The Debate Moves to Embryo Experimentation

by Louis Waller

Louis Waller holds the Sir Leo Cussen Chair of Law in Monash University, Melbourne, Australia. He was chairman of the Victorian Government's Committee to Consider the Social, Ethical and Legal Issues Arising from In Vitro Fertilization, 1982-84, and is chairman of the Standing Review and Advisory Committee on Infertility established under the Victorian *Infertility (Medical Procedures) Act* 1984.

Thousands of children have been born in Australia as the result of artificial insemination using donor sperm, still commonly called AID. Hundreds have been born as the result of in vitro fertilization (IVF), including a number utilizing donor sperm, a smaller number utilizing donor ova, and a few where the embryo formed in the laboratory was subjected to cryopreservation before its implantation.

Since 1982, there has been a series of Australian inquiries into the ethical, social, and legal aspects of the new birth technologies, especially in vitro fertilization. Each of the six States of the Commonwealth has initiated at least one such inquiry, in some form or another. The Victorian Government's Committee to Consider the Social, Ethical, and Legal Issues Arising from In Vitro Fertilization produced its Interim Report, September 1982, an Issues Paper on Donor Gametes in IVF in April 1983, its Report on Donor Gametes in IVF in August 1983, and its final Report on the Disposition of

Embryos Produced by In Vitro Fertilization in August 1984.

The most wide-ranging and also the most protracted inquiry has been in New South Wales, where the Law Reform Commission published its Report on Human Artificial Insemination in June 1986; it has yet to complete work on in vitro fertilization and surrogate motherhood arrangements. At the federal level, the Family Law Council, a statutory body established under the landmark *Family Law Act* 1975, published its report *Creating Children* in 1985, and in October 1986 the Australian Senate's Select Committee on the Human Embryo Experimentation Bill 1985 (the Harradine Bill) published its Report.

What led to these efforts? The short answer is public concern, often expressed in terms of "making life in a test tube." The extensive publicity that accompanied the first Australian IVF live-births meant that most people knew something of the process. There was certainly shared happiness in seeing a baby in the arms of a previously infertile couple. Furthermore, Australian scientists and doctors have been among the most prominent developers of the technology. Some of them had themselves called for regulations and for answers, especially to the questions of the status of the children born from the use of donor sperm.

The Main Concerns

As the birthplace of Australia's in vitro fertilization programs, Victoria has wrestled with many concerns about reproductive technology. In 1982, the Victorian IVF Committee, using it as an

Australian example, focused on assistance for infertile couples to establish their own families, on the one hand, and on the other, the future welfare of those children born as a result of IVF, and the intrusion of science and clinical medicine into the marriage relationship. The general opinion of the community, insofar as it could be gauged from scores of written submissions, the media, several public opinion polls, a public hearing, and interviews with interested experts—all filtered through the minds of the nine-member Committee and distilled in sustained debates—was that IVF in what was called "the most common situation" (where only the gametes of the spouses were used, and the embryos which were produced, or some of them, were transferred to the wife's womb), was clearly acceptable. All the reports on the subject that have thus far appeared in Australia have expressed that same general view.

Between 1983 and 1985, legislation was enacted at federal and state levels (but not in Queensland) to establish the relationship of father and child between the infertile husband (or, sometimes, permanent partner) and the baby resulting from AID, either with or without laboratory fertilization. In Victoria, and several other states that modeled their statutes on its *Status of Children (Amendment) Act* 1984, similar provision is made for cases where donor ova or donor embryos are employed.

The examination of the issue of donor gametes in IVF sharpened public concerns about donor anonymity and information. Sperm donors had been routinely assured of complete anonymity by those conducting AID programs in Australia. But, in contrast, legislation to give adopted persons some access to information about their natural parents had been enacted in England, and in Victoria (though there it remained unimplemented). This revealed "a substantial and growing view that the values of honesty and integrity are crucial to the creation of a happy family," as the Victorian IVF Committee put it, in its Report on Donor Gametes in IVF (1983). So it proposed that as well as the mandatory provision of nonidentifying information to all recipients of donor gametes, complete identifying information about donors whose gift resulted in a pregnancy should be stored in a Central Register, to be maintained by the Department of Health.

The Infertility Act of 1984

As is now well known, many of the recommendations made by the Victorian IVF Committee have been enacted into law in the *Infertility (Medical Procedures) Act* 1984. This statute is the only enactment of its kind in Australia, and in the common law world. The Victorian Committee's primary proposal was that a legislative framework was needed within which to express fundamental views and values on the new birth technologies. The Act's provisions dealing with experimentation on embryos have served as a focus for an extensive ongoing debate on that subject.

The Victorian legislation provides a comprehensive statutory scheme for the authorization and regulation of the new birth technologies, concentrating on IVF. It also provides for mandatory counseling for infertile couples and gamete donors in IVF programs, and for careful record keeping (including the establishment of a Central Register containing complete information on those gamete donors where successful pregnancies ensue, including AID as well as IVF procedures). It prohibits advertisements soliciting or offering surrogate mother services, and the payment or receipt of money for such services. It makes any surrogacy contract void, and therefore unenforceable in the courts. It does *not* prohibit embryo experimentation absolutely.

The statute does prohibit cloning and interspecies fertilization. It also seeks to implement the majority recommendation of the Victorian IVF Committee on human embryo experimentation, and its unanimous recommendation on the approval and scrutiny of that branch of scientific and medical experimentation. Section 6 of the Act prohibits experiments on embryos that destroy or damage them unless the particular experiment has been approved by the Standing Review and Advisory Committee on Infertility, itself established by the Act. Section

6(5) prohibits the fertilization of ova "except for the purposes of the implantation of embryos derived from those ova in the womb of that woman or another woman...." That means that destructive, nontherapeutic experiments may be approved only where spare or excess embryos formed in the course of an IVF program are used. The Standing Review and Advisory Committee has rejected one research proposal, which would have involved the fertilization of previously frozen ova, and the chromosomal analysis of the resultant embryos at the eight-cell (or later) stage. It has considered, and at the time of writing is completing its discussion of, a further proposal involving microinjection of single sperm into ova, with chromosomal analysis of the two pronuclei *before* syngamy, or fusion, of the separate male and female components. In its discussions on this subject, the Committee has necessarily considered *when* an embryo exists, in terms of both the expressions used in the legislation and the most recent understanding of the earliest stages of fertilization. Its work has been the subject of intense public and media interest, and has provoked a debate about embryo experimentation which embraces views that focus not only on the beginnings of human life, but also on the sources of gametes used in the experiments proposed, the needs and wishes of infertile couples and infertility support groups, and responsibility and accountability in the scientific and medical worlds.

Embryo Experimentation

In its Report in 1984, a majority of the Victorian IVF Committee said:

From a moral perspective it may be said that, regardless of the particular level of respect which different sections of the community would accord the embryo, this individual and genetically unique human entity should not be formed *solely* and from the outset to be used as a means for any other human purpose, however, laudable. Where the formation occurs in the course of an IVF procedure for the treatment of infertility, the reasons which lead

to the embryo's existence are not "means to an end" ones.

Its conclusion that an ethical distinction could be made between spare or excess embryos and those specifically produced for destructive experimentation was rejected by the Senate Committee, which seemed to emphasize the pragmatic difficulties and the ease of dishonestly avoiding the restriction. In the current debate, those issues have again been canvassed, but the question of according legal protection to the earliest stages of the fertilization process on the one hand, and only to post-fusion zygotes on the other, has occupied center stage.

The statutory establishment of an eight-person Standing Review and Advisory Committee on Infertility in Victoria is designed to provide the government, the legislature, and the community with information and advice on developments in the treatment and circumvention of infertility. Its work may serve as a model for other Australian jurisdictions, though its activities in 1986-87 in relation to embryo experimentation approvals has attracted critical comment from some research workers. Some of these critics now decry the enactment of any legislation in this field, suggesting that the only regulation necessary or appropriate is through institutional ethics committees, or in line with the guidelines promulgated in 1982 by the National Health and Medical Research Council (NH&MRC), responsible for major grant allocations in the field. On the other hand, an Australia-wide Round Table Conference on the Regulation of IVF and Related Research, convened in Canberra in July 1986 by the NH&MRC, while recognizing divergent views on the desirable means of achieving regulation, achieved consensus on the desirability of a uniform, or, at least, a coordinated and consistent approach to the *regulation* of the new birth technologies across the country.

The debate in Australia on the regulation of the new birth technologies will accordingly address the question of national, or uniform, enactments as well as controversial specifics such as the range of permissible experimentation on the earliest stages of fertilization. ■

Index